TEACHING THINKING SKILLS

A Series of Books in Psychology

Editors:

Richard C. Atkinson
Gardner Lindzey
Richard F. Thompson

TEACHING THINKING SKILLS:

Theory and Practice

Edited by

Joan Boykoff Baron
Robert J. Sternberg

W. H. Freeman and Company
New York

Library of Congress Cataloging-in-Publication Data

Teaching thinking skills.

  Includes bibliographies and indexes.
  1. Thought and thinking—Study and teaching.
I. Baron, Joan Boykoff. II. Sternberg, Robert J.
B105.T54T43 1986 160'.7 86-4776
ISBN 0-7167-1789-1
ISBN 0-7167-1791-3 (pbk.)

Printed in the United States of America

1 2 3 4 5 6 7 8 9 0 MC 5 4 3 2 1 0 8 9 8 7

To our children,
Michael and Jonathan Baron
and
Seth and Sara Sternberg

Contents

Preface

During the last few years, interest in the nature, assessment, and modifiability of higher order thinking skills has increased dramatically. This interest has manifested itself in several ways. First, there have been and continue to be numerous national and international conferences on thinking skills. Second, whole journal issues are being devoted to the topic (e.g., recent issues of the *Review of Educational Research* and *Educational Leadership*). Indeed, the publisher of the latter journal, the Association for Supervision and Curriculum Development, has made critical thinking skills its number one priority for educational development. Third, numerous books and articles are being published on the subject, including new programs for training these skills. Finally, school districts and consortia are sponsoring countless workshops on thinking skills.

The recent and fairly sudden surge of interest in higher order thinking skills can be explained in part by the national concern over poor test results. A flurry of high-level government-sponsored reports has indicated that thinking skills in children have reached an abysmally low level. For example, basing its conclusions on the results of the National Assessment of Educational Progress, the Education Commission of the States reported in 1982 that "the pattern is clear: the percentage of students achieving higher order skills is declining." Similarly, in 1985, the report of the Connecticut Assessment of Educational Progress to the Connecticut State Board of Education indicated that although students do well in reading for literal meaning, their performance drops substantially when they are asked to infer, integrate, and evaluate.

There is no question that many teachers and administrators want to improve the thinking of the children in their schools. Although the topic of teaching thinking has received new attention in recent years, none of the psychologists, philosophers, or educators most closely identified with the recent focus on thinking would contend that all of the ideas being put forward are new. Many of these ideas can be found in the writings of Plato, Aristotle, Dewey, William James, Piaget, and Thorndike. Nor is the goal of teaching thinking new. Socrates attempted it—with mixed results, judging by his ultimate fate—and more recently, the National Education Association asserted in a 1961 report that "the purpose which runs through and strengthens all other educational purposes—the common thread of education—is the development of the ability to think." What is new, however, is the fervor that characterizes recent attempts by cognitive psychologists, philosophers, and educators working together to move from the abstract to the concrete, from a theoretical understanding of ideas about teaching thinking to the more practical applications of these ideas to the classroom.

Teaching Thinking Skills: Theory and Practice presents twelve essays on the nature and instruction of thinking. All of the essays are by experts in the field of thinking and its instruction, but these experts represent diverse points of view, in particular, psychology (Bransford, Nickerson, Sternberg), philosophy (Ennis, Lipman, Paul, Swartz) and education (Baron, Perkins, Quellmalz). The book is divided into five main parts. Part I includes two essays (by Ennis and Nickerson) on the foundations of thinking skills and their instruction. Part II contains five essays (two by Perkins and one each by Quellmalz, Swartz, and Paul) on general approaches to the teaching of thinking skills. Part III includes three essays (by Lipman, Bransford and colleagues, and Sternberg) on programmatic approaches to the teaching of thinking skills. Part IV comprises just a single essay (by Baron) on evaluating thinking skills. Part V also contains just a single essay (by Sternberg) that integrates the preceding chapters.

This book is intended for educators, psychologists, philosophers, graduate students, and anyone else interested in the teaching of thinking skills. The book can serve as a main text in courses on teaching thinking and as a supplementary text in courses on thinking, educational psychology, instructional psychology, cognitive foundations of education, and the like. But more important, the book can stand on its own for those who wish to learn about the frontiers in teaching thinking skills. Although all of the essays are grounded in theories of thinking and instruction, they nevertheless deal with the application of these theories to practice. The book focuses jointly and interactively upon theory and practice, showing how theories of thinking can be put to work in classroom instruction.

The preparation of this book was inspired by the presentations made at a conference on thinking skills that took place in March, 1985 at Choate-Rosemary Hall in Wallingford, Connecticut. This conference was a program provided by the Connecticut State Department of Education under the Institute for Teaching and Learning. We are grateful to Gerald N. Tirozzi and Betty J. Sternberg for conceiving the idea of a statewide conference on thinking that would bring together a variety of theoretical and applied approaches. We thank Lorraine M. Aronson, Pascal D. Forgione Jr., Douglas A. Rindone, E. Jean Gubbins, and Mary Weinland for providing the encouragement and support necessary to make this conference a reality. We appreciate the conference planning and coordination of Dee Speese and the RESCUE staff in Litchfield, Connecticut. We thank Kathy Burke and Joyce Kovacs for their secretarial assistance and Grace Cole and Patti Gallucci for aiding in the preparation of conference materials.

As usual, Buck Rogers, psychology acquisitions editor for W. H. Freeman, made all of the steps in arranging publication of the book as easy as they could possibly be. And Georgia Lee Hadler, our editor, provided the highly structured yet flexible production schedule and well-chosen interventions that ensured the timely publication of this book.

And we thank all of those teachers and administrators whose efforts to teach thinking skills to their students have resulted in the kinds of theory, research, and practice that motivated this book.

Joan Boykoff Baron

Robert J. Sternberg

ROBERT J. STERNBERG
Department of Psychology
Yale University

Introduction

The goal of this book is to present a variety of approaches to the theory and practice of teaching thinking skills. To this end, we have assembled a group of contributors to the volume who represent a wide spectrum of approaches to teaching thinking. The chapters written by these contributors are divided into five parts.

I. Foundations of Thinking Skills and Their Instruction

II. General Approaches to the Teaching of Thinking Skills

III. Programmatic Approaches to the Teaching of Thinking Skills

IV. Evaluating the Teaching of Thinking Skills

V. Integration.

In Part I, the contributors discuss the foundations of thinking and its instruction. This part comprises two chapters.

In Chapter 1, "A Taxonomy of Critical Thinking Dispositions and Abilities," Robert Ennis defines critical thinking as "reasonable reflective thinking
that is focused on deciding what to believe or do." Ennis uses the term critical
thinking broadly, and his definition encompasses thinking skills in general.
He has three main goals in his chapter: (1) to present a model of the thinking
process; (2) to characterize the goals for a curriculum designed to teach thinking
skills; and, simultaneously, (3) to characterize the skills underlying thinking.
He divides these skills into two kinds: dispositions, which include attributes
such as seeking a clear statement of the thesis or question, seeking reasons,
and trying to be well informed; and abilities, which include attributes such as
focusing on a question, analyzing arguments, asking and answering questions
of clarification and/or challenge, and the like. Ennis's taxonomy of thinking
skills has greatly influenced teaching and the assessment of thinking and is
presented briefly but thoroughly.

In Chapter 2, "Why Teach Thinking?", Raymond Nickerson deals with
four main questions: (1) Is the teaching of thinking necessary? (2) What constitutes good thinking? (3) Why should we want students to become good
thinkers? and (4) What is the difference between thinking directed *by* goals
and thinking directed *at* goals? In answering the first question, Nickerson
concludes that students do not acquire high-level thinking skills easily or well
on their own or through ordinary instruction and hence would benefit from
the direct teaching of thinking. With respect to the second question, Nickerson,
like Ennis, characterizes attributes of good thinking, including attributes such
as using evidence skillfully and impartially, organizing thoughts and articu-
lating them concisely and coherently, and distinguishing between logically
valid and invalid inferences. Nickerson's list of attributes is shorter than Ennis's, but covers the same ground on a more macroscopic level. With respect
to the third question, Nickerson proposes four reasons for teaching thinking:
(1) to equip students to compete effectively for educational opportunities, jobs,
and recognition and rewards in today's world; (2) to render students better
citizens; (3) to contribute to the students' psychological well-being; and, most
important, (4) to turn students into rational thinkers, something we can ill
afford to ignore these days. Finally, with respect to the fourth question, Nickerson distinguishes between thinking that is directed by goals and thinking
that seeks to establish what one's goals should be.

In Part II, the contributors discuss general approaches to the teaching of
thinking skills that do not require the purchase or use of a prepackaged program
of instruction. Rather, the methods described are ones that teachers can use
to create thinking-skills curricula on their own.

In Chapter 3, "Thinking Frames: An Integrative Perspective on Teaching
Cognitive Skills," Perkins addresses three questions: (1) What constitutes bet-
ter thinking?, (2) By what process can people learn to think better?, and (3)
How can one tell whether a particular approach to teaching thinking is effec-

tive? Perkins addresses the first question by proposing that intelligence consists of three elements: power, tactics, and knowledge. He develops his answers to the second and third questions around this characterization and proposes several major points. First, the power aspect of intelligence will not improve substantially with practice. Second, the tactical repertoire comprises what Perkins refers to as thinking frames, or representations that organize the course of thought toward particular ends. Third, thinking frames vary in their generality and may be concerned with either the processes or the products of thought, the structural or textural features of process or product, and conceptual or other structures. Fourth, thinking frames may vary in their effectiveness. Fifth, there is a tradeoff between the generality of a thinking frame and its power to solve particular problems. Finally, bootstrapping frames can help one acquire larger repertoires of frames for thought.

In Chapter 4, "Knowledge as Design: Teaching Thinking through Content," Perkins continues his analysis of thinking skills by proposing a method for teaching thinking through particular content bases. He calls his method of teaching knowledge by design. The knowledge-by-design framework consists of four basic parts: purpose, structure, model cases, and arguments. Perkins provides a variety of instances of how these four basic parts can be used to teach thinking. For example, he considers something as ordinary as a thumbtack. To expand one's vistas on such a mundane object, one can think about its possible purposes, how its structure contributes to these purposes, what actual exemplars (model cases) of thumbtacks look like, and attributes of thumbtacks that make them useful for particular purposes, such as their price, durability, and the like (arguments). Perkins shows how his knowledge-by-design teaching techniques can be applied in virtually any subject-matter area to expand students' ability to think about the material at hand.

In Chapter 5, "Developing Reasoning Skills," Quellmalz presents a taxonomy of reasoning skills and her HOT (higher-order-thinking) method for teaching them. She suggests that the critical thinking skills proposed by philosophers map rather neatly into problem-solving processes and strategies identified by psychologists and suggests the form this mapping may take. She proposes that the main aspects of higher order thinking are (1) identification of the task or problem type, (2) definition and clarification of essential elements and terms, (3) judgment and connection of relevant information, and (4) evaluation of the adequacy of information and procedures for drawing conclusions and/or solving problems. She shows how these aspects of thinking are used in three subject-matter domains—natural science, social science, and literature—and proposes a process model for how these thinking skills can be combined. Finally, she describes in some detail how her HOT program has been used among young children to attain improvement in their thinking skills.

In Chapter 6, "Teaching for Thinking: A Developmental Model for the Infusion of Thinking Skills into Mainstream Instruction," Swartz describes his eclectic teaching-for-thinking method for infusing thinking skills into mainstream classroom instruction. The program is quite complete, involving both testing and extensive training in a variety of subject-matter areas. In the debate between those who argue for infusion and those who argue for a separate program for teaching thinking skills, Swartz comes out squarely in the former camp and moreover shows in detail just how infusion can be done in a way that reinforces thinking skills throughout the school curriculum.

In Chapter 7, "Dialogical Thinking: Critical Thought Essential to the Acquisition of Rational Knowledge and Passions," Paul elaborates his ideas about the importance of dialogical thinking—or seeing problems and their solutions from different points of view—to a program for teaching thinking skills. Paul notes that many of the problems used as bases for instruction in thinking courses are monological, that is, they can be easily solved within a single frame of reference. But he points out that most real-world problems are not monological but multilogical and that training in monological thinking can actually give students an unrealistic idea regarding what real-world problem solving is like. Paul gives numerous examples of dialogical thinking and how it can be taught in classroom settings.

Part III continues the theme of Part II, but is oriented toward specific, purchasable books and programs for teaching thinking skills. The contributors to this part outline some of the principles underlying their programs and summarize the nature of their respective programs for teaching thinking skills.

In Chapter 8, "Some Thoughts on the Foundations of Reflective Education," Lipman describes the basis and nature of his Philosophy for Children program. The goal of the program is to teach thinking skills by transforming the classroom into a community of inquiry based upon philosophical thinking principles. Lipman's model for how this can be done includes disciplinary and methodological sources of thinking, cognitive skills, mental activity, and dispositions. Although the Philosophy for Children program is conducted separately from typical classroom activity, the principles are applicable across content domains, and in fact different parts of the program actually draw upon different substantive disciplines for the teaching of thinking skills.

In Chapter 9, "Teaching Thinking and Problem Solving," Bransford, Sherwood, and Sturdevant outline the principles of Bransford and Stein's IDEAL Problem Solver program. The acronym IDEAL stands for five steps of the problem-solving process: *i*dentification of problems, *d*efinition of problems, *e*xploration of possible strategies for problem solving, *a*cting on these strategies, and *l*ooking at the effects of these strategies. Each of these steps is described in detail, and examples are given both of how the steps are applied in thinking and how the steps can be taught. This chapter goes beyond just describing the IDEAL program. For example, the authors also discuss the problem of inert knowledge (knowledge that is available to the individual but is not readily accessed from long-term memory) and the problem of teaching thinking across the full school curriculum.

In Chapter 10, "Teaching Intelligence: The Application of Cognitive Psychology to the Improvement of Intellectual Skills," Sternberg begins with a discussion of why intelligence is composed of more than what typical intelligence tests measure. He then describes ten typical fallacies that underlie many training programs for intellectual skills, such as that students should learn to read everything carefully, memorize a lot of new vocabulary, learn the best strategy for solving each problem, get lots of practice on various tests and testlike items, and use all of the information in the problem. Then he describes his program for teaching intellectual skills, *Intelligence Applied*. This program, based on Sternberg's triarchic theory of intelligence, seeks to train students in the basic processing components of higher order thinking, in applying these processes to relatively novel kinds of tasks and situations, in making these processes automatic in certain instances, and in applying the processes to everyday life. The program also includes a discussion of emotional and motivational blocks to the utilization of intellectual skills. Finally, Sternberg discusses some of the strengths and weaknesses of his training program.

Part IV consists of Chapter 11 by Baron, "Evaluating Thinking in the Classroom." Here Baron discusses some principles of evaluation and some of the obstacles to evaluation that can impede successful implementation of these principles. Although her chapter concentrates upon evaluation, it also includes many suggestions that will prove profitable for instruction. Moreover, Baron draws upon the preceding chapters in the book, showing how the principles she proposes relate to the specific ideas and programs presented earlier. The chapter thus provides a useful conclusion to the various contributions that constitute the main substance of the book.

Part V consists of Chapter 12, "Questions and Answers about the Nature and Teaching of Thinking Skills," in which Sternberg argues that, for the most part, the various approaches are compatible and deal with different aspects and methods of teaching thinking skills. Ultimately, the most profitable program of instruction will probably be one that combines the best elements of the various approaches. Major questions about thinking skills are posed and answered in the context of the book chapters.

Teaching Thinking Skills: Theory and Practice provides a comprehensive overview of the major modern viewpoints regarding the theory and practice of teaching thinking skills. The reader who completes the book will have an extensive and complete introduction to current views on this critical topic in education and psychological thought.

Part I

FOUNDATIONS OF THINKING SKILLS AND THEIR INSTRUCTION

ROBERT H. ENNIS
Illinois Critical Thinking Project
University of Illinois

A Taxonomy of Critical Thinking Dispositions and Abilities

In its 1983 pamphlet, *Academic Preparation for College*, the College Board listed reasoning as a basic competency. In *Action for Excellence*, the Task Force on Education for Economic Growth of the Education Commission of the States (1983) did likewise. The Rockefeller Commission on the Humanities (1980) and the Carnegie Foundation's Ernest Boyer (1983) placed heavy emphasis on critical thinking. The California State University system now specifies the study of critical thinking as a requirement for graduation. Statewide testing programs in California, Connecticut, Pennsylvania, and Michigan call for the testing of thinking or critical thinking at various levels in the public schools. The Education Commission of the States included higher order thinking skills as a topic in its large-scale assessment conferences this year and last year. The American Philosophical Association (1985) has urged philosophers to help with attempts to test for critical thinking and include critical thinking in elementary and secondary curricula, and has offered assistance in the coordination of such efforts. And in the elementary and secondary schools we find heavy current emphasis on the upper three levels (analysis, synthesis, and evaluation) of Bloom's taxonomy of educational objectives (1956). These are but a few examples of the attention thinking is receiving in educational circles nowadays.

But are all these people talking about the same thing? Initially this chapter will compare critical thinking with some other approaches to thinking. While there is a good deal of overlap, there are some advantages in focusing on critical thinking as opposed to other approaches. The bulk of the chapter will develop a conception of critical thinking.

"CRITICAL THINKING" DEFINED AND COMPARED

Critical thinking, as I think the term is generally used, is a practical reflective activity that has reasonable belief or action as its goal. There are five key ideas here: *practical, reflective, reasonable, belief,* and *action.* They combine into the following working definition: *Critical thinking is reasonable reflective thinking that is focused on deciding what to believe or do.* Note that this definition does not exclude creative thinking. Formulating hypotheses, alternative ways of viewing a problem, questions, possible solutions, and plans for investigating something are creative acts that come under this definition.

Critical thinking is not equivalent to the higher order thinking skills, in part because that idea is so vague. However, critical thinking, a practical activity, includes most or all of the directly practical higher order thinking skills. Furthermore critical thinking includes dispositions, which would not be included in a listing of skills.

Although too vague to provide the schools and colleges with specific guidance, the concept, *higher order thinking skills*, has performed the important function of reminding us that there is much more cognitive material to be acquired in school than banks of memorized and soon-to-be-forgotten facts. We may also add routine comprehension and application of principles to the set of items that higher order thinking skills are generally supposed to be higher than— that is, the set of skills that we are implicitly urged to go beyond in framing a curriculum that does justice to the full range of cognitive possibilities of students.

Perhaps you have noticed that I have just mentioned the lower three levels of Bloom's taxonomy: recall (which is misleadingly called *knowledge*), comprehension, and application. A principal function of Bloom's taxonomy, like that of the concept, *higher order thinking skills,* is to remind us that there is much more that the schools could be doing than promoting recall, routine comprehension, and application. Actually, in the minds of many educators, Bloom's top three levels (analysis, synthesis, and evaluation) *are* the higher order thinking skills, though some educators might supplement the top three levels with nonroutine practice of the next two lower levels, comprehension and application.

These upper levels of Bloom's taxonomy are one possible conceptualization of higher order thinking. But it provides too little guidance if its top three (or top five) levels are taken as the set of higher order thinking goals for the schools. First, the concepts are too vague as they stand. Take the concept *analysis*, for instance. Analysis of a chemical compound, analysis of an argument, analysis of one's opponent's weaknesses in a basketball game, analysis of a word, and analysis of the political situation in South Africa seem like such different activities that we must wonder just what in particular one is supposed to teach under the label "analysis."

Second, as one might expect from the first difficulty, the taxonomy is not accompanied by criteria for judging whether the activity is being conducted correctly. To teach higher order thinking skills one needs criteria for making such judgments.

Although there are other objections to using the Bloom taxonomy (see Ennis, 1981b; Furst, 1981; Nelson, 1981; and Seddon, 1978), I shall stop with these two. They at least establish legitimate doubts about the usefulness of Bloom's taxonomy as a detailed approach to higher order thinking skills. But do realize that Bloom only offered it as a set of types of objectives, not as a list of educational objectives.

"Critical thinking" seems to me to be a more appropriate label than "reasoning" for the items listed under "reasoning" by the College Board and the task force of the Education Commission of the States. For this reason and for the sake of simplicity, I shall henceforth use the term *critical thinking*.

"Informal logic," the name of a course often taught in philosophy departments to respond to the interest in learning to think better, seems also to cover the same basic ideas as "critical thinking." However, the name "informal logic" suggests that the content be offered in a separate course, or as part of a course, rather than infused in other subject matter areas. The label "critical thinking" has no such limitation. It can be used as the name of a separate course and the name of the thinking emphasis that one should find infused in other subject matter courses.

The process of reflectively and reasonably deciding what to believe or do can be broken down into a set of critical thinking dispositions, three basic areas of critical thinking ability, and an area of strategical and tactical ability in employing critical thinking. These dispositions and abilities are the fundamental elements in Table 1-1, entitled "Goals for a Critical Thinking/Reasoning Curriculum." (See Ennis, 1969, 1980, and 1981a for more interpretation of this outline than is possible here. But be warned that in those publications, I tried to impose a definition of critical thinking that is narrower than that which I am now employing. The current definition includes creative elements. The narrower one tried to exclude them. I abandoned the narrower one because, although it provides more elegance in theorizing, it does not seem to be in accord with current usage.)

The abilities in this outline are listed in an order in which they might appear in a critical thinking course at the college level. To incorporate them into the

Table 1-1 Goals for a Critical Thinking/Reasoning Curriculum

I. Working definition: *Critical thinking* is reasonable reflective thinking that is focused on deciding what to believe or do.

II. Critical thinking so defined involves both dispositions and abilities:
   A. Dispositions
      1. Seek a clear statement of the thesis or question
      2. Seek reasons
      3. Try to be well informed
      4. Use and mention credible sources
      5. Take into account the total situation
      6. Try to remain relevant to the main point
      7. Keep in mind the original and/or basic concern
      8. Look for alternatives
      9. Be open-minded
         a) Consider seriously other points of view than one's own (dialogical thinking)
         b) Reason from premises with which one disagrees—without letting the disagreement interfere with one's reasoning (suppositional thinking)
         c) Withhold judgment when the evidence and reasons are insufficient
      10. Take a position (and change a position) when the evidence and reasons are sufficient to do so
      11. Seek as much precision as the subject permits
      12. Deal in an orderly manner with the parts of a complex whole
      13. Use one's critical thinking abilities
      14. Be sensitive to the feelings, level of knowledge, and degree of sophistication of others
   B. Abilities
      1. Focusing on a question
         a) Identifying or formulating a question
         b) Identifying or formulating criteria for judging possible answers
         c) Keeping the situation in mind
      2. Analyzing arguments
         a) Identifying conclusions
         b) Identifying stated reasons
         c) Identifying unstated reasons
         d) Seeing similarities and differences
         e) Identifying and handling irrelevance
         f) Seeing the structure of an argument
         g) Summarizing
      3. Asking and answering questions of clarification and/or challenge, for example:
         a) Why?
         b) What is your main point?
         c) What do you mean by "_____"?
         d) What would be an example?
         e) What would not be an example (though close to being one)?
         f) How does that apply to this case (describe a counterexample)?
         g) What difference does it make?

Elementary clarification

Table 1-1 (*continued*)

h) What are the facts?

i) Is this what you are saying: "_____"?

j) Would you say some more about that?

4. Judging the credibility of a source
   a) Expertise
   b) Lack of conflict of interest
   c) Agreement among sources
   d) Reputation
   e) Use of established procedures
   f) Known risk to reputation
   g) Ability to give reasons
   h) Careful habits

5. Observing and judging observation reports; criteria:
   a) Minimal inferring involved
   b) Short time interval between observation and report
   c) Report by observer, rather than someone else (i.e., not hearsay)
   d) Records are generally desirable; if report is based on a record, it is generally best that
      1) The record was close in time to the observation
      2) The record was made by the observer
      3) The record was made by the reporter
      4) The statement was believed by the reporter, either because of a prior belief in its correctness or because of a belief that the observer was habitually correct
   e) Corroboration
   f) Possibility of corroboration
   g) Conditions of good access
   h) Competent employment of technology, if technology is useful
   i) Satisfaction by observer (and reporter, if a different person) of credibility criteria (item B4)

6. Deducing and judging deductions
   a) Class logic
   b) Conditional logic
   c) Interpretation of statements
      1) Double negation
      2) Necessary and sufficient conditions
      3) Other logical words and phrases: *only, if and only if, or, some, unless, not, not both,* etc.

7. Inducing and judging inductions
   a) Generalizing
      1) Typicality of data
      2) Limitation of coverage
      3) Sampling
   b) Inferring explanatory conclusions and hypotheses
      1) Types of explanatory conclusions and hypotheses
         a) Causal claims
         b) Claims about the beliefs and attitudes of people
         c) Interpretations of authors' intended meanings
         d) Historical claims that certain things happened
         e) Reported definitions
         f) Claims that something is an unstated reason or unstated conclusion

Basic support

Inference

Table 1-1 (*continued*)

- 2) Investigating
  - a) Designing experiments, including planning to control variables
  - b) Seeking evidence and counterevidence
  - c) Seeking other possible explanations
- 3) Criteria: Given reasonable assumptions
  - a) The proposed conclusion would explain the evidence (essential)
  - b) The proposed conclusion is consistent with known facts (essential)
  - c) Competitive alternative conclusions are inconsistent with known facts (essential)
  - d) The proposed conclusion seems plausible (desirable)
- 8. Making value judgments
  - a) Background facts
  - b) Consequences
  - c) Prima facie application of acceptable principles
  - d) Considering alternatives
  - e) Balancing, weighing, and deciding
- 9. Defining terms, and judging definitions in three dimensions
  - a) Form
    - 1) Synonym
    - 2) Classification
    - 3) Range
    - 4) Equivalent expression
    - 5) Operational
    - 6) Example–nonexample
  - b) Definitional strategy
    - 1) Acts
      - a) Report a meaning (reported definition)
      - b) Stipulate a meaning (stipulative definition)
      - c) Express a position on an issue (positional, including programmatic and persuasive definition)
    - 2) Identifying and handling equivocation
      - a) Attention to the context
      - b) Possible types of response
        - i) The simplest response: "The definition is just wrong."
        - ii) Reduction to absurdity: "According to that definition, there is an outlandish result."
        - iii) Considering alternative interpretations: "On this interpretation, there is this problem; on that interpretation, there is that problem."
        - iv) Establishing that there are two meanings of key term and a shift in meaning from one to the other
        - v) Swallowing the idiosyncratic definition
  - c) Content
- 10. Identifying assumptions
  - a) Unstated reasons
  - b) Needed assumptions; argument reconstruction

Advanced clarification

Table 1-1 (*continued*)

Strategy and tactics

11. Deciding on an action
   a) Define the problem
   b) Select criteria to judge possible solutions
   c) Formulate alternative solutions
   d) Tentatively decide what to do
   e) Review, taking into account the total situation, and decide
   f) Monitor the implementation
12. Interacting with others
   a) Employing and reacting to fallacy labels, including

1) Circularity	12) Conversion
2) Appeal to authority	13) Begging the question
3) Bandwagon	14) Either—or
4) Glittering term	15) Vagueness
5) Name calling	16) Equivocation
6) Slippery slope	17) Straw person
7) Post hoc	18) Appeal to tradition
8) Non sequitur	19) Argument from analogy
9) Ad hominem	20) Hypothetical question
10) Affirming the consequent	21) Oversimplification
11) Denying the antecedent	22) Irrelevance

   b) Logical strategies
   c) Rhetorical strategies
   d) Argumentation; Presenting a position, oral or written
      1) Aiming at a particular audience and keeping it in mind
      2) Organizing (common type: main point; clarification; reasons; alternatives; attempt to rebut prospective challenges; summary, including repeat of main point)

This is only an overall content outline. It does not incorporate suggestions for level, sequence, repetition in greater depth, emphasis, or infusion in subject matter area (which might be either exclusive or overlapping).

total curriculum of an elementary, secondary, or higher education system, we would probably have to foster these abilities several times at various levels of difficulty and in various subject areas in spiral curriculum fashion. The dispositions would be introduced when students are ready and would be continuously emphasized thereafter (see Ennis, 1985, for a discussion of the concepts of transfer, domain, and subject specificity associated with these curriculum ideas).

I have presented this prospective school curriculum organization vaguely, partly because there are various ways it could be done successfully and partly because much research and development is yet to be done. But it is at least clear that necessary elements include (1) *teachers* accomplished in critical thinking and their teaching areas who have time to explore new teaching ideas, (2) *materials* that the teachers can use for teaching (many materials are already at hand), (3) *administrators* sympathetic to the teaching of critical thinking, (4) the development of several different *pilot curricula* to be tried out in different school systems, (5) careful continual *evaluation* and recording of what occurs, and (6) *dissemination* of information about successful and unsuccessful efforts.

CRITICAL THINKING DISPOSITIONS

The first thirteen listed dispositions are essential for the critical thinker. The fourteenth disposition, to be sensitive to others, although not strictly speaking constitutive of critical thinking, is important for any critical thinker. Without it, critical thinking often comes to naught.

CRITICAL THINKING ABILITIES

The basic areas of critical thinking ability are *clarity, basis, inference,* and *interaction.* They are depicted in Figure 1-1, together with critical thinking dispositions.

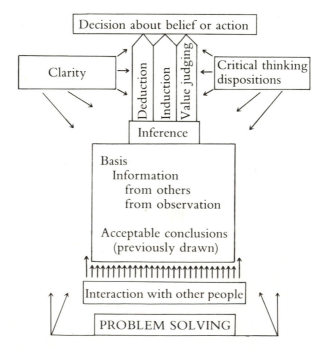

Figure 1-1 Constituents of critical thinking—in context (Robert H. Ennis, Illinois Critical Thinking Project).

These basic areas make intuitive sense. We want to be clear about what is going on. We want to have a reasonable basis for a judgment. We want the resultant inferring to be reasonable. We want the interaction with other people to be sensible. And we want those dispositions to be operative.

Let us now consider the four basic areas of ability in more detail. The following examples should help clarify this approach, perhaps on occasion challenge you, and support the point that there are many areas calling for critical thinking that are not subjects people are likely to have studied in school, thus requiring that we teach for transfer and that our efforts in school not be judged to have succeeded unless critical thinking instruction transfers to areas of practical concern.

I will use my experience as a juror serving on a murder trial to illustrate my contentions. Obviously there was no subject that I studied in school called *juries* or *killing*. Serving as a juror is an activity to which we want our critical thinking instruction to transfer.

We had to judge the credibility of witnesses; interpret a complicated set of criteria for murder and voluntary manslaughter; draw conclusions about the intentions, beliefs, and veracity of the defendant; and make a judgment about how the victim might have been stabbed. These are problems that were not covered in my school subjects, although I do not mean to imply that there is no room for critical thinking in school curricula. There is a leading place for it in all school subjects though this place is often neglected. In our school subjects we must not only teach students to think critically in each subject, but we must also teach for transfer to basic thinking tasks in life.

In what follows, I shall not exemplify every ability or criterion, but shall just provide a sampling to whet your appetite. The subject, critical thinking, is not fully covered in a one–semester college course; nor can this chapter cover it in detail.

Clarity

Because it involves a wide range of abilities, some of which are considerably more sophisticated than others, I have divided clarification into an elementary group (composed of the first three abilities) and an advanced group (the ninth and tenth abilities, which are dealt with later in this chapter).

Focusing

The first principle of clarification is *focusing on a question*. It includes identifying a problem, hypothesis, or thesis. When we are thinking critically about an hypothesis or thesis, a question is implied: Is the hypothesis (or thesis) acceptable?

In the jury trial, we focused on two questions: Did the defendant commit murder? Did she commit voluntary manslaughter? We first considered the proposition that the defendant committed murder. Usually a focus can be expressed as a proposition that is under consideration, but always in the form of a question. In any case, it is difficult to get anywhere or to know what is relevant without a focus.

Analyzing Arguments

A second sort of clarifying ability applies to any arguments offered in support of a proposition or an answer to a question. This second ability, *Analyzing arguments*, is actually a composite of many interrelated abilities, all of which can sometimes be quite difficult to apply. In my jury experience, we had to identify the conclusions of the defense and prosecuting attorneys, and of each other, in our arguments about whether the various criteria for murder were satisfied. (Note the overlap with focusing on a question. This is not an elegant list; it is a practical list.) We had to be clear about what reasons were offered and sometimes had to identify reasons that were not explicitly stated. We had to recognize as irrelevant a suggestion that one of the jurors made that the victim's body had been moved, and we had to see the structure of the prosecutor's total argument. The structure was suggested by a set of criteria for murder with which we were supplied. We had to see how those criteria fit together and how the prosecutor supported each one of the necessary conditions for a verdict of murder.

Here are the criteria with which we had to work:

To sustain the charge of murder, the State must prove the following propositions:

First: That the Defendant performed the acts which caused the death of the Victim, and

Second: That when the Defendant did so she intended to kill or do great bodily harm to the Victim, or she knew that her acts would cause death or great bodily harm to the Victim, or she knew that her acts created a strong probability of death or great bodily harm to the Victim, and

Third: That the Defendant was not justified in using the force which she used.

If you find from your consideration of all the evidence that each of these propositions has been proved beyond a reasonable doubt, then you should find the Defendant guilty.

If, on the other hand, you find from your consideration of all the evidence that any of these propositions has not been proved beyond a reasonable doubt, then you should find the Defendant not guilty.

These criteria make a complex whole. First of all each of the three major conditions is necessary for a verdict of guilty. This fact follows from the general direction, "If any of these propositions has not been proved beyond a reasonable doubt. . . ." Furthermore, the three are jointly sufficient for a verdict of murder, a fact that follows from the general direction, "If all have been proved beyond a reasonable doubt. . . ." The second condition is itself composed of six conditions, any of which is sufficient for the second major condition, but at least one of which is necessary for the satisfaction of that second major condition.

Those relationships were an essential part of the structure of the prosecutor's total argument. Furthermore, each attempted proof of each of the three major conditions had its structure. If we did not see how everything fit together, we could not have decided how to vote.

This example is more complex than we would use with elementary- or middle-school students, but it indicates a goal that we should have. We want our students to be able to handle such complex arguments by the time they are through school and are eligible to serve on juries.

Asking Questions

A third sort of clarifying ability—*asking appropriate clarifying questions*—is obviously an important critical thinking ability. One example: A juror asked, "What do you mean by 'proved beyond a reasonable doubt'?" Another: "Why do you think that she is guilty?"

Basis

Support for one's inferences come from three sources: statements made by others, observations, and inferences that one has made previously. Because inference is also a separate topic, I shall focus here on the first two sources.

Judging Credibility

Since a large share of what we come to believe has other people as its source, *the ability to judge the credibility of a source* is crucial. It is also an ability that can be fostered in elementary school (Schroeder, 1985), though, as with all of these abilities, there are sophisticated applications that are well beyond elementary-school students.

In the trial, we had to judge the credibility of the defendant when she claimed that the victim threatened to kill her, as well as the credibility of the pathologist, the detectives, and the policemen who testified. The credibility of witnesses is an overwhelming concern in the courtroom. Such criteria as expertise, lack of conflict of interest, reputation, and the use of established procedures are repeatedly employed. For example, the policemen testifying were asked by the defense attorney whether they were friends of the victim. To have been friends would have constituted a conflict of interest and would have been grounds for impugning their testimony.

Observing

Observation was also significant in the murder trial. We jurors were given the opportunity to visit the scene of the killing and were expected to observe the general layout of the house. The layout was crucial in understanding whether the defendant could have swung the knife at the victim the way she claimed and helpful in understanding how the events progressed that fateful evening.

The emphasis on records of observation was evident in the court's procedures because of the notorious unreliability of memories. The detective read from notes he took when he visited the scene, thus countering in advance a challenge based upon the fallibility of memory. This use of records is a significant criterion.

Inference

According to one rough categorizing scheme there are three somewhat overlapping and interdependent kinds of inference: deductive inference, inductive inference, and inference to value judgments.

Deducing

Deducing and judging deductions is sometimes underemphasized, in reaction to the overemphasis it has often received in the past. I mean to include its practical aspects, omitting the elegant systematization and symbolization procedures that abound in deductive logic courses (see Ennis, 1981c, for elaboration). Basically, deduction is concerned with whether something follows necessarily from something else. There are many ways in which this relationship plays a role in the other aspects of critical thinking. One example was in our judging whether the defendant had committed murder. Because we decided that no one of the six conditions in the second necessary condition was satisfied, it followed necessarily that we were to judge the defendant not guilty.

The role and interpretation of negation and multiple negation are aspects of deductive logic. Negation played a double role in a complex proposition offered by one juror: "The State has not proved beyond a reasonable doubt that she was not justified in using the force that she used." Dropping both negations here to simplify his statement would have been a serious error (resulting in his allegedly claiming that the State had proved beyond a reasonable doubt that she was justified in using the force that she used). A mechanical application of the rule, "Two negatives make a positive," might have produced such a result. One of the other jurors in effect did offer that mistaken simplification as an interpretation of the first juror's statement. Some sophistication in dealing with negation was needed.

Inducing

Inductive inference includes generalizing and inferring to hypotheses that are supposed to explain the facts. While the jurors were concerned with that specific case, we nonetheless employed many generalizations. The prohibition against hearsay evidence that was prominent in the trial is at least in part based upon a generalization: hearsay is often unreliable.

We use generalizations all the time. Here are two that I have often heard: "Cancer is associated with smoking," "Important things happen in groups of three." I am not endorsing either of these generalizations, but offer them to emphasize their importance in our lives and the importance of thinking critically in arriving at and assessing them.

The other type of inductive inference is inference to hypotheses that are supposed to explain the facts ("best-explanation inference"). The pathologist in the trial stated that the knife blow was only moderate in force. Part of her argument for this conclusion was that it *explained* why the depth of the wound was only $2\frac{1}{2}$ inches. Furthermore, there were no known facts that were inconsistent with the hypothesis. In addition, the alternative hypotheses were inconsistent with the facts. For example, the hypothesis that the blow was severe was inconsistent with the fact that the depth was only $2\frac{1}{2}$ inches together with the fact that there were no marks on the chest bones. If the blow had been severe, then the depth would have been more than $2\frac{1}{2}$ inches, since there were no marks on the chest bones. (Note the use of deduction in the rejection of this alternative hypothesis.) Last, the proposed conclusion was plausible. Thus, the four criteria for best-explanation inference (7b3 in Table 1–1) seemed to be satisfied.

In this example I have emphasized a critical thinking situation that we have not studied in school. But I do not wish to demean background knowledge of the area in which the critical thinking occurs. For example, it took an expert, the pathologist, to determine how difficult it is to slice through $2\frac{1}{2}$ inches of human flesh, an assessment with which the jurors had no experience. And the pathologist was better able than we to decide whether the conclusion was, on the whole, plausible. That sort of judgment requires experience and knowledge of a specific area.

Background knowledge is absolutely essential for critical thinking. The jurors had a great deal of the background knowledge that was required in the trial from dealing with all sorts of people in all sorts of situations in our daily lives. But we needed the expert's knowledge about knife wounds. So there we had to combine the criteria for credibility and the criteria for best-explanation inference.

The importance of background knowledge suggests that we cannot expect someone who is ignorant in a field to be good at making and judging best-explanation inferences. Background knowledge (often the subject matter we teach in school) is crucial. Thus critical thinking has both general and topic-specific components. Critical thinking principles and criteria are general; much of the background knowledge needed to apply them is specific to the topic (see Ennis, 1985, for a discussion of this relationship and its bearing on curriculum).

Inference to explanatory hypotheses can be quite simple in content. Consider, for example, an episode from "Sesame Street." Someone stole Bert's cookies. A witness reported that the thief had ears, hair, a nose, and a sweater that looked like Ernie's. The hypothesis that Ernie was the thief explained this evidence and Bert concluded that Ernie was the thief. But there was an alternative hypothesis that explained these facts. This alternative was that Cookie Monster disguised himself as Ernie and stole the cookies. This alternative was supported by Ernie's claim of innocence and the subsequent appearance of Cookie Monster stealing other cookies while disguised as Ernie.

You can see the role of the criteria for best-explanation inference here. The conclusion must explain the facts and not be inconsistent with any facts, there must be no plausible alternative explanations, and the conclusion should be plausible.

I am tempted to cite a number of examples from academic subjects, including an interpretation of Shakespeare's Iago in *Othello*, the charge that Napoleon's death was from arsenic poisoning rather than cancer, and Redi's experiments dealing with the allegedly spontaneous generation of maggots in meat. And I have one from the column of my favorite counselor, Dear Abby. These examples show the wide applicability of best-explanation thinking, but to conserve space I have not included them. I invite you to consider some hypothesis or thesis from a field of topic you know well and apply the four best-explanation criteria to it.

Making Value Judgments

The last of the three basic types of inference is *making value judgments*. One example of a value judgment that we employed in the trial was that a person in such circumstances should leave the scene, as she was able to do, rather than respond with violence. We employed this judgment in deciding that the third criterion for murder was satisfied—that she was not justified in using the force that she used.

Advanced Clarification

Defining Terms

A key aspect of advanced clarification is defining terms. The definition of "proved beyond a reasonable doubt" was a crucial topic in our deliberation. We disagreed about whether the State had proved beyond a reasonable doubt that the defendant was not justified in using the force that she used (the third criterion for murder and the fourth for voluntary manslaughter). Some jurors wondered what "proved beyond a reasonable doubt" means. We sent out to the judge to help us with this question, but his reply after a half-hour wait was that there is no definition of this phrase and that we should do the best that we can.

Because discussion was about to collapse, I suggested a definition that enabled us to carry on. With improvements that I have since added, mine went something like this: "To prove a proposition beyond a reasonable doubt is to offer enough evidence in its support that it would not make good sense to deny that proposition." This definition was not startling, but it was accepted by my fellow jurors, and we were able to continue the discussion.

There is much more to say about aspects of that definition episode, concerning at least the form of definition that I used, the kind of definitional act that I was performing, and the equivocation that I believe I avoided. But for now, I only want to make the point that definition was crucial in that jury's deliberations, as it is in many cases.

Identifying Assumptions

The jurors employed *assumption identification* (see Ennis, 1982, for elaboration) in examining each other's arguments. For example, one juror (who was holding that the defendant might have been justified) correctly identified another's assumption: "You're assuming that I have to prove that she was defending herself against attack. Rather, the State has to prove that she was not."

One assumption that we made and that we did not identify at the time was the value judgment I mentioned: A person in such circumstances should leave the scene, if possible, rather than respond with violence. Some people to whom I have since told this story have challenged this assumption. They believe a woman threatened with violence by a man should respond with violence, if she can, even if she is able to escape. Our verdict that she was guilty of voluntary manslaughter, then, rested on a debatable assumption.

Deciding on an Action: Problem Solving

Up to this point, we have focused on acquiring reasonable beliefs. Reasonable beliefs are sometimes valuable in their own right and sometimes valuable for the role they play in reaching reasonable decisions about what to do. So all of the previous material should be assumed to be relevant to *deciding on an action*. Voting that the defendant was not guilty of murder (but was guilty of voluntary manslaughter), and asking for a definition of "proof beyond a reasonable doubt" were actions the jurors took as a group.

Another way to organize an approach to critical thinking is in accord with the elements in the process of problem solving (11a–e in Table 1-1). Unfortunately, problem-solving approaches tend not to be concerned with criteria for making judgments—with how to tell whether the result of the thinking process is adequate. But their emphasis on the steps involved in the thinking process is valuable, so they are included as a way of organizing my approach to deciding on an action. By incorporating the material and criteria relevant to decisions about belief, I have added what amounts to an explicit concern with whether the problem solution is adequate.

Interacting with Others

Interacting with others in discussions, presentations, debates, and written pieces is crucial for critical thinkers. We jurors had to interact with each other, lay out arguments, and summarize positions. This all requirerd the practical application of the three constitutive areas of critical thinking ability: clarity, basis, and inference.

Employing Fallacy Labels

Knowing how to use and react to fallacy labels (e.g., circularity, appeal to authority, band wagon, etc.) is often helpful in dealing with other people though I will not discuss all the labels listed in Table 1-1. The labels serve as a quick way of communicating one's concern to others who know the meaning of the labels (though the application still requires defense). It is helpful to know the meaning of these labels, so that one is not intimidated in discussion by someone like William Buckley saying, in a manner I cannot imitate, "That's a *non sequitur*," which only means that the conclusion does not follow. The danger with fallacy labels is that they can be and are misused, because applying them with discretion is difficult and requires more than just knowing what they mean. For example, knowing that someone is appealing to an authority does not by itself entitle one to conclude that the appeal is fallacious. Much of our knowledge comes from authorities.

The field of critical thinking is sometimes organized in terms of fallacy labels (e.g., Johnson & Blair, 1983). I have not used this approach because some basic principles and criteria tend to be neglected by it, and because in practice there is so much danger of students' acquiring a superficial knowledge and labeling things fallacies that are not fallacies—legitimate appeals to authority, for example.

Interdependence

The abilities I have presented are, in practice, *interdependent*. They were presented separately for purposes of discussion and teaching. The actual practice of critical thinking (as exemplified by my jury experience) requires us to combine these abilities and to employ them in conjunction with the critical thinking dispositions and knowledge of the topic.

The Role of Dispositions

Critical thinking ability is not enough. One must have these critical thinking dispositions as well. The need for critical thinking dispositions was apparent in the jury situation, as well as in other situations. The jurors needed to and did seek a clear statement of issues ("What does 'proved beyond a reasonable doubt' mean?") and reasons ("Why do you think that she was not justified in using the force that she used?") and tried to be well informed (We even wanted to ask questions of the defendant, something that was prohibited by the court). But we did not always exhibit the dispositions. For example, not all the jurors thought that it was important to seek each other's reasons, and not all were open-minded all the time. Some did not try to see things from the point of view of the juror who wondered whether the State had proved beyond a reasonable doubt that the defendant was not justified in using the force that she used.

SUMMARY AND COMMENT

I have compared critical thinking with some other approaches: higher order thinking skills, Bloom's taxonomy of educational objectives, reasoning, informal logic, problem solving, and fallacies. Although all have value, critical thinking seems to be a better basis for an overall curriculum effort.

The jury example that I have presented has idiosyncracies. It is not representative in all respects of all critical thinking situations. But this example does show a socially significant activity that requires most of the components in this conception of critical thinking—and in a context that is not school subject matter. Let us work toward the goal of transferring our critical thinking instruction in and out of school subject matter to such contexts.

The significant features of this conception of critical thinking are

focusing on belief and action,

making statements in terms of things that people actually do or should do,

including criteria to help us evaluate results,

including both dispositions and abilities, and

being organized in such a way that it can form the basis for a thinking-across-the-curriculum program as well as a separate critical thinking course at the college level.

Its clarity and criteria make it superior to the Bloom taxonomy as an elaboration of higher order thinking and make it a necessary complement to most problem-solving approaches. It is directly applicable to our daily lives. Last, it is intended to be comprehensive. If it succeeds in being comprehensive, fine. If not, at least we have a basis for telling whether something has been left out, enabling us to better evaluate the conception and to improve upon it.

The outline presented here does not tell us how and when to teach what; it is only a first step in the development of a total curriculum. Much exploratory work needs to be done in that direction. But if we do not have an idea of where we want to go, we cannot know in which direction to take our first steps.

REFERENCES

The American Philosophical Association (1985). Board of officers statement on critical thinking. *Proceedings and addresses of the American Philosophical Association*, 58:484.

Bloom, B. S. (Ed.) (1956). *Taxonomy of educational objectives*. New York: Longmans.

Boyer, E. L. (1983). *High school*. New York: Harper & Row.

College Board (1983). *Academic preparation for college.* New York: College Entrance
    Examination Board.
Commission on the Humanities (1980). *The humanities in American life.* Berkeley, Calif.:
    University of California Press.
Ennis, R. H. (1969). *Logic in teaching.* Englewood Cliffs, N.J.: Prentice-Hall.
Ennis, R. H. (1980). A conception of rational thinking. In Jerrold Coombs (Ed.),
    Philosophy of education 1979. Bloomington, Ill.: Philosophy of Education Society.
Ennis, R. H. (1981a). Rational thinking and educational practice. In Jonas Soltis (Ed.),
    Philosophy and education (Volume 1 of the eightieth yearbook of the National Society
    for the Study of Education). Chicago: NSSE.
Ennis, R. H. (1981b). Eight fallacies in Bloom's taxonomy. In C. J. B. Macmillan
    (Ed.), *Philosophy of education 1980.* Bloomington, Ill.: Philosophy of Education
    Society.
Ennis, R. H. (1981c). A conception of deductive logic competence. *Teaching Philosophy,*
    4:337–385.
Ennis, R. H. (1982). Identifying implicit assumptions. *Synthese,* 51:61–86.
Ennis, R. H. (1985). Critical thinking and the curriculum. *National Forum,* 65:28–31.
Furst, E. J. (1981). Bloom's taxonomy of educational objectives for the cognitive do-
    main: Philosophical and educational issues. *Review of Educational Research,* 51:441–
    453.
Johnson, R. H., & Blair, J. H. (1983). *Logical self-defense.* Toronto: McGraw-Hill
    Ryerson.
Nelson, B. K. (1981). Hierarchy, utility, and fallacy in Bloom's taxonomy. In C. J.
    B. Macmillan (Ed.), *Philosophy of education 1980.* Bloomington, Ill.: Philosophy
    of Education Society.
Seddon, G. M. (1978). The properties of Bloom's taxonomy of educational objectives
    for the cognitive domain. *Review of Educational Research,* 48:303–323.
Schroeder, F. (1985). Unpublished personal communication.
Task Force on Education for Economic Growth of the Education Commission of the
    States (1983). *Action for excellence.* Denver, Colo.: Education Commission of the
    States.

Versions of this essay have been presented to three critical thinking workshops of the Community College Humanities Association Conference on Critical Thinking sponsored by Sonoma State University; the Connecticut Thinking Skills Conference sponsored by the State
of Connecticut; the Conference on Higher Order Thinking Skills sponsored by The Psychological Corporation; the Faculty Colloquium Series sponsored by the Department of
Educational Policy Studies of The University of Illinois; the Conference on Critical Thinking
sponsored by Christopher Newport College; the Curriculum Enhancement Workshop in
Philosophy sponsored by the State of New Jersey; and the annual meeting of the American
Federation of Teachers on July 11, 1985 in Washington, D.C. I am indebted to many participants in these conferences for their helpful suggestions.

RAYMOND S. NICKERSON

BBN Laboratories Inc.

Why Teach Thinking?

Most of the discussion about teaching thinking has focused on the question of *how*—How can thinking be taught?—and much discussion has centered on the relative merits of the various answers that have been proposed. In a sense, every program that has been developed to enhance thinking skills is somebody's answer to this question.

But the question of *why*, despite the fact that it logically precedes the question of how, has not received nearly as much attention. Perhaps the reason it has not received more emphasis is that the answer is considered to be obvious. Why teach thinking? Because everyone should know how to think and evidence indicates that many people do not, so it is the responsibility of the educational system to do something about it. Is there more to it than that?

I believe there is more to it than that. The answer is not self-evident and reflection on the question forces attention to some assumptions, matters of definition, and philosophical issues that deserve to be discussed.

IS IT NECESSARY TO TEACH THINKING?

One major assumption underlying interest in teaching thinking is that there is a need for such teaching. Is there any evidence that this assumption is correct? Surely, with or without special training, everyone thinks. We cannot make a similar claim about "doing" physics, chemistry, or mathematics, or even about reading and writing. One must be taught these things.

Not so with thinking. I mean to suggest by that assertion more than that our minds must have some content and that we cannot, at least for long, keep them blank. All of us compare, classify, order, estimate, extrapolate, interpolate, form hypoptheses, weigh evidence, draw conclusions, devise arguments, judge relevance, use analogies, and engage in numerous activities that are typically classified as thinking. This is not to say that we always do these things perfectly, or even that we typically do them all very well, but that we do them with or without prodding and the benefit of formal training. Descartes' famous dictum, "I think, therefore I am" might well have been turned on its head to "I am, therefore I think." If thinking is not a consequence of being, it is certainly a consequence of being human. We are wired to think, and we can no more avoid doing so than we can avoid breathing.

However, most of us who talk about teaching thinking would probably agree that what we need to teach, and to learn, for that matter, is not how to think in an absolute sense, but how to think more effectively—more critically, more coherently, more creatively, more deeply—than we often, perhaps typically, do. To be sure, all people classify, but not equally perceptively; all people make estimates, but not equally accurately; all people use analogies, but not equally appropriately; all people draw conclusions, but not with equal care; all people construct arguments, but not with equal cogency.

The fact that we think spontaneously does not prevent us from succumbing to the stratagems of hucksters and demagogues; nor does it ensure the consistent rationality of our behavior. Indeed, the list of documented ways in which our reasoning commonly goes astray is a long one (Nickerson, Perkins & Smith, 1985; Nisbett & Ross, 1980; Tversky & Kahneman, 1974). What is especially troublesome is our apparently pervasive proclivity to bias our interpretation of evidence in favor of our own preferences and preestablished conclusions.

Moreover, there is little evidence that students acquire good thinking skills simply as a consequence of studying conventional course materials. Although domain-specific knowledge is essential to good thinking within a domain, it is not sufficient to assure that good thinking will occur. As Glaser (1985) puts it:

> A student does not tend "naturally" to develop a general disposition to consider thoughtfully the subjects and problems that come within the range of his or her experience; nor is he or she likely to acquire knowledge of the methods of logical inquiry and reasoning and skill in applying these methods, simply as a result of

having studied this subject or that. There is little evidence that students acquire skill in critical thinking as a necessary byproduct of the study of any given subject. (p. 27)

In other words, if students are to acquire good thinking skills in the classroom, explicit attention will have to be given to that objective; it is not likely to be realized spontaneously or as an incidental consequence of attempts to accomplish other goals.

WHAT CONSTITUTES GOOD THINKING?

If one accepts this view, the problem becomes that of being sufficiently explicit about what constitutes good thinking to determine whether any changes that are effected through educational efforts are in fact changes for the better. I use the vague term *good* in preference to the various other familiar qualifiers—critical, creative, reflective, effective, dialectical—because it connotes something desirable without predisposing us to focus on some types of thinking and ignore others. But what do we mean—what should we mean—by good thinking?

My stereotype of a good thinker can be characterized in terms of knowledge, abilities, attitudes, and habitual ways of behaving. Here are some of the characteristics that would be on my list:

uses evidence skillfully and impartially;

organizes thoughts and articulates them concisely and coherently;

distinguishes between logically valid and invalid inferences;

suspends judgment in the absence of sufficient evidence to support a decision;

understands the difference between reasoning and rationalizing;

attempts to anticipate the probable consequences of alternative actions before choosing among them;

understands the idea of degrees of belief;

has a sense of the value and cost of information, knows how to seek information, and does so when it makes sense;

sees similarities and analogies that are not superficially apparent;

can learn independently and, at least equally importantly, has an abiding interest in doing so;

applies problem-solving techniques appropriately in domains other than those in which they were learned;

can structure informally represented problems in such a way that formal techniques (e.g., mathematics) can be used to solve them;

listens carefully to other people's ideas;

understands the difference between winning an argument and being right;

recognizes that most real-world problems have more than one possible solution and that those solutions may differ in numerous respects and may be difficult to compare in terms of a single figure of merit;

looks for unusual approaches to complex problems;

can strip a verbal argument of irrelevancies and phrase it in terms of its essentials;

understands the differences among conclusions, assumptions, and hypotheses;

habitually questions one's own views and attempts to understand both the assumptions that are critical to those views and the implications of the views;

is sensitive to the difference between the validity of a belief and the intensity with which it is held;

can represent differing viewpoints without distortion, exaggeration, or caricaturization;

is aware of the fact that one's understanding is always limited, often much more so than would be apparent to one with a noninquiring attitude; and

recognizes the fallibility of one's own opinions, the probability of bias in those opinions, and the danger of differentially weighting evidence according to personal preferences.

This list is extensive enough to make the point that if we accept it—incomplete as it is—we must acknowledge that there is a considerable difference between good thinking and the kind of thinking that most of us habitually do.

WHY TEACH THINKING?

Why should we want students to become good thinkers? One possible answer is so that they will be equipped to compete effectively for educational opportunities, jobs, recognition, and rewards in today's world—or to put it more succinctly, so that they will have a better chance of being successful. This is a pragmatic answer that seems to be implicit in much of the discussion of the need to do a better job of teaching thinking.

While this answer has some merit, it can be challenged. What is the evidence that good thinkers get better jobs and are more successful in general than less good thinkers? Goodlad (1980) has observed that few employers pay for such activities as contemplating, questioning, and inquiring, and that many discourage them. Clearly, some jobs require skill at certain types of thinking (e.g., troubleshooting and problem solving), but whether people who make a habit of thinking deeply and reflectively are, in general, more valued employees or more successful employers than those who do not seems to me to be an open question. Brown and Saks (1984), speaking from the vantage point of economists thinking in terms of costs and benefits to society as a whole, assert flatly that "there is no obvious economic argument for maximizing the reasoning skills of the population" (p. 572).

A second possible answer is that good thinking is a prerequisite for good citizenship. This is reminiscent of Jefferson's forceful arguments for public education. To cite some more recent writers: Glaser (1985) suggests that critical thinking ability "helps the citizen to form intelligent judgments on public issues and thus contribute democratically to the solution of social problems" (p. 27), and Postman (1985) says simply that there can be no liberty for a community that lacks the critical skills to distinguish lies from truth.

The promotion of good citizenship is a laudatory reason for teaching thinking and one that would undoubtedly be widely supported. I would certainly want to be counted among its endorsers, because I believe that, at least in a democracy, citizens have an obligation to think deeply about significant issues. But we must acknowledge that there may be differences of opinion from time to time as to what constitutes good citizenship. Thinking is not always rewarded by society, nor does it always contribute to peace and tranquility. As evidence that independent thinking may be less highly valued by society than is sometimes acknowledged, Clifford (1985) points to the reaction of American public opinion to the independent thinking by young people in the 1960s and 1970s. Nor is ours the only society that has not always been appreciative of people who think for themselves. We need only remind ourselves of how the Athenians treated perhaps their greatest thinker during the golden days of Greece.

If we assume that critical thinking is not the norm, which is to say that most people do not engage in it habitually, then it follows that people who do acquire the habit of thinking critically will, by definition, think uncommon thoughts. It should not be surprising if more than occasionally they hold opinions that differ from those that prevail within the culture.

A third possible answer to our question is that the ability to think well contributes to one's psychological well-being; good thinkers are more likely to be well-adjusted individuals than not-so-good thinkers. I doubt if anyone knows whether this is true. We can point to numerous examples of great thinkers who have maintained very positive outlooks and have lived life with inspiring enthusiasm; on the other hand, we have no trouble finding others whose reflections brought them to the brink of despair.

I suspect, but certainly cannot document, that good thinkers are likely, on balance, to find life more interesting and rewarding than less good thinkers, but I would not want to try to justify the teaching of thinking skills on this basis alone because I believe there is some chance that by teaching a person to think, we increase the opportunities for conflict both within the individual and between him or her and society.

But conflicts that arise as a consequence of thinking deeply about issues probably ought to arise. And if thinking sometimes gives one pain instead of pleasure, that is part of the price of being human. John Stuart Mill (1863/1939) thought about the fact that more highly developed mental faculties implies greater vulnerability to disappointment and suffering of various types and came to the conclusion that "It is better to be a human being dissatisfied than a pig satisfied; better to be Socrates dissatisfied than a fool satisfied" (p. 902). He acknowledged that the pig or the fool might see things differently, but questioned whether anyone in possession of the higher faculties would voluntarily give them up in exchange for greater happiness at a different level of existence.

A fourth possible answer to the question of why we should want students to become good thinkers, and one I find quite compelling, is that we cannot afford for them not to do so. We currently face some very complex and threatening problems—that much is obvious. Perhaps the most frustrating, and frightening, aspect of the world situation is the possibility that the main impediment to progress is irrational human behavior. Our precarious situation is not due to lack of raw intelligence or technological know-how. To the contrary, some of the most troublesome aspects of the situation are direct consequences of our cleverness and technological wizardry. We are now smart enough to destroy ourselves as a species and, unless we learn to be better thinkers in a broad sense, we may well do so.

The answer to our question that I find most compelling has little to do with the practical advantages of being able to think well, either for individuals, for the society to which they belong, or for the world; it has much to do, however, with what we are, and, even more, with what we might aspire to be.

We call ourselves Homo sapiens, in our conceit some would say. Whether we deserve this appellation or not, there can be no question about the importance of cognition to our lives. No other species relies less on instinct and more on its ability to learn, and to think in the broadest sense. We want students to become good thinkers because thinking is at the heart of what it means to be human; to fail to develop one's potential in this regard is to preclude the full expression of one's humanity. Thinking well is a means to many ends, but it is also an end in itself.

A DISTINCTION

The purpose of listing the representative characteristics of a good thinker at the beginning of this chapter was to include a rather broad spectrum of capabilities and qualities to make the point that good thinking has many facets. It involves careful listening, logic, reflection, contemplation, self-assessment, and much more. Assertions about thinking often seem to be based on a conception of thinking that includes some of these aspects but not others.

In proposing that we need to become better thinkers in a broad sense, I have in mind a distinction that is difficult to capture in a word or two. Certain contrasts come to mind, including problem-solving versus problem-finding, thinking directed *by* goals versus thinking directed *at* goals, thinking *within* value systems versus thinking *about* value systems, and safe thinking versus risky thinking. None of these contrasts quite captures the distinction I want to make, but in combination they come close.

One way to illustrate the distinction is with reference to goals. One type of thinking, which we might refer to as thinking directed *by* goals, focuses on the question: Given a goal, how am I to accomplish it? Inventiveness shows itself here in one's ability to come up with novel and effective means to a specified end. Critical thinking in this case is necessary to evelute the possibilities that come to mind.

There can be no doubt of the importance of this type of thinking. By definition, people who are good at figuring out how to reach specified goals are more likely to attain those goals than are people who are less skillful in this regard. Moreover, goal-oriented thinking lends itself to analysis and the formulation of methods that can be described and, presumably, taught. Problem-solving heuristics such as those described by Polya (1957) and by Newell and Simon (1972) illustrate my point.

The idea of teaching problem-solving skills is not controversial. Differences of opinion on the subject center on questions of method, not the need. To be sure, we must acknowledge that effective thinking in the sense of applying resources to the accomplishment of specific goals can be done in the service of bad goals as well as of good ones. The ingenious criminal who plots the perfect crime and carries it out must be considered an effective thinker in this sense. But this fact does not negate the importance of teaching this type of thinking. We can and should take the same attitude toward teaching this type of thinking that we take toward the teaching of other procedural skills. When one learns mathematics, chemistry, or physics, one acquires knowledge and skills that can be applied to a wide variety of objectives, both good and bad. The fact that mathematics can be applied to socially unacceptable ends is seldom used as an argument against teaching the subject. If such an argument were considered legitimate, there is hardly any area of human knowledge to which it could not be applied. Any risks inherent in helping people to be more effective in thinking directed by goals are no different, in principle, from the risks inherent in the teaching of any other useful knowledge or skills.

A second type of thinking, which we might refer to as thinking directed *at* goals, involves the question of what one's goals should be, or that of whether any particular goal deserves one's allegiance. Here the question is not how to attain a goal, but what goals are worth attaining. The challenge to the thinker—and the teacher—is more profound, because the criteria for judging the quality of one's thinking are not so clear. Effectiveness cannot be measured with the simple yardstick of success in reaching a stated goal, because the worthiness of the goal is itself the object of thought. This kind of thinking comes closer to what is usually meant by critical or reflective thinking (although the correspondence is not perfect because one can think critically or reflectively about means as well as ends). And the idea of teaching students to engage in it is controversial.

I believe that often, when people in positions of authority (parents, teachers, managers, military leaders) say that they wish that the people over whom they have authority (children, students, employees, subordinates) could think, they mean that they wish their charges or subordinates were more skillful at accomplishing goals set, or at least endorsed, by their superiors. Seldom do they have in mind a concept of thinking that is sufficiently broad to include the questioning of the goals themselves and the authorities that have set them.

But the ability to think deeply, critically, and creatively about goals is essential, and its cultivation becomes increasingly imperative in view of the rapid advance in technological know-how. As Norbert Wiener (1964) once put it:

> As engineering technique becomes more and more able to achieve human purposes, it must become more and more accustomed to formulate human purposes. In the past, a partial and inadequate view of human purpose has been relatively innocuous only because it has been accompanied by technical limitations that made it difficult for us to perform operations involving a careful evaluation of human purpose. This is only one of the many places where human impotence has hitherto shielded us from the full destructive impact of human folly. (p. 64)

It is easy to be platitudinous here. Of course we want young people to think about goals, to be questioning, to form their own opinions, and to arrive at their own values. We want them to think critically and reflectively in the most general sense, to look for evidence of the truth or falsity of assertions, to judge arguments on their merits and not on the basis of who has made them. How could we want it to be otherwise? On the other hand, we try to transmit to young people (especially our own children, if we are parents) certain values; we try to instill in them our own views of right and wrong, our own sense of justice, equity, and fairness; and we hope desperately to be successful. We do want them to make up their own minds on issues that matter; but we are not indifferent to the conclusions they draw, and in particular we do not want them to arrive at positions that we ourselves find ethically or morally repugnant. We see the value of traditions and recognize their importance to the stability of society, even perhaps when we cannot fully justify them on rational grounds.

This is not a new dilemma. The ancient Athenians, to whom we owe such an intellectual debt, knew it well. Socrates and his followers struggled with the question of how to assure that democracy does not dissolve into anarchy. While prizing their status as free men, and—in Socrates's case, at least—preferring death to any curtailment of freedom of speech, they recognized that unconstrained liberty can easily become chaos, which breeds demagoguery and tyranny. How do we deal with this problem? How do we promote an attitude of critical inquiry on the one hand and a healthy respect for valued tradition and legitimate authority on the other?

Several writers have addressed this issue more or less directly. I will cite two for purposes of contrast. Goldman (1984) sees some danger in cultivating in the young a spirit of critical inquiry:

> The inherent skepticism of the [Socratic] method can easily turn to nihilism: its openness to new visions and revisions may erode standards and disorient and alienate its disciples. . . . A proper education of the young must begin with a firm grounding in the nature and values of our culture. Without teaching the rules of the game and the lay of the land, we handicap the young and threaten the continuity of the society. (p. 60).

To be sure, Goldman notes that, in imposing a culture and its standards on the young, we must be ready to give good reasons for the standards and to discuss them openly: "On the other hand, in these early years we should not take the initiative to demonstrate inconsistencies, and other inadequacies in the belief systems we are helping to inculcate" (p. 60).

In contrast, Scriven (1985) takes the position that training in critical thinking, which should be seen as the primary task of education, should involve "highly controversial issues of considerable personal, social or intellectual importance that are not seriously addressed in the regular curriculum" (p. 12). And he strongly urges that exposure to controversial issues include hearing conflicting points of view about real issues from people who hold those points of view: "The real case, in dealing with controversial issues is the case as put by real people who believe in what they're saying" (p. 9). Scriven notes that it is unrealistic to expect a viewpoint on a controversial issue to be represented fairly by one who opposes it.

In a nutshell, the dilemma is: How do we teach students to think independently and to arrive at their own conclusions when we are not indifferent to the conclusions they draw? And on issues of substance, we seldom are indifferent, nor should we be. This is a difficult question, but, I believe, an answerable one. The essential ingredients, I would argue, are intellectual honesty and the careful use of language. One need not apologize for having strong beliefs provided that one can give reasons for them and that one recognizes them to be beliefs. There is a great difference between saying "X is the truth" and "X is what I believe to be true, and here is why." Moreover, there is a difference between trying to convince a person of the plausibility of a belief and insisting that he or she accept the belief because you assert it to be true.

I see no conflict between teaching moral and ethical principles that one believes and at the same time promoting an inquiring and reflective attitude. To do this effectively undoubtedly requires considerable intellectual honesty and maturity on the part of the teacher. One must, in fact, display the traits that one hopes to foster among one's students, which is to say, one must try to use evidence skillfully and impartially, be willing to suspend judgment in the absence of sufficient evidence to support a decision, understand the difference between reasoning and rationalizing, recognize the fallibility of one's own opinions, and so on.

SUMMARY

The question "Why teach thinking?" has many answers. How reasonable one finds any particular one of them is likely to depend on how one conceptualizes thinking or what aspect(s) of thinking one wishes to emphasize. Increasing people's problem-solving skills may well increase their earning power. Getting people to be more observant may enrich their lives aesthetically. We should not be surprised if the acquisition of better listening skills improves one's social interactions. Learning to look at controversial issues from other people's points of view should have a similarly beneficial effect. Learning to analyze arguments and evaluate them critically should make one less susceptible to manipulation and brainwashing, as should an awareness of the various alogical approaches that can be used to influence behavior and mold beliefs.

Becoming more critically reflective may very well make one more likely to challenge established ideas, institutions, and ways of doing things. But that can be seen as unfortunate only by those who believe that the old ideas, institutions, and ways are impossible to improve upon. And if that belief is true, we are in serious trouble indeed.

While we share much with the rest of the animal kingdom, we are unique in the degree to which our behavior is cognitively, as opposed to instinctively, controlled. We have options and the ability to choose. We are capable of anticipating the consequences of our choices and of evaluating our options before we select among them. We are able not only to contemplate the past, but to imagine a variety of possible futures. We are not constrained to see things from our own peculiar vantage points only, but are capable of at least trying to see them from specific other people's points of view.

We are *capable* of these things, but these capabilities need to be cultivated because we are also capable of blindly following authority, acting without thought for the consequences of our actions, having our opinions molded and our behavior shaped by illogical arguments and alogical persuaders of an astonishing variety of types, believing the future will be what it will be and taking no steps to make it what it could be, and failing to make any effort to see things from other people's points of view.

If we are serious about teaching thinking, we must try to learn to be better thinkers ourselves. We must be prepared to have our own beliefs and opinions compete in the marketplace of ideas. Our conception of a thinking person must recognize that not all thinking people will think alike. They will not all come to the same conclusions on a given set of issues. They will certainly not all have the same insights, nor will they be inventive or creative in the same ways. Perhaps all that we can expect is that they will share a love of truth and a commitment to rationality, but that is a very great deal indeed.

We must try to teach thinking in the broadest sense. The risks associated with not doing so are unacceptable. And our hope must be that students will learn far more than we yet know how to teach.

REFERENCES

Brown, B. W., & Saks, D. H. (1984). An economic view of the acquisition of reasoning skills: Agenda for research in the information age. *Review of Educational Research.* 54:560–576.

Clifford, G. (1984). Buch and Lesen: Historical perspectives on literacy and schooling. *Review of Educational Research,* 54:472–500.

Glaser, E. M. (1985). Critical thinking: Educating for responsible citizenship in a democracy. *National Forum,* 65:24–27.

Goldman, L. (1984). Warning: The Socratic method can be dangerous. *Educational Leadership,* 42:57–62.

Goodlad, J. (1980). What schools should be for. *Learning,* 9:38–43.

Mill, J. S. (1863/1939). Utilitarianism. In E. A. Burtt (Ed.), *The English Philosophers from Bacon to Mill,* New York: Random House, 1939.

Newell, A., & Simon, H. A. (1972). *Human problem solving.* Englewood Cliffs, N.J.: Prentice-Hall.

Nickerson R. S., Perkins, D. N., & Smith, E. E. (1985). *The teaching of thinking.* Hillsdale, N.J.: Erlbaum.

Nisbett, R., & Ross, L. (1980). *Human inference: Strategies and shortcomings of social judgment.* Englewood Cliffs, N.J.: Prentice-Hall.

Polya, G. (1957). *How to solve it* (2nd ed.). Princeton, N.J.: Princeton University Press; New York: Doubleday.

Postman, N. (1985). Critical thinking in the electronic era. *National Forum,* 65:4–8.

Scriven, M. (1985). Critical for survival. *National Forum,* 65:9–12.

Tversky, A., & Kahneman, D. (1974). Judgment under uncertainty: Heuristics and biases. *Science,* 185:1124–1131.

Wiener, N. (1964). *God and golem, inc.* Cambridge: MIT Press.

Part II

GENERAL APPROACHES
TO THE TEACHING
OF THINKING SKILLS

3

D. N. PERKINS
Graduate School of Education
Harvard University

Thinking Frames: An Integrative Perspective on Teaching Cognitive Skills

We live in a time of ripeness for education. Although teachers ever since Socrates have aspired to show students how to think intelligently and apply what they have learned, today we have a sharpened awareness both of how hard that goal is to achieve and how we might achieve it. Several recent trends have fueled the current consciousness that teaching better thinking is a primary aim of schooling. The back to basics movement of the 1970s mustered efforts to improve low-level skills of reading, writing, and arithmetic. However, students' persistent shortfall in such areas as making inferences from reading, writing pointedly and persuasively, and solving word problems in mathematics became apparent: After tracking the ebb and flow of students' performance over decades, the National Assessment of Educational Progress detected a decline in some higher order skills (Mullis, 1984), although the decline was modest compared to the difference between actual performance and what would be ideal. Several national reports on schooling highlighted how much rote work and how little cogitation occurred in the typical school day (e.g., Boyer, 1983; Goodlad, 1983; National Commission, 1983; Sizer, 1984).

Even as the problem became apparent, philosophers, psychologists, and educators had been developing a better understanding of thinking and its difficulties along with tactics to foster the development of thinking skills. The state of the art today, as seen in recent overviews, is much improved over a decade ago (Chipman, Segal, & Glaser, 1985; Nickerson, Perkins, & Smith, 1985; Segal, Chipman, & Glaser, 1985). The commitment of many individuals to work in this area did not so much follow from recent criticisms of education as precede and parallel them. The result is a confluence of better technical knowledge about thinking and its teaching together with the social impetus to apply that knowledge.

But this combination of knowledge and enthusiasm in a way is an embarrassment of riches. Although much has been said about teaching thinking in recent years, far less has been resolved. The sources just mentioned testify to the bewildering variety of approaches that has gained attention. Although numerous methods are available, few have been subjected to thoroughgoing formal assessments. Although in some cases positive results have emerged upon posttesting, rarely do follow-up studies examine whether these results survive over time or transfer to other areas of application. Teachers and school administrators find themselves in the midst of ferment: full of the will to do something, faced with an abundance of choices, but ill prepared to make those choices well.

The framework presented in this chapter may help those caught in this very real dilemma. It offers a broad account of the nature of intelligence and provides some general critical principles for choosing among alternative approaches to building intellectual abilities. At the same time, a caution is due: No small set of general principles can take the place of good judgment in deciding between two roughly similar approaches, one of which might be much better crafted. This perspective provides a guide, but not a substitute, for careful, responsible thinking.

With that caveat in mind, let us seek answers to three questions: What constitutes better thinking? By what process can people learn to think better? How can one tell whether a particular approach to teaching thinking is effective?

WHAT CONSTITUTES BETTER THINKING?

Intelligence is a much more complicated and malleable human trait than many people suppose. We must avoid the narrow reading of intelligence as IQ. Instead, intelligence can be defined as intellectual competence, that is, whatever makes people more effective thinkers: academic skills, good practical everyday problem solving, good judgment in dealing with one's own affairs and conducting oneself with others, and so on.

Three daily ways of talking about intelligence provide a good introduction to three positions that contemporary psychologists hold about the nature of intelligence. When we say someone is "a real brain," "a powerful thinker," or has "a lot of brain power," the idea is that some brains are more powerful engines than others. In contrast, a good deal of folk advice reflects a tactical view of intelligence: "look before you leap," "a penny saved is a penny earned," "the wheel that squeaks gets the grease." A third view of intelligence appears in such phrases as "the voice of experience" or "the wisdom of years." The notion here is that competence rests in extensive knowledge of and hands-on experience with the particular activity in question. Let us examine what psychology has to say about each position.

Three Definitions of Intelligence

Intelligence as Power

Arthur Jensen is perhaps the best-known exponent of a power perspective on intelligence. He holds that intelligence fundamentally is a matter of the precision and efficiency of the neurophysiological computer in our heads. As evidence, Jensen offers a series of experiments with a choice-reaction-time task, a mechanical test of reflexes that does not demand thinking in any ordinary sense. Subjects' scores on this test correlate somewhat with subjects' scores on standard IQ measures. Jensen's interpretation is that conventionally mea-sured intellectual competence reflects the raw computational power of the brain as measured by relatively primitive tasks such as choice-reaction time. Jensen also notes that extensive practice with the choice-reaction time task does not enhance performance and implies that the basal efficacy of the brain does not improve with practice, at least in the short term (Jensen, 1984).

Another psychologist who has taken a power perspective on intelligence is Howard Gardner, who proposes that people have seven distinct intelligences—including linguistic, logical-mathematical, and musical—rather than the one unitary intelligence proposed by Jensen and many other psychologists (Gardner, 1983). Like Jensen, Gardner thinks that a person's basal intelligence in an area sharply influences the person's capacity to develop skills. However, Gardner believes that special instructional techniques, for instance, the Suzuki method in violin, can lift a person well beyond his or her initial potential under normal conditions of exposure or education.

Intelligence as Tactics

Other contemporary psychologists emphasize a tactical approach to intel-lectual competence, holding that good thinking is based in large part on the repertoire of strategies one can deploy for a given task. For instance, research on retardates has shown that their poor performance on simple memory tasks largely reflects the lack of simple strategies for memorizing that normal young-sters have acquired; when taught such strategies, retardates do nearly as well as normal individuals. This demonstrates that a tactical rather than a brain-power deficit explains their immediate problem with memory (Baron, 1978). Teaching college students a repertoire of problem-solving strategies can dramatically improve their mathematical problem solving (Schoenfeld, 1982; Schoenfeld & Herrmann, 1982). Teaching poor readers tactics for focusing on key information and anticipating the sorts of questions that get asked in school can substantially improve reading performance (Palinscar & Brown, 1984). Teaching strategies for analyzing and generating designs can greatly improve students' ability for common-sense invention (Bolt Beranek & Newman, 1983; Perkins, 1984). Research has yielded ample evidence that careful instruction in well-chosen tactics can enhance performance considerably.

Intelligence as Content

A third perspective on intellectual competence highlights the role of context-specific content knowledge. As used here, content knowledge includes both facts and know-how, or in more technical terms, propositional and procedural knowledge. The classic experiment demonstrating the importance of such knowledge concerns chess, a game that seems to demand good logical reasoning. However, research has disclosed that chess masters' skill involves a large repertoire of configurations of pieces and patterns of play quite specific to chess (Chase & Simon, 1973; de Groot, 1965). Chess masters perceive the layout of the pieces and plan courses of play by thinking in patterns that novices lack. Research on expertise in other domains has also disclosed the importance of highly context-specific content knowledge. Knowing the facts is not enough; people need domain-specific ways of organizing perceptions and attacking problems. Domains that have been studied include physics (e.g., Chi, Feltovich, & Glaser, 1981; Larkin, 1983), mathematics (e.g., Schoenfeld, 1982; Schoenfeld & Herrmann, 1982), music (Hayes, 1981), and computer programming (Soloway & Ehrlich, 1984). Hayes (1981) argues that acquiring sufficient content repertoire to attain expertise in a domain requires very extensive practice, on the order of ten years of continuous involvement.

The Tactics—Content Continuum

Because activities like playing chess plainly involve tactics in some sense of the word, one may question whether the division between tactics and content proposed here draws a sharp line. Indeed there is no such line. Think of the contrast between tactics and content as a continuum of knowledge. At the tactical extreme are very general tactics that cut across domains, such as making a plan or trying to relate this problem to one that has already been solved. In the middle are domain-specific but still rather general tactics such as trying to control the center in chess. At the content extreme one finds low-level and very particular knowledge, such as, in mathematics, number facts or memorized theorems from plane geometry. So long as one bears in mind this continuum, the tactics—content contrast will cause no mischief.

Teaching for Tactics

So which is correct, the power, the tactical, or the content perspective? All are right. Each perspective has its body of evidence that cannot readily be dismissed. Intelligence evidently is a complex phenomenon, a compound of very different elements. As a reminder of this complexity, the following equation is useful:

$$\text{Intelligence} = \text{Power} + \text{Tactics} + \text{Content}$$

That is, intellectual competence on a certain task depends on the power of one's neurological computer, the tactical repertoire one can bring to bear, and a stock of context-specific content and know-how. (A point of caution: Read the + metaphorically as taken together with.)

What are the implications for education? In a phrase, teach for tactics. The power side of intelligence does not seem subject to improvement in the short term, although nutritional factors and exposure to an intellectually demanding environment may yield gains in the long term (Schooler, 1984). As to content, education routinely has placed its bet there without winning payoffs. Furthermore, we need to remember that extensive content knowledge accumulates slowly and only contributes to long-term intellectual competence. So the best opportunity for education is to build students' tactical intelligence.

The Use of Artifice

The notion that people use tactics to improve their minds is another aspect of our reliance on technical means to get things done. We live by artifice. How fitting, then, if better thinking should prove to be another occasion for artifice. Of course, we are not especially conscious of the artificial nature of good thinking. Neither are we particularly conscious of the artifices that sustain our life-styles from moment to moment. Without thinking, we become accustomed to such good habits of mind as planning, being careful, checking our work, anticipating other people's feelings, speaking in ways that take into account the listener's level of knowledge, or giving ourselves time to ponder an important decision rather than proceeding impulsively. Such straightforward mental moves are artifices, inventions to make the best of our minds, just as much as shoes are artifices to make the best of our feet.

Yet many people do not think as well as they could because their thinking is not artificial enough in the right ways. There are many good tactics with which most people are not familiar. But there is a more significant problem: Some important patterns of thinking run contrary to the human grain. It is easy enough to develop one's preferred side of a case, but paying careful heed to the other side of the case does not come readily. Given a problem, people immediately and often appropriately start to think of solutions, but sometimes the better move is to consider the problem itself. How is it defined? Can it be redefined? How can it best be represented? Is it necessary to solve the problem at all, or can one achieve the larger aim by going around the problem?

Challenging one's assumptions is another uncomfortable move. Although we spontaneously take a lot for granted, and in many situations should for the sake of efficiency, circumstances arise where the tacit assumptions need to be questioned.

Some have proposed that better thinking is made of more and better tactics. Efforts to develop thinking skills should provide such tactics by means that ensure their retention and fluent, widespread application, matters not to be taken for granted. The term artificial intelligence normally refers to research by computer scientists attempting to program computers to display intelligent behavior; computer chess is a common example. But just as nature has anticipated human invention on so many fronts—the sonar of bats or the jet propulsion of squid, for example—so nature has done as much for the practice of thinking itself. Our natural ways of thinking are for the most part artificial—contrivances learned from others or invented by oneself to put our minds to good use. To become better thinkers, students need to think more artificially.

Choosing the Right Approach

Here are two critical principles to help in making decisions about approaches to teaching thinking.

Critical principle: Beware of approaches that rely mostly on exercises to enhance thinking; look for the teaching of tactics.

Most approaches to developing thinking teach tactics, but some highlight mental muscle building through exercise. Such approaches tacitly, and sometimes explicitly, adopt a power model of intelligence. But evidence shows that the basal power of the brain does not change readily. Moreover, well-designed tactical instruction includes plenty of practice so that students get the benefit both of practice and tactical guidance, so why settle for exercise alone?

Critical principle: Beware of approaches that rely mostly on immersion in content to enhance thinking.

This is the conventional ploy of education. Certainly some programs of instruction involve students much more richly and substantively in the content of a discipline than do others. However, such instruction does not necessarily highlight the tactical side of the discipline. Without such an emphasis, gains are likely to be slow.

Teaching Tactics Yields Intellectual Gains

Some might doubt these critical principles on the grounds that occasionally people do seem to make general intellectual gains from exercises or content-rich instruction over a relatively short period. To be sure, some do, but not as often or reliably as one would like. Because the power and content components of intelligence change slowly, such gains must reflect acquisition of tactics. Where do the tactics come from? Some people invent them for themselves, stimulated by exercises and rich content, and so improve their thinking. But most do not, especially among less able students. Evidence presented later argues that, in general, learners simply cannot be relied upon to invent their own tactics without some guidance.

Thinking Frames

Because tactics are so important, we must define the term as clearly as possible. The everyday term tactics is vague and narrow in certain ways that encourage the introduction of a new, more refined concept—thinking frames—which is defined as *a guide to organizing and supporting thought processes*. The examples of tactics already given plainly satisfy this definition. "Look before you leap," for instance, advises one to take the time to think ahead. "Consider both sides of the case" likewise urges one to think about both sides of a situation, not just one's preferred side.

Although the term thinking frames may be new, the concept is not. There are many episodes in intellectual history where people set out to devise or extract thinking frames from common practice. Aristotle's enumeration of syllogistic forms as the basis for reason, Bacon's effort to set out principles of scientific inquiry, and Schoenberg's self-conscious formulation of twelve-tone music are three examples.

Moreover, two suggestive metaphors come with the term thinking frames. As any photographer knows, the frame of the viewfinder organizes the image within it, creating a visual statement where, without the frame, one might see only clutter. And as any builder knows, the frame of a building supports its totality. Both metaphors highlight a crucial feature of thinking frames: They support and organize thought but they do not do the thinking. They are guides, not recipes.

BY WHAT PROCESS CAN PEOPLE LEARN TO THINK BETTER?

Acquiring Frames

The story so far has concerned what tactical intelligence is made of, but not how people get more of it. The learning process, too, requires attention. Three broad aspects of learning can be distinguished, each one constituting a bottleneck in building a larger repertoire of thinking frames. They are:

Acquisition. The learner acquires an initial mastery of the thinking frame, understanding it and applying it to simple cases, although often in a belabored way.

Making automatic. After some practice, the learner becomes able to apply the frame with fluency in simple cases, although if one makes the cases difficult enough naturally the learner will not be as facile.

Transfer. The learner applies the frame across a wide range of contexts, some remote from the original context of learning.

The rest of this section will explain the acquisition bottleneck.

Soaking Up Does Not Occur

Perhaps the simplest question one might ask about initial acquisition is "Where does the frame come from?" There are three answers. Learners might become acquainted with a frame through direct instruction, they might invent it for themselves, or they might "soak it up" from an enriched atmosphere, without the frame ever taking the form of an explicit representation.

Here a crucial and perhaps controversial claim needs to be made: Soaking up does not occur. People do not learn subliminally. Any frame or other chunk of information that a person acquires originally takes the form of an explicit, although not necessarily verbal, representation in the person's mind. The evidence of this phenomenon is complex and scattered. Ericsson and Simon (1984) build a careful case for the crucial role of explicit representations during thinking and learning.

There is a common-sense objection to the notion that soaking up does not occur: People often learn from enriched home or school environments, even in the absence of explicit instruction in thinking frames. The answer to this is that enriched contexts stimulate frame invention. The learner can gain many minor and occasional major insights by generalizing or analogizing from whatever happens in the enriched context, but the learner's active engagement is required for extracting lessons from the context. Soaking up supposedly operates by itself. But active engagement, especially the right sort of active engagement, cannot be counted upon and plainly often does not occur.

An Experiment in Soaking Up

In an experiment on the teaching of mathematical problem solving conducted by Alan Schoenfeld (1979) the students were divided into two groups. One group studied a series of worked-out solutions to problems that demonstrated certain problem-solving techniques; however, the materials did not identify the problem-solving techniques. Another group studied the same series of solutions with overlays that highlighted the tactics being used. Both groups practiced solving problems. Whereas the second group showed marked gains in problem-solving performance, the first showed none at all. Other studies suggest that modeling alone, without making explicit the principles modeled, leads to less and sometimes *no* learning (Palinscar & Brown, 1984).

Teaching Frames Explicitly

In general, frame acquisition involves many potential bottlenecks—for example, complexity and subtlety of the frame in question or the learner's prior knowledge of frames taken for granted by the new frame. But above all, one must be sure that the learner has a good chance of arriving at the frame. Because soaking up does not occur and people do not invent their own frames reliably, instruction should either teach frames explicitly or make a special effort to promote frame invention. Simply enriching the context with modeling—the "actions speak louder than words" theory—is not enough.

Critical principle: Efforts to develop thinking should either teach frames directly or do something beyond enrichment in general and modeling in particular to provoke students to invent their own frames. The latter is much trickier.

Making Frames Automatic

Making a frame automatic means practicing the frame until its application in simple cases becomes fluent. To understand this bottleneck, it is important to recognize why fluency plays an important role in building a learner's intelligence. One simple answer is that fluency together with precision make for efficiency. But the matter actually concerns the limited capacity of human short-term memory, or working memory as it is often called.

The Role of Memory

When addressing any task, we have to hold certain things in mind—our goal, our immediate intentions, information we have just arrived at that needs to be used in the next step, and so on. Such information may never pass into long-term memory; in a matter of minutes the phone number you looked up will have disappeared from your mind, although you hold it in working memory long enough to dial. The problem is that working memory has a rather limited capacity, usually said to be about seven chunks of information plus or minus two in an adult, with considerably less available capacity in children (Brainerd, 1983; Case, 1984; Miller, 1956).

This implies a bottleneck in learning a thinking frame. A freshly acquired frame of any complexity will occupy considerable space in working memory. The learner may have stored the words or images that make up the frame in long-term memory, but not typically the patterns of action needed to apply the frame. When putting the frame to work, the learner must laboriously remember what the frame says to do and do it piecemeal with great attention. At the same time, the learner must also hold the problem to which the frame is being applied.

There are two important consequences of these needs. First, the learner cannot benefit from the full power of the frame until it has been made automatic, because until then it takes up some of the working-memory space needed to hold complicated problems. Second, if led too quickly to attempt solving such problems, the learner may miss the opportunity to make a frame automatic because he or she is unable to practice on the problems effectively for lack of sufficient working memory to hold both a problem and the frame in mind at once. Some instructional approaches escalate the difficulty of the examples too quickly, thus undermining the process.

Ensuring That Frames become Automatic

Since making frames automatic has such importance, what can be done to ensure that it occurs? One appropriate tactic is practice on examples so easy that they hardly exercise the real potential of the frame. It is difficult to say how much trivial practice will suffice but if problem difficulty escalates so quickly that many students have trouble by the time they hit the third or fourth example, there was not enough trivial practice. Another useful tactic helps the student manage the memory demands of the frame by external aids. For instance, a poster on the wall outlining the key elements of a frame can provide a ready reminder; students need not distract themselves from a problem by trying to remember the frame but can simply refer to its elements as needed. However, this route requires taking pains that students ultimately do internalize the frame rather than always relying on the poster. Otherwise, when the poster is taken down or the students leave the room, the students no longer have the frame available to them.

Practicing Frames

Making application of a frame automatic is important because it frees up working memory and allows learners to attempt solving problems of substance. Practice is the solution, but it must be enough practice to make application automatic in straightforward cases, and practice of the sort that students can genuinely carry out.

Critical principle: In assessing an approach, look for practice on trivial examples or for practice with external reminders together with later weaning from dependency on those reminders.

Transferring Frames

The third bottleneck concerns transferring frames from the context of acquisition to different contexts of application. This clearly is a crucial problem: Education ideally aims not at the final exam but at the applications the students may make of what they have learned in further study and outside of school. For instance, problem-solving frames acquired in mathematics should carry over to physics and chemistry class, as well as beyond the walls of the school to engineering, business, and other contexts. Transfer is all the more important with stand-alone courses designed to teach thinking skills. Such courses occur apart from instruction in the various subject matters, yet typically they aim to improve students' performances in those subject matters.

High-road and Low-road Transfer

It is natural to assume that when students learn something in one context that is relevant to another, transfer happens spontaneously. Unfortunately, considerable contemporary evidence argues against this comfortable view. Transfer occurs far less often or readily than one might think (e.g., Belmont, Butterfield, & Ferretti, 1982; Pea & Kurland, 1984a, b; Scribner & Cole, 1981). According to Salomon and Perkins, this happens because most instructional situations do not meet certain conditions for transfer (Perkins & Salomon, 1986; Salomon & Perkins, 1984). They identify two distinct mechanisms for transfer. High-road transfer occurs by way of mindful abstraction from the context of learning and application to another context. It demands the conscious effort of the learner in seeking generalizations and applications beyond the obvious, an effort few features of conventional education encourage. There is evidence that self-monitoring of one's problem solving process abets high-road transfer (Belmont, Butterfield, & Ferretti, 1982; Schoenfeld, 1978).

"Low-road" transfer occurs spontaneously when a performance made automatic in one context gets triggered in another context resembling the first. For instance, if you know how to drive a car, you do not have to reason out how to drive a pickup truck. There are minor differences, but the familiar pattern of steering wheel, gear shift, and so on evokes your car driving habits and, fortunately, they suit the truck well enough. But this transfer depends on the truck being very like the car. Low-road transfer reaches only so far as perceptual similarities obtain. Broad low-road transfer calls for varied practice that samples a wide range of possible applications. Unfortunately, here again conventional education tends to fall short: Most practice involves a rather narrow range of traditional types of examples. Consider, for instance, the stereotyped genres of word problems in arithmetic and algebra: age problems, mixture problems, time-rate-distance problems, and so on.

Promoting Transfer

Many instructional programs designed to develop thinking skills take no more care to establish the conditions for transfer than does traditional education. Accordingly, transfer becomes a third bottleneck on the way to mastering of general-purpose thinking frames and a concern in assessing any approach to teaching thinking.

Critical principle: Examine whether an approach promotes high-road transfer by emphasizing self-monitoring and the deliberate abstraction and application of frames across different contexts or promotes low-road transfer by varied practice designed to sample widely potential applications or both.

How Can One Tell Whether a Particular Approach to Teaching Is Effective?

We have already begun to answer this question in the previous section: An effective approach must pay heed to the pitfalls of acquisition, automatization, and transfer. However, besides these concerns about the learning process, we also must examine critically the frames to be learned.

Using a Variety of Frames

The single most important characteristic of thinking frames is their startling variety. Some thinking frames cut across domains, whereas others contribute to a particular discipline. Some concern the process of thought, whereas others address the organization of products of thought. Some concern major chunks of a process or product, whereas others pertain to style or texture. A brief exploration of three such contrasts—general versus specific, process versus product, and structure versus style—is in order, lest we fall into too narrow a concept of tactical intelligence. Bear in mind that these are not the only dimensions along which thinking frames vary, but they may be enough to underscore the point that thinking frames are not all of a kind. Quite the contrary, the tactical side of human intelligence reflects a startling diversity of artifices that direct our minds toward effective thinking.

General versus Specific

A frame like "look before you leap" finds some application in nearly any context. However, many frames apply principally within particular domains or disciplines. For example, "simultaneous linear equations" is a problem-solving frame that contributes mostly to mathematics and the hard sciences. "Gain control of the center" is a frame that applies to chess and military contexts but not to many others.

Process versus Product

Some thinking frames recommend a process to be followed. The "prewrite, write, rewrite" formula espoused by some writing instructors is a simple example. However, other thinking frames recommend that one's product display a particular organization. The topic-sentence-elaboration form for a paragraph is one example; the thesis-argument-counterargument-rebuttal-conclusion form for an essay is another. Note that these, unlike process frames, do not advise you to do things in a certain order. You may write the body of a paragraph first and then edit in a topic sentence, outline some of your arguments first and then, with them in mind, formulate your thesis precisely enough to stand at the beginning of your essay. In general, many disciplines have product frames that help to guide and sustain thinking. Other examples are the form of proof in plane geometry; sonnet, villanelle, and other poetic forms; and fugue, rondo, sonata, and other forms in music.

Structure versus Style

Some thinking frames concern the overall structural organization of a process or product. "Prewrite, write, rewrite" recommends a certain process organization, while "thesis, argument, counterargument, rebuttal, conclusion" recommends a certain product organization. Other frames prescribe a style that infuses the process or product. For example, in free writing one is supposed to let the thoughts flow—a process style. As to product style, different writing styles are suitable for different purposes: rich or lean, precise or loose, complex or simple, and so on.

Broadly speaking, what psychologists refer to as cognitive styles are process styles that cut across domains. For instance, a person with an impulsive cognitive style reaches decisions quickly, often too quickly, while a person with a reflective cognitive style reaches decisions more deliberately and cautiously, perhaps, in the extreme, too cautiously (Kagan, 1965; Kagan & Kogan, 1970). In general, our everyday language provides numerous terms to serve as thinking frames for characterizing and recommending for or against styles of thought: loose, rigid, precise, divergent, narrow, broad, fluent, and so on.

Avoiding Rigidity

Just what *is* the thinking frame when one has a complex tactic? Suppose, for instance, a general strategy consists of five component strategies; is each substrategy a frame or just the whole? Or suppose one has a piece of advice consisting of a visual image coupled with a verbal moral? Which is the frame? In both cases, both. In the first instance, one can speak of a frame with subframes, just as one speaks of a strategy with substrategies. Fussiness about whether the frame is the part, the whole, the words, or the image does not suit the purpose of introducing thinking frames as a broad notion that stretches the boundaries of what we normally refer to as tactics or strategies.

With such clarifications in mind, another pointer follows:

Critical principle: A comprehensive program should involve frames of many kinds—process and product, structure and style, general and special purpose. Beware of narrowness in programs.

Packaged programs that teach thinking skills usually concentrate on general or specific process frames, neglecting product and style frames. While no one program with a modest number of lessons can attempt everything, it is wise to remember that tactical intelligence spans far more than most tactically oriented approaches reflect.

Using Effective Thinking Frames

Just as some designs for chairs, airplanes, or cameras serve better than others, so do some thinking frames. Not all thinking frames help their users. Counterexamples come easily to mind. Many a student has fallen into the study formula, "Read the text over and over." Research shows that this frame prescribes a particularly poor method of study. Indeed, better retention results if one spends well over 50 percent of the time reviewing the text mentally rather than rereading it (Higbee, 1977). Research on informal reasoning suggests that naive reasoners use a "makes sense" criterion of truth, pursuing a line of argument only until it seems to make sense without probing it for weaknesses (Perkins, 1985b; Perkins, Allen, & Hafner, 1983). This frame fosters faulty reasoning and ill-founded beliefs. Dweck and Licht (1980) argue that many students suffer from an image of learning as an "either you get it—if you're smart enough—or you don't" process, a frame that naturally impairs their progress.

Therefore, we need to ask whether the frames taught in a particular approach are likely to do their job. While figuring out what makes a good frame cannot be answered by a formula, here are some general concerns.

Leverage

Does the frame in question provide leverage on the desired performance? This cannot be taken for granted. One useful test asks whether the frame bears *directly* on the target performance. For instance, although many have felt that teaching formal logic should improve everyday reasoning, most patterns of formal logical inference rarely occur in pure form in everyday reasoning (Perkins, 1985a; Perkins, Allen, & Hafner, 1983). Some target performances have been investigated enough to reveal a fair amount of information about the sorts of frames that might be helpful, for example, studying (e.g., Higbee, 1977; Palinscar & Brown, 1984; Robinson, 1970; Schmeck, 1983), mathematical problem solving (e.g., Polya, 1954, 1957; Schoenfeld, 1980, 1982; Wickelgren, 1974), problem solving in physics (e.g., Chi, Feltovich, & Glaser, 1981; Larkin, 1983), informal argument (e.g., Ennis, 1969; Ennis, Chapter 1, this volume; Perkins, Allen, & Hafner, 1983; Toulmin, 1958; Toulmin, Rieke, & Janik, 1979), creative thinking (e.g., Lenat, 1983; Perkins, 1981, 1984) and meta-cognitive control strategies (e.g., Flavell, 1981; Lawson, 1984; Robinson, 1983).

However, in many areas, we know much less from empirical work about what might serve well. Moreover, even when relevant research exists, the technical accounts are not always easy to obtain or interpret. By and large, the individual faced with a practical decision in a school context must rely on good judgment, remain aware of the risks, and expect to revise decisions on the basis of experience in his or her setting.

When, What, and How

Most approaches to building thinking skills that teach tactics tell you *what* tactics to use, but not always *when* or *how*. Consider the matter of *when*, for example. Many efforts to teach critical thinking strategies do not deal extensively with when one should undertake a careful critical analysis of an issue. Not only do many trivial decisions not require such depth, but, by failing to distinguish when careful thought can contribute, this method of instruction runs the risk of resulting in students dropping the tactics altogether. A similar story applies to the *how*. For instance, in encouraging young reasoners to think about the other side of the case, instructors may neglect to give them means of distancing themselves and generating alternate arguments. To generalize, a good thinking frame should cover what action is to be taken when and how. Many efforts to teach thinking fall short in this area.

Complexity and Organization

The specific content of frames aside, the decision maker also can look for instruction that teaches an ensemble of frames that are neither too simple nor too complex. For instance, a course of instruction that does nothing but emphasize the imperative "Think!" is not beneficial. Likewise, such broad and folksy bits of advice as "Look before you leap" or "A stitch in time saves nine" do not do much good. At the other extreme, some approaches to teaching thinking emphasize long lists of forty or more principles that learners are supposed to take to heart during a semester course. Few students can internalize so much general guidance that quickly. When the ensemble of frames being taught appears somewhat complicated, one saving feature to look for is organization. Are the principles sorted into categories, ordered by priority, cast into a hierarchy? Any such structure will make the complexity more manageable.

Self-monitoring and Management

Particular tactics can be used more effectively if accompanied by frames that keep one alert to what one is doing and what one's options are (Belmont, Butterfield, & Ferretti, 1982). For instance, students can be encouraged to ask themselves every five or ten minutes, "Am I making progress? If not, should I change directions, try a new approach? What are my options right now?" (Schoenfeld, 1980). In general, some emphasis on self-monitoring and management should be part of any instruction in thinking skills.

Generality–Power Tradeoff

Sometimes what a frame is good for depends on what you want. The generality–power tradeoff is a widely recognized relationship between the generality and power of thinking tactics. As a rule of thumb, the more general the thinking frame, the more weakly it serves any given application. For instance, very general rules of problem solving such as "try to relate the problem to one you have already solved" find wide application and offer some help, but do not suddenly empower one to solve numerous problems in math or chess or chemistry that one could not manage before. In contrast, a field-specific frame such as the notion of energy balance in physics may do just that for its particular range of application. Most stand-alone programs designed to teach thinking skills teach general frames and therefore offer modest gains across a wide front (but see the cautions about transfer in a previous section). Efforts to integrate the teaching of thinking skills with the subject matters can offer much more field-specific thinking frames and hence potentially can boost performance in particular fields. Deciding which to attempt or whether to try for both involves both priorities and available resources.

Bootstrap Frames

The discussion of the generality-power tradeoff addressed short-term benefits. But there is a complicating factor: Some general frames, although only modestly empowering in the short run, may prove excellent investments in the long run exactly because they help learners to expand their frame repertoires. Frames concerning learning strategies pay for themselves not so much during the week or month in which they are acquired as during the years that follow. Like compound interest, they increase the learner's intellectual capital. The tactic "try to make up a tactic and use it" is another simple example. If you practice that tactic persistently, you may have difficulty making up a good tactic on any one occasion, but gradually your repertoire of tactics will grow. Such frames may be called *bootstrap frames*, because they help to lift a frame repertoire by its own bootstraps.

Many approaches to fostering the development of thinking include bootstrap frames. Examples include the four design questions at the center of the knowledge as design approach to subject matter instruction (Perkins, 1986; Perkins, Chapter 4, this volume), the operations of selective encoding, comparison, and combination (Sternberg, 1985; Sternberg, Chapter 10, this volume), strategies for self-monitoring (e.g., Belmont, Butterfield, & Ferretti, 1982), key cognitive styles (e.g., Baron, 1978), and others. In general, high priority should be given to including at least some bootstrap frames in any approach, although including *only* bootstrap frames may be unwise, because of the short-term generality-power tradeoff.

Finding Frames That Work

More might be said about the sorts of frames that serve the learner well. However, the foregoing points will do for a first take on the vexing problem of assessing what frames an approach to teaching thinking offers. One might sum up the implications as follows.

Critical principle: consider whether the frames will really help.

Some particular questions to ask in applying this principle are:

1. Do the frames provide genuine leverage on the task?

2. Do the frames specify what to try, when to try it, and how?

3. Is the ensemble of frames well-organized and not too large?

4. Is there provision for self-monitoring and management?

5. Does the approach offer the generality-power tradeoff you want?

6. Are some of the frames bootstrap frames?

MAKING SENSE OF MAKING MINDS

Answering the Three Questions

Teaching thinking is a matter of making minds. The framework presented here is a small offering toward making sense of this process of shaping minds, along with some criteria for judging what might be better and worse ways of making minds. At the outset, three key questions were mentioned. Broad answers to those questions have been offered along the following lines.

What Constitutes Better Thinking?

Intelligence in the sense of general intellectual competence can be considered a compound of neurological power, tactical repertoire, and context-specific content as expressed in the metaphorical equation Intelligence = Power + Tactics + Content. The power aspect of intelligence may not improve much with practice, especially in the short term. However, both tactics and content can be learned. One's tactical repertoire consists of thinking frames, a term chosen to embrace a broader range than is generally connoted by the term tactics. Thinking frames are extremely varied and function by supporting and organizing thought.

By What Process Can People Learn to Think Better?

The analysis of intelligence into power, tactics, and content suggests that enhancing people's tactical repertoire provides the best educational opportunity, considering the resistance to change and the time needed to acquire a rich base of content knowledge. This means that people need to learn thinking frames. One can analyze the learning process into three aspects.

Acquisition. Frames are acquired by (a) direct instruction, formal or informal, or (b) invention by the learner, often provoked by an enriched context, but not by (c) learners unconsciously soaking up frames from context.

Making references automatic. To function well, frames need to operate automatically to relieve requirements on working memory. This can happen by (a) practice on very simple examples or (b) practice with memory supports that are eventually withdrawn as the performance is internalized.

Transfer. Transfer of frames tends not to occur spontaneously. Transfer can be encouraged by (a) explicit guidance toward high-road transfer, fostering self-monitoring of problem-solving processes, abstraction of frames, and applications in new contexts, or (b) varied practice that widely samples the range of potential applications to promote low-road transfer.

How Can One Tell Whether a Particular Approach to Teaching Thinking Is Effective?

The critical principles advanced earlier call for review. First of all, one can examine the frames an approach teaches.

Varied frames. Favor a rich combination of approaches that includes a variety of types of frames—process and product, structure and style, and so on.

Effective frames. Favor frames that genuinely offer leverage on the task, specify what to try, when to try it, and how, and provide a well-organized ensemble.

Generality-power tradeoff. Consider what generality-power tradeoff suits the situation in question.

Bootstrap frames. Use bootstrap frames, which foster the learning of other frames. These include frames for cognitive control and for learning.

The Process of Learning

Just as important as what frames should be learned is the process of learning, where other hazards appear.

Acquisition. Use approaches that teach frames directly. View with caution approaches that rely on provoking students to invent their own frames: The provoking must involve more than just practice and an enriched context of modeling. Do not rely on approaches that only emphasize practice, with its tacit power theory.

Making performance automatic. Be sure that an approach provides for making the frames automatic through practice with very simple examples or by external frame reminders withdrawn as frames become internalized.

Transfer. Encourage transfer by explicitly promoting high-road transfer through emphasis on self-monitoring and deliberate abstrction and application or by explicitly promoting low-road transfer through practice on a variety of examples that include a wide range of potential applications. Ideally, both roads can be taken at once—if time allows.

Making minds is a much more serious enterprise than making book or beds, something quite as sensitive and substantive as making babies. Of course, those involved in education take only a modest share of the responsibility. Our minds are made in many ways—by genetic influences, patterns of early parenting, the imprint of culture, favorite toys. But what happens in classrooms helps shape minds, whether by art or accident. The aim must be for more art and less accident. The responsibility is a serious and exciting one, and current science gives no safe formula for sure bets. Perhaps the framework offered here will provide educators and others encountering this new domain of teaching thinking with some creative impetus and a critical guide.

REFERENCES

Baron, J. (1978). Intelligence and general strategies. In G. Underwood (Ed.), *Strategies in information processing* (pp. 403–450). London: Academic Press.

Belmont, J. M., Butterfield, E. C., & Ferretti, R. P. (1982). To secure transfer of training instruct self-management skills. In D. K. Detterman & R. J. Sternberg (Eds.), *How and how much can intelligence be increased?* (pp. 147–154). Norwood, N.J.: Ablex.

Bolt Beranek and Newman, Inc. (1983). *Final report, Project Intelligence: The development of procedures to enhance thinking skills.* Cambridge, Mass.: Bolt Beranek and Newman, Inc.

Boyer, E. (1983). *High school: A report on secondary education in America.* New York: Harper & Row.

Brainerd, C. J. (1983). Working-memory systems and cognitive development. In C. J. Brainerd (Ed.), *Recent advances in cognitive-developmental theory: Progress in cognitive development research* (pp. 167–236). New York: Springer-Verlag.

Case, R. (1984). The process of stage transition. A neo-Piagetian viewpoint. In R. J. Sternberg (Ed.), *Mechanisms of cognitive development* (pp. 19–44), New York: W. H. Freeman and Company.

Chase, W. C., & Simon, H. A. (1973). Perception in chess (Cognitive Psychology, 4:55–81.

Chi, M., Feltovich, P., & Glaser, R. (1981). Categorization and representation of physics problems by experts and novices. *Cognitive Science,* 5:121–152.

Chipman, S. F., Segal, J. W., & Glaser, R. (Eds.). (1985). *Thinking and learning skills: Research and open questions* (Vol. 2). Hillsdale, N.J.: Erlbaum.

de Groot, A. D. (1965). *Thought and choice in chess.* The Hague: Mouton.

Dweck, C. S., & Licht, B. G. (1980). Learned helplessness and intellectual achievement. In J. Garbar & M. Seligman (Eds.), *Human helplessness.* New York: Academic Press.

Ennis, R. H. (1969). *Logic in teaching.* Englewood Clifs, N.J.: Prentice-Hall.

Ericsson, K. A., & Simon, H. A. (1984). *Protocol analysis.* Cambridge: MIT Press.

Flavell, J. H. (1981). Cognitive monitoring. In W. Patrick Dickson (Ed.), *Children's oral communication skills* (pp. 35–60). New York: Academic Press.

Gardner, H. (1983). *Frames of mind.* New York: Basic Books.

Goodlad, J. I. (1983). *A place called school: Prospects for the future.* New York: McGraw-Hill.

Hayes, J. R. (1981). *The complete problem solver.* Philadelphia: Franklin Institute.

Higbee, K. L. (1977). *Your memory: How it works and how to improve it.* Englewood Cliffs, N.J.: Prentice-Hall.

Jensen, A. R. (1984). Test validity: *g* versus the specificity doctrine. *Journal of Social and Biological Structures,* 7:93–118.

Kagan, J. (1965). Individual differences in the resolution of response uncertainty. *Journal of Personality and Social Psychology,* 2:154–160.

Kagan, J., & Kogan, N. (1970). Individuality and cognitive performance. In P. Mussen (Ed.). *Carmichael's manual of child psychology* (Vol. 1). New York: Wiley.

Larkin, J. H. (1983). The role of problem representation in physics. In D. Gentner & A. L. Stevens (Eds.), *Mental models.* Hillsdale, N.J.: Erlbaum.

Lawson, M. J. (1984). Being executive about metacognition. In J. R. Kirby (Ed.), *Cognitive strategies and educational performance* (pp. 89–110). New York: Academic Press.

Lenat, D. B. (1983). Toward a theory of heuristics. In R. Groner, M. Groner, & W. F. Bischof (Eds.), *Methods of heuristics* (pp. 351–404). Hillsdale, N.J.: Erlbaum.

Miller, G. A. (1956). The magical number seven, plus or minus two: Some limits on our capacity for processing information. *Psychological Review,* 63:81–87.

Mullis, I. V. S. (1984). What do NAEP results tell us about students' higher order thinking abilities? Paper prepared for the Wingspread Conference on Teaching Thinking Skills. Wingspread Conference Center, Racine, Wisconsin.

National Commission on Excellence in Education (1983). *A nation at risk: The imperative for educational reform.* Washington, D.C.: U.S. Department of Education.

Nickerson, R., Perkins, D. N., & Smith, E. (1985). *The teaching of thinking.* Hillsdale, N.J.: Erlbaum.

Palinscar, A. S. & Brown, A. L. (1984). Reciprocal teaching of comprehension-fostering and comprehension-monitoring activities. *Cognition and Instruction,* 1:117–175.

Pea, R. D., & Kurland, M. D. (1984a). *Logo programming and the development of planning skills.* Paper presented at the Conference on Thinking, Harvard Graduate School of Education, Cambridge.

Pea, R., & Kurland, M. D. (1984b). On the cognitive effects of learning computer programming. *New Ideas in Psychology,* 2:137–168.

Perkins, D. N. (1981). *The mind's best work.* Cambridge: Harvard University Press.

Perkins, D. N. (1984). Creativity by design. *Educational Leadership,* 42:18–25.

Perkins, D. N. (1985a). Reasoning as imagination. *Interchange,* 16:14–26.

Perkins, D. N. (1985b). Post-primary education has little impact on informal reasoning. *Journal of Educational Psychology,* 77:562–571.

Perkins, D. N. (1986). *Knowledge as design.* Hillsdale, N.J.: Erlbaum.

Perkins, D. N., Allen, R., & Hafner, J. (1983). Difficulties in everyday reasoning. In W. Maxwell (Ed.), *Thinking: The frontier expands* (pp. 177–189). Philadelphia: Franklin Institute.

Perkins, D., & Salomon, G. (1986). Transfer and teaching thinking. In D. Perkins, J. Bishop, J. Lochhead, (Eds.). *Thinking: Progress in research and teaching.* Hillsdale, N.J.: Erlbaum.

Polya, G. (1954). *Mathematics and plausible reasoning* (2 vols.). Princeton, N.J.: Princeton University Press.

Polya, G. (1957). *How to solve it: A new aspect of mathematical method* (2nd ed.). Garden City, N.Y.: Doubleday.

Robinson, E. (1983). Metacognitive development. In S. Meadows (Ed.), *Developing thinking: Approaches to children's cognitive development* (pp. 106–141). New York: Methuen.

Robinson, F. P. (1970). *Effective study*. New York: Harper & Row.

Salomon, G., & Perkins, D. N. (1984). *Rocky roads to transfer: Rethinking mechanisms of a neglected phenomenon*. Paper presented at the Conference on Thinking, Harvard Graduate School of Education, Cambridge.

Schmeck, R. R. (1983). Learning styles of college students. In R. F. Dillon & R. R. Schmeck (Eds.). *Individual differences in cognition* (Vol. 1, pp. 233–270). New York: Academic.

Schoenfeld, A. H. (1978). Presenting a strategy for indefinite integration. *American Mathematical Monthly*, 85:673–678.

Schoenfeld, A. H. (1979). Explicit heuristic training as a variable in problem solving performance. *Journal for Research in Mathematics Education*, 10:173–187.

Schoenfeld, A. H. (1980). Teaching problem-solving skills. *American Mathematical Monthly*, 87:794–805.

Schoenfeld, A. H. (1982). Measures of problem-solving performance and of problem-solving instruction. *Journal for Research in Mathematics Education*, 13:31–49.

Schoenfeld, A. H., & Herrmann, D. J. (1982). Problem perception and knowledge structure in expert and novice mathematical problem solvers. *Journal of Experimental Psychology: Learning, Memory, and Cognition*, 8:484–494.

Schooler, C. (1984). Psychological effects of complex environments during the life span: A review and theory. *Intelligence*, 8:259–281.

Scribner, S., & Cole, M. (1981). *The psychology of literacy*. Cambridge: Harvard University Press.

Segal, J. W., Chipman, S. F., & Glaser, R. (Eds.), (1985). *Thinking and learning skills, Relating instruction to research* (Vol. 1). Hillsdale, N.J.: Erlbaum.

Sizer, T. B. (1984). *Horace's compromise: The dilemma of the American high school today*. Boston: Houghton Mifflin.

Soloway, E., & Ehrlich, K. (1984). Empirical studies of programming knowledge. *IEEE Transactions on Software Engineering, SE-10*(5), 595–609.

Sternberg, R. J. (1985). *Beyond I.Q.: A triarchic theory of human intelligence*. New York: Cambridge University Press.

Toulmin, S. E. (1958). *The uses of argument*. Cambridge, England: Cambridge. University Press.

Toulmin, S. E., Rieke, R., & Janik, A. (1979). *An introduction to reasoning*. New York: Macmillan.

Wickelgren, W. A. (1974). *How to solve problems: Elements of a theory of problems and problem solving*. New York: W. H. Freeman and Company.

This chapter was prepared at Project Zero of the Harvard Graduate School of Education, with support from National Institute of Education grant number NIE-G-83-0028, *Learning to Reason*. The ideas expressed here do not necessarily reflect the positions or policies of the supporting agency.

4

D. N. PERKINS
Graduate School of Education
Harvard University

Knowledge as Design: Teaching Thinking Through Content

Two current trends make these times especially promising for education and educators. First, recent reports criticizing our nation's schools have aroused public awareness and support of education. Second, advances in theories of thinking and learning, together with a number of practical experiments, suggest that thinking can be taught. The two trends go hand in hand because a principal criticism has been that education is too fact oriented and mindless—just the sort of shortfall that attention to the teaching of thinking might remedy.

By itself, however, this sense of support and direction does not amount to a solution or even to a clear definition of the many problems educators face. Therefore, it's useful to highlight a pair of problems posed by contemporary criticisms of education and the aroused interest in teaching thinking. I call them the problems of disconnected knowledge and teaching thinking out of context.

As to disconnected knowledge, students often receive knowledge disconnected from features that make it understandable and meaningful. For instance, in math it's common to learn concepts without knowing their purposes; often those purposes only unfold as the student progresses through the system of mathematical concepts under study. For example, when you learn the Pythagorean theorem, you usually learn little about the pervasive role it plays in many aspects of mathematics. When you study history, you frequently find scant attention paid to the evidence underlying an historical fact or interpretation. To be sure, a certain amount of ground needs to be covered and one cannot stop to justify every point. Still, the extreme disconnection from argument is striking: Students may come to know something about history, but not much about historical thinking. Science instruction routinely pays insufficient attention to examples and images that make the concepts under study vivid and concrete and impart an intuitive grasp of them. For example, few students, even at the college level, have a good sense of how an object in free fall behaves. They may have learned the equations, but not what those equations mean dynamically. While I have referred to disconnection from purposes in the context of mathematics, from arguments in the context of history, and from examples and images in the context of physics, such gaps clearly are not limited to those specific subject matters.

The emphasis on themes such as purpose, arguments, and images is connected to current efforts to teach thinking skills. Perhaps the teaching of thinking in primary school, secondary school, and college could alleviate this problem of disconnected knowledge. Unfortunately, the solution is not that simple. Most efforts to teach thinking skills take the form of stand-alone courses rather than instruction integrated with the teaching of content. They do not teach thinking in context, but on the side. What are the benefits and risks of teaching thinking out of context?

One practical advantage is that teaching a single course is far simpler than revitalizing the style of instruction throughout a curriculum. Another is that academic courses are not the only occasions for thinking in students' lives. Some stand-alone courses designed to teach thinking skills potentially impact on home problems, career decisions, and other issues beyond the immediate compass of their schooling. Still another is that several stand-alone courses exist and there is even evidence that some are effective in meeting their immediate objectives, although questions of long-term impact and transfer usually go beyond the available data.

However, there is another side to the argument. Placing all our bets on stand-alone thinking courses entails certain risks and misses certain opportunities. The principal risk is the problem of transfer. Contemporary research shows that instruction offered in one context often does not transfer to other contexts, so that thinking skills taught out of the context of subject matter instruction may well have little impact on performance in the subject areas. Sometimes such impact may occur, but despite these exceptions, the difficulty is very real. In contrast, teaching thinking through content dissolves the whole problem of transfer.

As to the opportunity, teaching thinking through content promises far more exposure and practice during the course of education than stand-alone courses are likely to provide. Politically and practically, it's hard to imagine a primary school or secondary school curriculum with more than a couple of one-year stand-alone courses on thinking. On the other hand, a high percentage of routinely taught courses might involve some teaching of thinking in context.

Taken together, the problems of disconnected knowledge and teaching thinking out of context pose an interesting challenge for education. Many teachers, working in their own ways, infuse their content instruction with attention to critical and creative thinking. But this harvest of talent will not in itself provide a philosophy and methodology that can be disseminated. Then how in general can we teach thinking in context in such a way that knowledge gets connected to the aims, images, and arguments that make it meaningful? The problem might be addressed in many ways, one of which is known as knowledge as design.

A THEORY OF KNOWLEDGE FOR TEACHING THINKING

Many approaches to teaching thinking have at their core theories of thinking, problem solving, creativity, or other traits and abilities of the mind. My philosophy differs from these in beginning with a theory of knowledge that concerns not what people should do to think well but what constitutes knowledge. Such an approach lays a good foundation for any method that aims to integrate the teaching of thinking with subject-matter instruction, because subject-matter instruction deals with the knowledge and know-how of particular fields.

The theory of knowledge in question is simple from the standpoints of philosophy and psychology. It holds that understanding any piece of knowledge or any product of human intellect involves viewing it as a design, a structure shaped to a purpose. In particular, understanding involves being able to answer four design questions about the object in question:

What is its *purpose* (or purposes—there may be more than one)?

What is its *structure*?

What are *model cases*?

What *arguments* explain and evaluate the object?

The more deeply a learner explores these four questions, the better the understanding.

For example, consider a simple object like a thumbtack. What is its purpose? To attach papers or other light penetrable objects to bulletin boards and other penetrable surfaces. What is its structure? A wide round head affixed to a short prong. What are the model cases? Here one would show an actual example if thumbtacks were new to the group in question; but thumbtacks are so familiar that this is not needed. What are the arguments? For a simple explanatory argument, the head is wide to provide a comfortable platform for the thumb and a large surface to hold papers without the papers ripping off the tack easily. The short shaft allows the tack to penetrate up to its head readily and hold papers firmly against the bulletin board or other surface. The point permits the tack to penetrate easily. For a simple evaluative argument, thumbtacks are cheap, handy, and easy to insert; but they can create holes in walls, sometimes are hard to remove, and when lost on the floor, they may get stuck in the soles of your shoes or, worse yet, in bare feet.

This brief exploration of a thumbtack seems straightforward, but how often do we examine the ingenuity behind the ordinary objects around us? Moreover, we can carry the analysis much deeper. There is a physics of thumbtacks worthy of the attention of students who may wonder whether the theories in a textbook pertain to anything between planets and atoms. The point of the tack concentrates the force applied by the thumb onto a very small area, yielding a very high pressure. This principle helps the tack penetrate a hard surface. The slanting sides of the prong taper to a point, exemplifying the principles of a wedge: The taper pushes the material of a penetrable surface to the sides with much more force than would a more abrupt taper because of the wedge effect. Students with the mathematical background can calculate the gains resulting from the concentration of pressure and the wedge effect. All this is an extension of the explanatory argument begun with simple comments about the flat head and the pointed shaft.

The Wide Applicability of Knowledge as Design

Of course, a theory of knowledge worth its salt has to deal with a far greater range of items than household gadgets. Many examples will appear in the following pages, but pointing out that the four design questions make sense for a variety of academic topics will do for now. For example, is it meaningful to ask about the purpose, structure, model cases, and arguments for a political system like democracy? Yes, the purpose has to do with governing and human rights, the structure involves elections, model cases include the United States, and the arguments include the trade-off between the advantages and abuses of centralized power. Can one reasonably ask the design questions of a scientific theory like Newton's laws? To be sure, this purpose involves explaining a range of dynamic phenomena, the equations give the structure, model cases include the orbits of the planets, and the arguments include the empirical evidence for the soundness of the laws. What about a sonnet? The purpose concerns poetic expression, the structure, classic sonnet form, model cases include Shakespeare's "That time of year . . ." and arguments about the form involve the trade-off between lost freedom and gained guidance provided by a formal structure.

Perhaps these examples suffice to suggest that the design questions find application in nearly any academic context. But how do they address the two problems described at the outset—disconnected knowledge and teaching thinking out of context? As to the first, notice that the design questions dealing with purpose, models, and arguments concern the very problems of disconnection. Instruction organized around the design questions does not permit neglect of the purposes of theorems, the evidence for historical facts and interpretations, or model cases exemplifying principles of physics. In education, we almost always attend to the structure of what's being taught—the form of the theorem, the outline of an historical event, the formulas of a physical theory—and in this way answer the structure question. But the other three design questions too often are ignored.

As to teaching thinking, steps in that direction are built into the design questions. Simply asked one by one, they provide a guide to analyzing objects as concrete as thumbtacks and as abstract as theorems. Attention to explanatory and evaluative arguments yields a focus on critical thinking. Examination of model cases and the general structure they exemplify helps students pass between concrete examples and abstractions and facilitates the acquisition of abstractions. The accent on knowledge as design opens the way for students to participate in the designing of pieces of knowledge such as simple theories and other products of mind such as poems. Finally, other tactics of thinking, such as heuristics for problem solving, can be learned and understood through the framework; after all, a problem-solving heuristic itself is a design shaped to help us to solve a certain sort of problem. If one thinks of it as a mental screwdriver, one can understand it in terms of the same four design questions one applies to a physical screwdriver.

The following sections examine how some of this translates into classroom practice. Since there are so many possibilities, the emphasis here falls on applications that foster understanding and critical thinking, leaving applications that focus on creativity to another occasion. (At the same time, note that critical and creative thinking are not entirely separate; good critical thinking is creative in its insights, whereas good creative thinking invariably involves critical appraisal and improvement of the product in progress.)

One last comment before taking up some applications: Notice that the first two sections of this chapter covertly use the four design questions as their organizing framework. Each begins with an exploration of purpose, continues with a description of some structure, offers model cases, and closes with explanations and justifications. Knowledge as design is a framework as well suited to explaining itself as to explaining other things. That same straightforward pattern is repeated in the sections that follow.

EXPLICATING A CONCEPT

Teachers often need to explicate a difficult or confusing concept to students. Such a challenge frequently arises in mathematics, which seems to have more than its share of such concepts. The four design questions provide a systematic way of examining a concept and trying to make it plain. Consider the familiar case of explaining and justifying why a negative number times a negative number yields a positive number.

We know about positive numbers times positive numbers and about positive times negative and negative times positive numbers. There's one more combination we need to worry about: a negative number times a negative number. How does that come out? And why do we need to concern ourselves with it at all?

Purpose

Let's take the second question first. One reason we have to worry about it is that it's there. You can write down a problem like $-3 \times -5 = ?$. If you can write the problem, it's nice to know a way to solve it. Another reason is that sometimes cases arise where the natural thing to do is to multiply a negative times a negative, so you need to know the results.

Structure

Now there's no secret about the rule, and you'll just need to learn it. A negative number times a negative number yields a positive number. For example, $-3 \times -5 = +15$. Very simple. The question is: Why that rule?

Models

Let's look at some model cases, remembering that multiplication is just repeated addition; 3 times 5 is just 3 added 5 times. Natural situations for a positive times a positive come up often. For instance, you get your allowance of $3 five times and you gain $15. Occasionally cases of a negative times a positive arise. For instance, you lose your $3 allowance five times for misbehavior; that's $-3 \times 5 = -15$. You're short $15 you otherwise would have had. Occasionally cases of a positive times a negative arise, too. For instance, your parents forget your $3 allowance five times; that's *not* repeating your allowance five times, or $3 \times -5 = -15$. Again you're short $15.

Now what about a negative times a negative? Well, suppose that for misbehavior your parents want to withhold your allowance five times. But they forget. That's -3, the withheld allowance, $\times -5$, *not* repeating the withholding five times, $= +15$, you gain $15. What's going on here is very simple. A negative times a negative is a case of double reversal. One thing in the situation reverses things once, but something else in the situation reverses things again, so you're back to a positive. Let's make a table of the model cases we've discussed to see how it all works out (Table 4-1).

Here are a few more examples of negative times positive and positive times negative situations.

George is a gambler. When he's on a winning streak, he wins $400 per day. But when he's on a losing streak, he loses $400 per day. Suppose George is on a losing streak and goes gambling for five days. How much does he lose? Now suppose George is on a losing streak but he has the sense to stay home. How much does he save in this double reversal situation?

Alice wants to lose weight. Every day that Alice jogs, she loses 3 ounces. Suppose Alice jogs 7 days; how much does she lose? Now suppose Alice skips her jogging for 7 days. How much does she *not* lose? To put it another way, how much more does she weigh than she would have if she'd jogged?

Argument

We've talked about examples of a negative times a negative, but we haven't justified the rule. How do we know it's right? Well, the examples themselves tell us something—it makes sense that a negative times a negative would be a positive. Remember: If Alice loses 3 ounces per day when she jogs but gets lazy for a week and doesn't jog, that's $-3 \times -7 = +21$ ounces she's heavier than she would have been. That's some justification.

Let's look a little more carefully at the justification issue simply in terms of numbers. You have a problem like $-3 \times -7 = ?$. What are your choices? You certainly want the answer to come out -21 or $+21$, or you wouldn't be multiplying. So which is it? Think of it as a design problem: Which rule is going to work out best in the long run?

Let's try the negative rule and see if it gets us into trouble. Let's say that $-3 \times -7 = -21$. Now this is a little odd because we already have agreed that $-3 \times +7 = -21$; repeating -3 seven times certainly yields -21. So if we say that we get -21 from -3 and -7 too, it's as though the sign of the 7 doesn't make any difference. Now we probably don't want that to happen; $+7$ is a lot different from -7 and it ought to make a difference whether you have a $+7$ or a -7 when you multiply. If we use the rule that a negative times a negative is positive, it *does* make a difference. We have $-3 \times +7 = -21$, but $-3 \times -7 = +21$. In other words, examples like the case of Alice or the case of the allowance aside, we only have a couple of design options for de-

Table 4-1 A Model Case of a Negative Times a Negative

No reversal	Get your allowance	$3		5	times	gain	$15
		+3	×	+5		=	+15
One reversal	Cancel allowance	$3		5	times	short	$15
		-3	×	+5		=	-15
Another reversal	Get your allowance	$3 forgotten		5	times	short	$15
		+3	×	-5		=	-15
Both reversals	Cancel allowance	$3 forgotten		5	times	gain	$15
		-3	×	-5		=	+15

ciding what rule we want. The option that a negative times a negative yields a negative leads to a strange situation; that leaves us with the other option: a negative times a negative yields a positive.

Of course, none of this is a mathematical *proof* that a negative times a negative is a positive. The rule can be proved formally if the level of sophistication of the group warrants it.

Querying the Design Questions

This example of seeking to make a concept clear by applying the four design questions brings up some questions of its own.

Isn't this a great deal of work just to get across the rule that a negative times a negative yields a positive? I intend to teach an understanding of the rule. The rule alone could be taught by rote much more efficiently. Probably there is not enough school time to teach everything with full understanding, so we have to choose where to make that effort. This rule of arithmetic might be one such place, but the same principles of knowledge as design apply to whatever you choose.

Skilled teachers often present something in this manner anyway, don't they? Indeed they do, a point that helps to justify the knowledge as design approach. Teachers often make the purposes of something plain, state the structure clearly, and give model cases and a justification. This also is a characteristic of good expository writing; examine the work of a writer who writes very clearly and you will find that the writer usually touches on all four points. The themes of purpose, structure, model cases, and argument are natural parts of what it routinely means to be clear about something.

Then why spell out the four questions? Because, as a matter of fact, although we sometimes spontaneously pay heed to them, very often we do not. This results in the problem of disconnected knowledge in education discussed earlier.

So all we need to do is stick to the questions? Unfortunately, it's not that simple. To use the questions well in explicating a concept, we have to invent clear statements of purpose, structure, models, and arguments. The four design questions provide a framework within which to proceed but do not reduce teaching to a formula because they require us to generate precise answers to the four questions. This is unfortunate because it calls for effort but fortunate because it forces us to strive to teach for meaning and not take a cookbook approach.

STUDENT DESIGN ANALYSES

Involving Students in Knowledge as Design

The previous section emphasized that teachers employing the design framework to explicate concepts need to work out design analyses of the concept in question. Of course, we also would like to engage the students in developing such analyses. Education should not be solely a matter of serving up knowledge on a platter but should involve students themselves in the process of investigative thinking. The four design questions provide a convenient framework for accomplishing that purpose.

One straightforward plan is as follows.

1. Invite students to write brief analyses of an ordinary object considered as a design, stating its purpose and discussing why and how well the object is designed to serve that purpose.

2. Introduce the four design questions by modeling an example on the blackboard; then ask the students to write another analysis, using the design questions as headings.

3. Introduce a design analysis sheet that gives explicit guidance about what to put down and in what proportions; have the students write two or three anlayses using this form.

4. Wean the students of the sheet, asking them to keep its basic structure in mind but to write analyses without looking at it.

5. Carry this style of analysis over to nonconcrete designs that are reasonably accessible.

An Application: The Bill of Rights

Let us see what these five steps might look like in a particular case.

Step 1.   Writing about Something as a Design

The teacher asks the students to write about a pair of scissors as a design, stating its purpose and explaining the manner in which its structure serves that purpose and how effectively it works. The students are given 10 minutes to write for this and subsequent exercises; the time limit keeps the pace up.

Step 2.   Introducing the Design Questions

The teacher introduces the four design questions as a way to help in thinking about designs. The teacher analyzes a towel on the blackboard, providing some answers and calling on the class for others. Then the teacher asks the students to write another 10-minute analysis, using the four design questions as headings. This time the students analyze a blackboard eraser.

Step 3.   Introducing the Design Analysis Sheet

It's hard to convey to students how much one can say about an everyday object and how to relate the argument to the structure by explanation. A form like that in Table 4-2 provides a visual organization that helps the students to achieve a new level of elaboration. The teacher hands out copies of the design analysis sheet and models filling one out, addressing the example of a wash-cloth. Then the students do another 10-minute analysis, this time using the form and analyzing a cup and saucer.

Step 4. Fading the Design Analysis Sheet

The teacher announces that while it's good to have a form for clarity, but one cannot carry around a form all the time. The teacher then asks the students to write three more analyses overnight, using common household objects (for instance, chairs, bookmarks, or staircases, but not the insides of television sets or stereos). For each analysis, they can look at the design analysis sheet before starting but must not look at it while writing; rather, they should try to re-member its rough style and lay out their analyses similarly. Again, the students are to do each analysis in just 10 minutes.

Step 5. Escalating to More Abstract Topics

The previous step prepares the students to attempt analyses of more abstract objects, for example, the Bill of Rights. The next day, the teacher announces

Table 4-2 Design Analysis Sheet

Purpose(s)	Design: _____ Model (image or examples)
1. _____	
2. _____	
3. _____	
4. _____	
5. _____	
Structure (name parts, materials, shapes, and other features; if the name is ambiguous, label the model, too)	Argument 1: Explain how feature helps
1. _____	_____
2. _____	_____
3. _____	_____
4. _____	_____
5. _____	_____
6. _____	_____

Table 4-2 (*continued*)

7. _____	_____
8. _____	_____
9. _____	_____
10. _____	_____
11. _____	_____
12. _____	_____
13. _____	_____
14. _____	_____
15. _____	_____

Argument 2: Evaluate pros	Cons
1. _____	_____
2. _____	_____
3. _____	_____
4. _____	_____
5. _____	_____
6. _____	_____
7. _____	_____
8. _____	_____
9. _____	_____
10. _____	_____
11. _____	_____
12. _____	_____

Argument 3: State deep principles	Other design(s) with same principle(s)
1. _____	_____
2. _____	_____
3. _____	_____
4. _____	_____
5. _____	_____
6. _____	_____

that not only concrete objects, like pencils and chairs, but also any product of human ingenuity can be analyzed as a design. The teacher chooses as examples the articles of the Bill of Rights. (The Bill of Rights as a whole could also be analyzed, with less attention to the individual articles, of course; the teacher treats the articles separately in order to get more mileage out of the example.)

Table 4-3 A Blackboard Analysis of the First Amendment of the Bill of Rights

Purposes:	To ensure basic freedoms.
	To protect citizens from abuse by government powers.
	To make sure citizens have access to information.
Models:	For instance, a newspaper can criticize the government.
	You can sue the government.
	You can have a meeting or talk over whether government is doing a good job.

Structure with explanations:

Freedom of religion:	Because many governments have a state religion and suppress minority religions.
Freedom of speech:	Because many governments prevent people from speaking out against them so they don't receive criticism to improve themselves.
Freedom of press:	Because you can't have a democracy without people being informed; some governments manipulate people by mis-informing them.
Right of assembly:	People have to be able to meet together to plan and take united action; some governments don't allow this to pro-tect themselves.
Right of petition:	Many governments that injure you can just ignore your com-plaints; but this says that your case will be heard on its merits.

Pros:	Lack of opposition.
	Recourse when you feel you have been wronged.
	Opportunity to change the system.
	Feel freer.
	Leads you to think more about your role in society.
	More straight information available.
	Harder for government officials to be dishonest.
Cons:	In emergencies, government has less control.
	You have more burdens to bear as a citizen.
	Information more confusing, conflicting, with no one party line.
Deep principles:	To guarantee a right, put it in writing.
	Other examples: written laws and contracts.
	Don't just grant power; explicitly limit power.
	Other examples: Can't make your kids work in factories.

Following the layout of the design analysis sheet from memory, the teacher leads the class in an analysis of the First Amendment:

> Congress shall make no law respecting an establishment of religion or prohibiting the free exercise thereof; or abridging the freedom of speech, or of the press; or the right of the people peaceably to assemble, and to petition the Government for a redress of grievances.

The analysis in Table 4–3 might accumulate on the blackboard.

After modeling such an analysis on the blackboard, the teacher asks the students to write analyses of the Second Amendment, concerning the right to bear arms. The students have about 15 minutes to do this. Then the teacher discusses their ideas. Finally, the teacher asks the students to write two or more analyses for the next day, choosing any two of the remaining amendments of the Bill of Rights.

Why should one use the five steps sketched above or some similarly organized sequence? Often students have difficulties addressing abstractions such as articles of the Bill of Rights. So one first introduces the design questions and the design analysis sheet with concrete familiar objects. The students could, of course, use the design analysis sheet all of the time, but that creates a dependency. To encourage internalization of the questions and format, the teacher asks the students to learn the rough layout of the sheet and proceed freehand with their exercises. The teacher introduces time limits and stresses productivity to promote an initial fluency with design analyses. With a little practice and concentration, and working with a concrete object, it's possible to list at least 20 points about a concrete design, and sometimes up to 50, in a period of 10 minutes, including purpose points, structure points, models, and arguments.

CLASSROOM DISCUSSION

Classroom discussions are an important part of many instructional settings. The question is, how to conduct them so that they involve most of the students, proceed in an organized way, and penetrate beneath the surface of a topic.

The framework of the four design questions offers some help here. Of course, discussions can proceed in many useful ways. One involves the straightforward treatment of the design questions. The teacher takes special care with the argument question, pushing the discourse as deep as the students' responses and time allow.

An Application: The Physics of Frisbees

Imagine, for instance, a discussion in a science class where a student has brought in a frisbee as an example of something that flies. The student's frisbee provides a model. Suppose that brief conversations about purpose and structure are behind us and the teacher turns to argument.

Teacher: Okay, let's consider some explanation now. Why is the frisbee built this way? Look back at our list of structural features on the blackboard and see if you can explain one of them. Why is the frisbee designed the way it is? I'd like to see almost everyone's hand up with one idea. (*Here the teacher asks open-ended questions and urges all students to devise an answer. After pausing until most hands are up, the teacher calls on students.*)

Student 1: Well, it's round so you can spin it.

Teacher: Okay. How many other people were thinking something like that? (*Calling for a show of hands here, the teacher acknowledges other students who thought of the same point.*) Now let's take this a little further. Could you spin it if it weren't round?

Student 1: No. Well, I guess you could. But it wouldn't work very well?

Teacher: How come? What would go wrong?

Student 1: It would flop around; it wouldn't sail smoothly.

Teacher: Can you give another model case of that?

Student 1: Well, I can't think of anything.

Teacher: Can anyone think of an example of something shaped like a frisbee a little bit, but not round? What has a rim like a frisbee but isn't round?

Student 2: Maybe the lid of a shoe box. You know, it's shaped like a rectangle but it has sides like a frisbee.

Teacher: And what would happen if you spun it like a frisbee?

Student 2: Well, it wouldn't go very far.

Teacher: Why not?

Student 2: I don't know. I guess it's not so heavy. The air slows it down maybe.

Teacher: Good. Anyone else have some ideas about why it slows down?

Student 3: It doesn't spin well because the sides of the box lid hit the air.

Teacher: Good point. When it's not round, the sides hit the air and slow it down. That's a reason for a frisbee being round. But that leads to another question: Why is spin so important? (*No one raises a hand.*) Let me ask the question this way, and again I'd like almost everyone to think of an answer. What happens if you throw a frisbee without spinning it, versus throwing the frisbee with a spin? (*Most hands go up.*)

Student 4: It flops if you don't spin it. So I guess the spinning keeps it straight.

Teacher: How many other people had a similar answer? (*Several raise their hands.*) Anyone have a different answer?

Student 5: It's like a gyroscope that we studied last week.

Teacher: That's very good. How many others noticed that connection? (*Two or three hands go up.*) Could you explain?

Student 5: Well, we learned that the gyroscope effect keeps something in the same position, so it doesn't tilt or wobble. So the gyroscope effect keeps the frisbee from toppling over.

Teacher: Very good. So a frisbee is round so it can spin fast without slowing down when it's edges hit the air. And it needs to spin to keep it from tumbling. What about some other feature on the structure list? Who has an explanation for something else? Let me see almost everyone's hand.

Student 6: It's hollow underneath. You can hook your fingers into the rim and that helps you to spin it hard.

Teacher: A good point. Who else thought of that? Very good. Anything else about shape?

Student 7: It's rounded on top. I mean it isn't perfectly flat. That maybe helps it to fly.

Teacher: Can you think of anything else that's sort of rounded on top and flies?

Student 7: An airplane wing?

Teacher: A very interesting idea. Anyone else have that one? So a frisbee is a kind of a spinning wing. The spinning keeps it straight and the wing shape helps it to stay up. How much does that shape help it to stay up, though? (*No answer.*) Can anyone think of other things you can throw somewhat like a frisbee? Maybe we can see whether they fly just as well.

Student 8: A discus.

Student 9: A tin can lid. You can throw those by spinning them.

Teacher: Interesting examples. I wonder if we can see whether the rounded shape of a frisbee really gives it more lift than something that's flat.

Student 10: But a discus is pretty heavy; so are tin can lids.

Teacher: That's a good point. When you worry about a difference like that, you're worrying about what scientists call control of variables. That means that when you're making a comparison, you want it to be fair. If you're comparing how much the rounded top helps, you don't want the comparison messed up by other differences, like weight. So a discus is a good idea but, thinking about it, we see it's too heavy. Is there any way we could make a fairer comparison? Could we test the frisbee against itself somehow?

Student 11: How about cutting off the rim?

Teacher: Could be. A good idea. You're thinking up ways to compare it with itself. Let's think if it's a fair comparison.

Student 11: I guess not. Cutting off the rim would make it lighter.

Teacher: Well, that's a point. Can we test it against itself without making it lighter?

Student 12: How about throwing it upside down? If the rounded top really helps it to stay up, it shouldn't fly as well upside down.

Teacher: That's a good idea. Is it a fair comparison?

Student 12: Sure, because it weighs the same right side up and upside down.

Teacher: Okay, so we have a good idea for controlling the variables. It's a fair test because everything is the same except what we're interested in—the rounded top. We have a frisbee here, so let's try the experiment.

Several features of this discussion make for good pedagogy. The structural description of the frisbee leads to efforts to explain why it is built as it is. Physical principles get introduced through analyzing a concrete familiar object and trying to explain why it behaves as it does. The issue of experimental control of variables comes up naturally as part of the effort to compare a frisbee with similar objects to see what difference the rounded top makes. The teacher underscores the general principle. In effect, the frisbee, like the thumbtack, is a little package of physics waiting to be unwrapped. Well-conducted classroom dialogue can engage the students in the process of unwrapping.

READING BY DESIGN

Reading discursive material presents students and teachers alike with a perennial problem: How can one read mindfully? Perhaps the most hazardous aspect of this problem is that students often do not recognize it. Reading as many students practice the activity simply means reading to learn what the source says in a relatively rote fashion, without transforming it, relating it to other matters, or viewing it critically. The four design questions again offer assistance: They can be employed as a framework for reviewing what one has read. To see how, we first have to examine a preliminary issue: the notion of a claim as a design.

Analyzing a Claim as a Design

Claims are very important elements in human discourse. They are the vehicles for conveying knowledge about the state of the world, mathematical truths, scientific theories, religious and moral tenets, philosophies of life, and many other parts of the conceptual reality we construct through experience and interaction with others. Considerable intellectual activity centers on claims, much as a game of tennis centers on the ball. We advance, retract, demonstrate, rebut, invent, revise, hedge, strengthen, and otherwise operate on claims. What is more natural, then, that we should want a useful way of understanding what a claim is?

Few will be surprised at this point by the suggestion that a claim can be understood as a design, with a purpose or purposes, structure, model cases if the claim is at all general, and arguments. Consider, for example, an advertising claim. Clearly the claim has a purpose—to sell the product. Its structure is the broad form the claim takes; perhaps it seeks to sell the product in question by extolling the product's virtues or by projecting an image of what users of the product are like. Model cases often are shown in advertisements along with the claim; a common example is the use of a picture of a car that looks as sleek as the advertising claim asserts. Finally, the arguments category applies in at least two ways. First of all, there is the question of the truth of the claim, a matter often at issue in advertising. Second, the efficacy of the claim merits consideration: True or not, does it sell the product?

If advertising claims fairly transparently count as designs, what about more academically oriented claims, say the claim that IQ is inherited, to choose a controversial one. Again, the design questions make sense. What is the purpose of such a claim? Purpose can be interpreted in the sense of aim and import. The IQ claim aims to integrate and summarize a large body of data concerning human intellectual functioning and the influence on it of heredity versus environment. If true, the claim has important applications for schooling, marriage practices, the teaching of thinking, and diverse other circumstances. As to structure, not that much need be said about a simple, clear, and brief claim, such as "the salt shaker is on the table," but a claim like "IQ is inherited" begs for sharpening (how much of the IQ is inherited?) and explicating (what does it mean to say that IQ is inherited?). As to arguments, clearly the principal issue here is the adequacy of the supporting evidence.

Perhaps the sample cases of the advertising and IQ claims suffice to show how sensible it is to treat claims as designs. It's easy to add a general justification, too. Consider the circumstances under which we coin claims. We do not do so idly, just for the sake of listing truths. If that were our only concern, we could start with $1 + 1 = 2, 1 + 2 = 3$, and continue to produce an infinity of truths of no interest. Instead, we conceive, refine, and advance claims to serve such purposes as persuading, clarifying, integrating, informing, and so on. Recalling the definition of design given earlier—a structure shaped to a purpose—we see that claims fit the formula perfectly.

An Application: Newspaper Editorials

Let us consider the case of newspaper editorials. A teacher may ask his or her students to read editorials, but what are the students to do with what they have read? The students can isolate the key claims and analyze them as designs.

What is it like to do this? Consider as an example a news analysis by Ed Siegel in the Boston *Globe* for Wednesday, February 20, 1985. The editorial carried the provocative title "Westmoreland turned victory into a defeat." The teacher asks the students to read the editorial, isolate a key claim, and analyze it as a design. A student might produce the following analysis.

Key claim: Westmoreland ended up worse off than if he had never sued.

Purpose: Sums up the situation for readers. Sells papers because people like to read about upsets.

Structure: Pretty much what it says. Westmoreland shouldn't have sued, because he lost. That is, things went against him. He had to make a deal to stop the trial or lose. If he hadn't sued, no one would know how the trial went.

Model cases: For example, in another article on the same page, the foreman of the jury said, "People were dug in both ways, but the end result probably would have been a verdict in favor of CBS" and "I was impressed by Westmoreland . . . I wanted to believe him and yet the evidence was so strong against him, I was leaning the other way."

Arguments: The article points out that Westmoreland had a lot of sentiment in his favor before the trial. CBS really looked bad, because CBS was careless in making the documentary. The problem was that some of the witnesses said things that meant Westmoreland really did distort things. Westmoreland and his lawyer say that the trial went okay. CBS agreed to stop the trial and they made a statement that was an apology. But CBS says it wasn't an apology at all. It doesn't sound like an apology either. Nobody is fooled.

This example is somewhat weak so as not to raise false expectations. In fact, some students will even find it difficult to extract the key assertion or assertions from an article or editorial. Even when a student can carry out the basic steps of a design analysis for an article, there is no guarantee of crisp writing or great penetration. At the same time, the proper comparison is: What does the same student do without the help of the design questions? Try the experiment. Ask students to extract a key assertion from an article and explore it in writing, without giving them the design framework as guidance. You will find that most students write very little, for want of an organized way of approaching the task.

The basic tactic of knowledge as design is to provide a framework that can help to organize a student's approach to nearly any academic task in a way that does justice to its subject-matter content. As stressed earlier, depth and subtlety will come from practice and the teacher's help toward deeper arguments, finer-grained expressions of structure, and so on. In this spirit, the foregoing example represents only one way that the design questions can be used in reading-oriented activities. Another is to analyze different types of articles as designs. Newspaper articles, for instance, have a definite structure designed to deliver the basic and most recent information first and provide background and details later on for the reader who wants to continue. Yet another activity is to follow the students' analysis of a form like the newspaper article with an assignment to write in that form, using the analysis as a guide.

STRATEGIES BY DESIGN

The knowledge as design framework can be adapted to many sorts of intellectual performances. But other strategies for thinking and learning certainly are also useful. The world of thought is complex and the many strategies are needed to manage it. Therefore, it's natural to ask about the relationship between knowledge as design and some other strategy that seems to be worth teaching.

Knowledge as design provides a metastrategy for teaching any particular strategy. After all, a strategy itself is a design—a structure shaped to a purpose. What better way to make that strategy understandable to students than to present it by means of another strategy devised for just such a purpose.

Looking for Counterexamples

Consider for example a very simple but powerful strategy: looking for counterexamples. This strategy appears constantly in the writings of philosophers, who, in examining assertions critically, almost reflexively reach for potential counterexamples to test the soundness of assertions. Counterexamples are important because our intuitions about common sense claims and the meanings of words often are not realistic. For instance, in some research that colleagues and I have done on informal argument, people asked to think about a question sometimes mention the premise, "Art is creative." To be sure, we associate art with creativity. Indeed, popular books and even some textbooks attach the label creative to art activities as though any art activity, no matter how preprogrammed, were creative simply by virtue of being an art activity.

It's exactly in such circumstances that one needs to reach for counterexamples to test the soundness of an association. Is art in general creative? What about the art of people who display their wares at shopping malls? What about the pictures of big-eyed dogs? What about the products of the French academies with their slick classicism? What about the admittedly often enjoyable seascapes that sit over the fireplaces of a million homes? Once one asks the right question, it becomes evident that a great deal of art is not particularly creative at all.

Suppose, then, that in the context of a social studies class we want to introduce the critical thinking principle of looking for counterexamples. We can treat it as a design, as follows.

Purpose

The teacher points out that we often accept plausible claims uncritically, without examining them. The teacher lists some claims that at first glance might seem sound but, the teacher forecasts, actually are questionable.

Democratic governments guarantee individual freedom.

Kids usually rebel against their parents.

Kids usually don't rebel against their parents.

Problems of inflation are due to poor money management by governments.

Unions and management can't get along.

Freedom of speech means you can say anything you want.

The teacher has chosen the claims carefully so that they are subject to counterexamples from the students' general knowledge or recent studies. The teacher points out explicitly that we need tactics for thinking critically about sweeping statements, some of which may be true but many of which are not.

Structure

The teacher suggests that one of our basic tools in critical thinking is the counterexample: thinking of cases from our knowledge and experience that oppose the claim in question.

Models

The teacher leads an effort to find counterexamples for each of the assertions listed on the blackboard. With the teacher's encouragement, the students find two or three counterexamples for each claim.

Argument

The teacher points out that these sweeping claims prove indefensible when one examines them critically through the use of counterexamples. The teacher highlights the key point: Our intuitive first reaction to a claim may not correspond with reality. Our intuitions can mislead us. To check our the truth of a claim we need to criticize it. One way to do that is to try to think of counterexamples. The teacher encourages the students to think of the counterexample tactic as a design for taking apart and investigating claims.

Of course, this is only one example of the use of counterexamples. Certainly the teacher must emphasize the application of the strategy or the strategy will not be remembered and used. For another instance, a teacher might offer the further lesson that the impact of counterexamples depends on how extreme the statement in question is. Does it say "always such and such," "usually such and such," "sometimes such and such?" In the first case, one clear counterexample refutes the claim, in the second, commonplace counterexamples are needed, while the third stands against all counterexamples, so long as some positive cases can be found.

The Advantages of Treating Strategies as Design

The case of the counterexample provides a straightforward instance of using the knowledge as design approach to teach another thinking strategy. If one wanted to, one could even think of the counterexample strategy as part of knowledge as design in another sense, namely an elaboration of the argument question. But my point is that it does not matter whether the new strategy fits somewhere within the four design questions or not. Any strategy is itself a design and can be so treated in instruction.

Several advantages accrue from employing the design framework to teach strategies. They result from the pointedness of the design questions themselves.

The approach makes explicit the strategy's purpose, structure, model cases, and argument. As stressed earlier, we often but not always include all four elements. This is as true in the teaching of strategies as in teaching conventional content. Often, strategies are taught without justification or without being clear about their purpose and, especially, their applicability. Not only common sense but also the research literature argues that the more explicitly a strategy is understood, the more likely it is to be used and used well. Presenting strategies by means of knowledge as design fosters such understanding.

AN OVERVIEW OF KNOWLEDGE AS DESIGN

The previous sections offered a sampling of instruction guided by knowledge as design. Like any brief sampling, this one has its drawbacks. While certain points are highlighted, applications demonstrated, and issues examined, inevitably others are neglected. Perhaps it's useful to close this introduction to knowledge as design with a brief overview of several aspects of the approach. For more details, see my book, *Knowledge as Design* (1986) cited in Chapter 3.

The Range of Knowledge as Design

A natural question to ask of any approach to fusing the teaching of thinking with subject matter instruction concerns its range: What content, ability levels, age levels, and so on, does it suit?

Content

Knowledge as design suits most academic content. It induces a shift in emphasis in the way some kinds of content are taught. In history, for example, knowledge as design makes room for historical facts but would introduce considerable historical argument and interpretation. Such shifts are intentional. They favor connected knowledge in contrast to a scattered rote-learned repertoire of facts and principles.

Applicability to Natural Phenomena

Natural phenomena are not designs, since they are not structures shaped to a purpose. To be sure, an atom or the solar system has a structure, but the structure reflects the laws of physics and not a design process (unless by a religious interpretation). So how can we use knowledge as design with natural phenomena? One way is to discuss a design that depends upon the phenomenon in question; the frisbee, for example, depends on gyroscopic action. Another is to discuss not the phenomenon itself but our theory about it, which is a design. For example, in teaching about the solar system one might focus on the heliocentric theory as a design that makes sense of certain observations.

Age

The approach was designed for learners from about five years of age through adulthood. Five-year-olds can think about simple questions regarding the purpose, structure, and pros and cons of household or classroom gadgets; they benefit from explicit attention to purpose, structure, models, and argument in explaining concepts, although of course one has to take care not to exceed their capacity for complexity and abstraction. Among college students, the same broad framework can be applied to advanced topics in mathematics, physics, literary criticism, history, and so on.

Academic Ability

The approach suits learners from the slow to the very able. The emphasis on concrete examples and explicitness should help some slower students.

Nonacademic Applications

Although academic applications have been emphasized here, the patterns of thinking highlighted in knowledge as design apply directly to many out-of-school contexts. For example, a person might critically appraise vacation plans, candidates for a position, career possibilities, or a potential purchase decision by clarifying the purposes, elaborating the structure of the circumstances, recalling or imagining model scenarios, and developing an argument out of pros and cons.

Creative and Critical Thinking

Knowledge as design provides a framework for creative as well as critical thinking. The design questions offer a guide to designing something: What is its purpose? How can it be structured? What model scenarios might you imagine or act out to see how well an idea would work? What arguments pro and con can you find for that approach? Now choose an approach, elaborate its structure, and look at arguments for its details. Design-oriented activities can be given in any subject matter. For just one example, in English, after students have learned a few general points about the designs of classification systems, the teacher can ask them to develop a classification system for the sources of slang terms, using ordinary dictionaries, dictionaries of slang, and their own common sense about contemporary speech.

Accommodating Strategies and Skills

Knowledge as design can be used as a framework for teaching strategies and skills. Any thinking or learning strategy is itself a design—a design for thinking or learning better—and as such lends itself to presentation and explication by means of the knowledge-as-design framework. Procedures such as long division are designs; discussing them from that standpoint can help students to understand their rationale and deal with them more effectively.

Encouraging Development

The examples discussed in this chapter involve relatively straightforward and simple applications of the knowledge-as-design framework. However, the framework allows considerable development that can help learners look more deeply into a subject. For example, the argument category extends into a comparative consideration of different forms of argument, their relative strengths and weaknesses, and suitable occasions for using them.

The Style of Knowledge as Design

Some stylistic features of knowledge as design are apparent from the examples given earlier. Nonetheless, it may be helpful to spell out certain characteristics, because careful attention to them can yield successful applications of the approach.

Saturation with Design Questions

As the examples illustrate, teaching according to knowledge as design involves saturating the instruction with the design questions, which keep recurring in various guises, sometimes explicitly and sometimes implicitly. Such persistence fosters comfort and facility with the approach, as well as ensuring connected knowledge moment to moment.

Generative for Students

The approach emphasizes the production of ideas, such as creative proposals, critical assessments, etc. The teacher constantly raises questions. Fluency and flexibility in generating ideas are encouraged.

Generative for Teachers

Knowledge as design is presented here as an approach, not a curriculum. Teachers applying it to reconceive the knowledge and know-how they want to convey in design terms. Often this is rather easy. Sometimes it can be hard; finding a good model for an abstract concept or explicating the broad purpose of a theory can call for considerable thought. It should almost always be interesting.

Overlap of Design Categories

This issue has not come up in the examples, but deserves mention here. In classroom discussions or other contexts, sometimes questions arise about which design question something fits under. For instance, are details about the earth's orbit a model case of Newton's laws or an argument for Newton's laws? The answer is that both are possible. Sometimes a model case also provides evidence. Sometimes an argument may dwell on the purpose of the design in question. In general, the approach works best if its key terms are used with some respect for their meanings but without fussiness. Extended discussion about borderline or mixed cases proves distracting.

Diversity to Promote Transfer

The diverse applications illustrated here show that the framework fits in many contexts. It's better to apply the framework in varied contexts at the same time, either within a single course or, if it can be arranged, cutting across courses. This practice in varied contexts fosters transfer of learning, one of the fundamental difficulties in the teaching of thinking skills. Considerable research suggests that transfer often does not occur spontaneously and requires calculated provocation.

Explicitness

Knowledge as design promotes explicitness about the design questions and viewing knowledge and other products of mind as designs. This can get tedious and calls for occasional leavening. In general, students will benefit from labeling and description of purpose, structure, model cases, and arguments that are presented in a clearly organized fashion.

A Provisional Spirit

From the perspective of a design philosophy, any design is provisional. The good designs serve well for now and may survive forever, but an ingenious mind may come along and improve or replace them. Paper clips or computers may look quite different in a year, a decade, or a century. When we view knowledge as design, knowledge inherits this provisional spirit. Knowledge and know-how also are provisional human constructs. Some pieces of knowledge and know-how may well survive forever; the earth was once thought to be flat and is now known to be round, and nothing is likely to change our minds. But current economic principles, or Einstein's theory of relativity, or our understanding of prehistoric migrations to the Western hemisphere, or the status of Robert Frost among poets may well be notions that will be remade by future inquiry. The provisional constructive nature of knowledge is an important metalesson of knowledge as design.

The same provisional posture applies to knowledge as design itself—as an approach to instruction. If you were working with paper clips or the theory of relativity, you would respect the thought that lay behind either and not change them casually. But neither would you view them as given and forever fixed in principle. Likewise with knowledge as design. Take seriously the four questions and the means of applying them outlined here. If they do not entirely suit your needs or contexts, tinker. To say otherwise would be to harbor within knowledge as design an autocracy that denies its spirit.

This chapter was prepared for the Connecticut Thinking Skills Conference, March 11–13, 1985, Wallingford, Connecticut. Some of the ideas discussed were developed at Project Zero of the Harvard Graduate School of Education, with support from National Institute of Education grant number NIE-G-83-0028, *Learning to Reason*. The ideas expressed here do not necessarily reflect the position or policies of the sources of support.

5

EDYS S. QUELLMALZ

School of Education
Stanford University

Developing Reasoning Skills

To develop students' reasoning skills, school systems must launch systematic programs that combine a coherent framework of skills with sound instruction and assessment. Concepts of critical thinking and reasoning skills domains vary widely, however, and methods for teaching and testing thinking are not well developed. Furthermore, schools' commitment to higher order thinking has been largely rhetorical, while curriculum development has been infrequent and ineffective.

But the times are "a-changin." Educators and the public sense that the challenge and fun of spirited classroom discussion and projects have been stifled by deadly drills to cover the basics. Moreover, several national reports have called for attention to higher order skills and presented irrefutable evidence that American students do poorly on tests of their reasoning. The report of the National Assessment for Educational Progress (1981) on the 1979–1980 assessment of reading and literature states:

Responses to assessment items requiring explanation of criteria, analysis of text or defense of judgment or point of view were in general disappointing. Few students could provide more than superficial responses to such tasks, and even the "better" responses showed little evidence of well-developed problem-solving strategies or critical thinking skills. (p. 2)

Furthermore, in the highly influential study of secondary schools by the Carnegie Foundation, Ernest Boyer (1983) states:

Clear writing leads to clear thinking; clear thinking is the basis of clear writing. Perhaps more than any other form of communication, writing holds us responsible for our words and ultimately makes us more thoughtful human beings. . . . (p. 90)

Writing is an essential skill for self-expression and the means by which critical thinking also will be taught. (p. 176)

Therefore, evidence is accumulating that our students need instruction on higher order skills and that writing and sustained discussion are essential activities for fostering critical thought. In this chapter, I will propose a framework for focusing on a fundamental set of reasoning skills and discuss some current attempts to address these skills. I will recommend ways to design tasks to test higher order skills and describe instructional activities that employ writing as a vehicle for promoting skill development. The goals and approaches derive from theory and research in critical thinking, problem solving, instruction, and assessment.

FUNDAMENTAL HIGHER ORDER THINKING SKILLS

Philosophical and Psychological Models

The disciplines of philosophy and psychology have contributed greatly to current conceptions of thinking and reasoning. Philosophy has provided definitions of formal and informal reasoning and criteria for their appropriate use. Philosophers frequently apply critical skills in the analysis of arguments. Psychologists, on the other hand, focus more on the methods and underlying cognitive operations involved in using particular combinations of reasoning skills to address academic, practical, or novel problems. Philosophers tend to focus on the features and quality of the *products* of critical thinking, whereas psychologists focus on components of the *process*. Although experts within these fields use different terminology, careful comparisons of the concepts of critical thinking, inquiry, and problem solving from these disciplines reveal substantial overlap.

Within the field of philosophy, John Dewey (1933) defined the reflective thinker as one who carefully and persistently examines an action, proposal, or belief and uses knowledge to test consequences and possible solutions. B. O. Smith (1953) emphasized the judgmental dimensions of critical thinking, that is, "what a statement means and whether to accept or to reject it." For over two decades, Robert Ennis has elaborated on Smith's definition. Currently, Ennis classifies critical thinking into skill clusters that involve clarifying issues and terms, identifying components of arguments, judging the credibility of evidence, using inductive and deductive reasoning, handling argument fallacies, and making value judgments. In addition, he has described a set of dispositions that characterize the critical thinker (Ennis, 1962, 1985).

Psychologists have also studied higher order reasoning. Their research adds to the skills identified by philosophers and places the skills into processing frameworks. Psychologists who study intellectual development cite logical reasoning as one aspect of general intelligence. Piaget put logical reasoning within the last stage of development, formal thought. As a consequence, some educators and psychologists have identified logical skills as inappropriate for younger learners. Recent theory and research have shown this practice to be unjustified (Ennis, 1975; Linn, 1983).

Guilford, too, has offered a set of skills as components of intelligence. Of the 120 abilities in his structure-of-intellect model, the areas of cognition, evaluation, and convergent and divergent production all present tasks that require sets of reasoning skills identified by philosophers and other psychologists (Guilford, 1956).

Sternberg's triarchic theory of intelligence describes the three basic mental processes of knowledge acquisition, performance, and executive processing. Within these basic components, the subroutines of analysis, comparison, inference, and evaluation play essential roles (Sternberg, 1985).

In a different vein, psychological research on problem solving has revealed that the psychological processes of analysis, comparison, induction, and deduction are called upon in the course of identifying the nature of a problem, accessing appropriate information, connecting and using information to solve the problem, and evaluating the success of the solution. This problem-solving framework seems to hold for generalized problem solving as well as for domain-specific tasks (Bransford & Stein, 1984; Chi, Glaser, & Rees, 1982; Newell & Simon, 1976).

Merging the Models

If we consider how the critical thinking skills proposed by philosophers relate to psychology's general problem-solving model and its probable required cognitive operations, we can begin to identify a core of thinking and reasoning skills that are common to theory and research in the two disciplines.

Table 5-1 compares the components of reasoning extracted from the literatures of philosophy and psychology. The list of clarification skills proposed by philosophers includes identifying or formulating a question, analyzing major components, and defining important terms. These skills are also identified within the problem-solving paradigm. The cognitive procedures or processes that probably are necessary to carry out these tasks involve analysis (to identify distinctive components and terms of a problem or argument) and comparison (to determine that these elements fit a particular type of problem). Similarly, the skills identified by philosophers that involve judging the credibility of support, sources of evidence, and observations are comparable to the procedures in the problem-solving paradigm that involve identifying appropriate information and relevant knowledge networks and procedural routines (content and procedural schemata). These acts, in turn, require the underlying cognitive operations of identifying component information/evidence (analysis), typing the evidence (comparison), and judging its quality (evaluation). Also closely related are the inferential skills identified by philosophers and psychologists when students employ inductive and deductive skills to connect or use information and evidence as they attempt to reach a conclusion or solve a problem and when they evaluate the adequacy of the solution or conclusion. Throughout problem solving, metacognitive, self-monitoring processes are activated to evaluate progress.

Table 5-1 Comparison of Reasoning Skills Proposed in Psychology and Philosophy

Critical Thinking Skills (Philosophy)	Problem-solving Strategies (Psychology)	Probable Dominant Cognitive Processes (Psychology)
Clarification: Identify or formulate a question	Identify the problem Identify essential elements and terms	Analogical Analysis and comparison
Analyze major components		
Define important terms		
Judge credibility of support, the source, and observations	Identify appropriate information, content, and procedural schemata	Analogical Analysis and comparison; component evaluation
Inference Deduction Induction Value judgments Fallacies	Connect and use information to solve the problem	Infer/interpret relationships among components
Use criteria to judge adequacy of solution	Evaluate success of the solution	Evaluate effectiveness of specific and general strategies

It is important to note that none of the three lists in Table 5-1 is intended to propose a hierarchy. Research on on-line problem solving in a variety of tasks has repeatedly revealed that component skills may be used repeatedly during all stages of the problem-solving process. Therefore, attempts to designate difficulty levels or hierarchical stages to skills are unwarranted. Some evaluative tasks are much easier than analytical tasks, and two analytical tasks may demand different approaches or skills, depending upon the scope and complexity of the problem or argument.

Presently, a number of writers argue emphatically that critical thinking and problem solving and inquiry are, in fact, quite different. Some stress the evaluative dimension of critical thinking, limiting it to reactions to the thoughts of others. The Ennis outline, however, broadens this narrow view to encompass construction of one's own arguments. The philosophical term, critical thinking, often refers to both generalized thinking skills and critical skills in the social sciences and humanities. On the other hand, psychologists use the term problem solving to refer to generalized strategies and specific procedures within mathematics or science. Regardless of the particular terminology used, both philosophy and psychology seem to reference a central core of higher order thinking skills as well as a basic set of underlying operations that students must use to apply these skills.

Devising a Skills Framework

I propose that we abandon polarizing debates and focus instead on identifying a manageable framework of common skills that clearly generalize across academic and practical areas. If we hope to teach students to develop generalized

Table 5-2 Higher Order Thinking Strategies and Processes

Strategies

Students engage in purposeful, extended lines of thought where they:
   Identify the task (or type of problem)
   Define and clarify essential elements and terms
   Gather, judge, and connect relevant information
   Evaluate the adequacy of information and procedures for drawing conclusions
      and/or solving problems
In addition, students will become self-conscious about their thinking and develop
   their self-monitoring problem-solving strategies.

Processes

Cognitive	Metacognitive
Analysis	Planning
Comparison	Monitoring
Inference/Interpretation	Reviewing/Revising
Evaluation	

and specialized reasoning strategies, we must provide them with a coherent skills framework that will help them understand how these general and specific strategies relate to each other and how they can be brought to bear upon academic, life, and novel tasks.

Therefore, the framework that has evolved in my work over the last few years derives from the concepts of higher order thinking shown in Table 5-1. The definition of higher order thinking skills that has helped us devise our testing and instructional efforts merges the problem-solving paradigm of psychology with the critical thinking concepts of philosophy (Table 5-2).

I propose that the goal of higher order thinking is for students to engage in purposeful, extended lines of thought in which they use problem-solving strategies and become skillful in monitoring, evaluating, and improving those

Table 5-3 Examples of Applications of Higher Order Reasoning Skills in Three Subject Domains

	Science	Social Science	Literature
Analyze	Identify the components of a process or the features of animate and inanimate objects	Identify the components of an argument or the elements of an event	Identify the components of literary, expository, and persuasive discourse
Compare	Compare the properties of objects or events	Compare the causes and effects of separate events and of social, political, economic, cultural, and geographic features	Compare meanings, themes, plots, characters, settings, and reasons
Infer	Draw conclusions, make predictions, pose hypotheses, tests, and explanations	Predict, hypothesize, conclude	Explain characters' motivations in terms of cause and effect
Evaluate	Evaluate the soundness and significance of findings	Evaluate the credibility and significance of arguments, decisions, and reports	Evaluate form, believability, significance, completeness, and clarity

strategies. Furthermore, the cognitive operations and metacognitive components involved in the thinking strategies become targets for instruction. The problem-solving and component cognitive skills are common to several concepts of higher order thinking and represent a tractable number of skills to emphasize in testing and instruction. Furthermore, as Bloom (1971) noted, these fundamental "ways of knowing" exist as distinct methods of inquiry and problem or task types in academic disciplines. Analysis, comparison, inference, and evaluation are significant task types or activities. Table 5-3 suggests how these basic cognitive operations are significant activities for understanding, interpreting, and evaluating academic subject matter. For example, analyses of a process, an argument, or a literary piece are familiar activities in science, history, and literature. Similarly, inferring the consequences of an experiment, a political action or the motives of a character are significant tasks.

In academic subjects, we often compare the attributes of two specimens, the causes of two civil wars, or the themes of stories. Moreover, analogical reasoning is used in functional life problems, such as when shoppers compare cereals or when inventors develop their ideas. Evaluations of scientific conclusions, historical significance, and literary worth, as well as health care plans or football teams, are recurring academic and life activities. Therefore, the framework of higher order thinking skills presented in Table 5-2 seems a useful heuristic for considering skills to teach and test. These general skills are applicable to academic, life, and novel problems.

CURRENT ATTEMPTS TO ASSESS HIGHER ORDER THINKING SKILLS

Recognition of the need to focus on higher order thinking skills is beginning to surface in the educational objectives targeted for assessment at the national, state, and district levels. After years of stressing the basics, departments of education are moving toward accountability for higher level skills as well.

In their renewed emphasis on higher order skills, some testing programs are exploring testing formats that depart markedly from standard fare. The California Assessment Program's new eighth-grade history/social science test will measure students' critical thinking skills in both multiple-choice and essay formats (Kneedler, 1985). (See Table 5-4.) In the essays, students are not asked just to recognize strong and weak reasoning; instead, they are expected to explain their critiques of complete, but flawed, arguments or construct reasoned positions of their own. Also, students may be given extended time (several periods) to sift through and gather historical information relevant to a particular issue. Some activities may permit group problem solving such as debates or mock trials, culminating in individually written briefs. These critical thinking skills, drawn primarily from those assembled by Robert Ennis, divide critical thinking into three components of a problem-solving paradigm: defining problems, judging information related to the problems, and solving problems and drawing conclusions. Plans to extend the assessment to grades three, six, ten, and twelve are in progress.

In an assessment that served as a pilot of direct writing assessment for the eighth grade, the California Assessment Program asked students not only to write persuasive, expository, and narrative essays based on their background experience, but also to write essays in which they interpreted passages from science, social science, or literature. For example, students were asked to compare pioneer and modern food, predict the consequences of disrupting a food chain, or infer a character trait. These kinds of writing assignments take students beyond simple recall and summarizations of their knowledge; the assignments challenge them to interpret and evaluate and, just as important, to explain and defend their reasoning.

The state of Connecticut is also addressing higher order thinking skills as they pertain to academic disciplines and apply more generally. The most recent Connecticut Assessments of Educational Progress tests in social studies, English language arts, and science required a statewide sample of students in grades eight and eleven to use a variety of higher order reasoning processes to perform such tasks as designing and conducting an experiment and writing a persuasive essay (the latter was also administered to a grade four sample). The new Connecticut Mastery Tests in reading, mathematics and writing to be administered to all students in grades four, six, and eight in October, 1986

Table 5-4 Critical Thinking Skills Process Model for History/Social Sciences from the California Assessment Program

Defining and clarifying the problem
    Identify central issues or problems.
    Compare similarities and differences.
    Determine which information is relevant.
    Formulate appropriate questions.
    Express problems clearly and concisely.

Judging information related to the problem
    Distinguish among fact, opinion, and reasoned judgment.
    Check consistency.
    Identify unstated assumptions.
    Recognize stereotypes and cliches.
    Recognize bias, emotional factors, propaganda, and semantic slanting.
    Recognize value orientations and ideologies.

Solving problems/drawing conclusions
    Recognize the adequacy of data.
    Identify reasonable alternatives.
    Test conclusions or hypotheses.
    Predict probable consequences.

will include additional critical thinking and reasoning skills, e.g., reading items to measure evaluative comprehension (Table 5-5); mathematics items to measure conceptual understandings and problem-solving skills, and the production of an essay (or story) in order to evaluate each student's ability to produce a focused, well-organized and elaborated piece of writing.

What is notable about these state assessment efforts is that they attempt to clarify vague notions of higher order thinking. The specifications of frameworks and component skills that will be tested provide teachers and students with a finite set of instructional targets. In addition, the tasks used to test the skills can serve as examples of the kinds of problem types students are expected to master. As we well know, higher order skills currently receive little attention in classroom questioning, activities, textbooks, or tests. When higher order questions do occur, they often concern specific, isolated skills; they seldom ask students to sustain a line of reasoning in order to draw a conclusion or explain a judgment. Worse yet, although many significant interpretive and evaluative problems permit multiple interpretations or solution paths and require orchestration of a set of component judgments to arrive at a conclusion or solution, the one-right-answer format and piecemeal testing of components dominates. If we intend to offer alternatives to these limited tasks that may well become models for classroom assignments, our test tasks must represent a range of significant reasoning assignments that teachers are responsible for instructing.

RECOMMENDATIONS FOR THE DESIGN OF HIGHER ORDER THINKING TASKS

To help students develop reasoning skills within standard school subjects, we should begin by identifying significant problem types that require use of higher order skills. Table 5-3 suggests some generic examples; subject matter specialists can readily identify more. Given the findings from cognitive research that skilled individuals store knowledge in networks classified by problem or task types, the goal should be to identify important recurring issues within a

Table 5-5 Evaluative Comprehension Objectives Proposed for Connecticut's Fourth-Grade Mastery Test in Reading

Recognize statements of fact and opinion

Judge the authority or validity of evidence

Judge the consistency, relevance, and logical order of statements in a passage

Judge the suffiency of support based upon evidence or reasoned judgment field, then to generate sets or pools of these tasks to be used in instruction and assessment.

The tasks should emphasize use of a full problem-solving process, rather than drill on isolated components. In literature, we would be more interested in asking students to connect multiple descriptions of a character's actions and feelings that contribute to his or her character trait or type (What kind of a person was X?) than in asking for low-level, local inferences (when George smiled, how did he feel?). Also, there should be a heavy proportion of tasks that will permit multiple interpretations or solutions (Was Jack guilty of murder when he chopped down the beanstalk?). Furthermore, such tasks should ask students to explain the bases for their conclusions orally or in writing.

A particularly serious problem in the design of higher-order instructional and assessment tasks is the failure to build generalization and develop transfer. We should be asking students to generalize their reasoning strategies systematically and deliberately within similar problems (What kind of person was Othello?). We should also be asking them to transfer their strategies to other situations in which they apply (What kind of person was Hitler?).

Finally, we should be designing instructional assignments and test tasks that elicit metacognitive skills. We can ask students to identify the type of problem and its distinctive elements. Given a particular sort of problem, we can ask them to document their planning thoughts or steps. We can also ask them how they would change their approach if presented with a similar problem.

STRATEGIES FOR DEVELOPING INSTRUCTION OF HIGHER ORDER THINKING SKILLS

Approaches to teaching higher order skills are as varied as the concepts of the skills. Perhaps the most dismaying, but accurate, characteristic of instruction in this arena is its absence. Reasoning skills are procedural routines that are seldom made explicit to students or teachers. Reasoning skills are not usually the focus of an instructional activity or unit; they are assumed to be induced by students as they engage in assorted assignments. Although some students become proficient problem solvers or critical thinkers without direct instruction and without being able to explain their strategies, we have mountains of test data to document that most students of all ages do not perform well on higher order tasks.

One apparent reason for skill deficiencies is lack of time spent on a task. If students do not engage in discussions and assignments requiring sustained inquiry, they will not learn inquiry skills. If students receive only occasional assignments requiring higher level skills, they are unlikely to acquire strategic patterns. Furthermore, if occasional higher level assignments require different patterns of reasoning, students will have difficulty establishing the skill constructs, particularly if required reasoning skills are not identified and discussed. In short, macropatterning of assignments intended to promote higher order thinking should deliberately include concentrated, focused sets of lessons during the skill-acquisition phases, then provide systematic maintenance, generalization, and transfer activities. The scope and sequence of reasoning skills instruction is not currently evident in most curricula and is the Achilles's heel of most published Band-Aid programs. The effectiveness of such adjunct, generalized programs depends very heavily upon systematic reinforcement and specific application of reasoning skills within ongoing curricula. However, neither teachers nor students seem to feel comfortable when asked to bridge the gap between general discussions of reasoning strategies and their appropriate areas of application. More explicit engineering seems necessary.

The place to begin is with a coherent, manageable skills framework that delineates the reasoning skills and relevant problem types. The framework can then serve as a template for analyzing how the skills and problem types are represented in courses of study and curriculum materials. Higher order skills and activities may appear in existing resources, but sporadically or superficially. Therefore, surveys of available resources should include evaluations of the scope and quality of instruction on these skills. My analysis of social studies texts used in grades three through twelve in a large urban district revealed that the ever-present questions at the end of the chapter asked very few high-level questions. More important, the texts seemed to predigest information about social and historical events and issues by presenting summaries of what happened and why without providing any of the background information that would allow students to understand, much less interpret or evaluate, the situations. Often texts provided insufficient detail about events to sustain extended discussion or higher order processing.

When texts do provide sufficient content, the identification of sections that lend themselves to sustained reasoning activities can be especially useful to teachers. Table 5-6 is an example of a scheme I designed for a critical thinking project in the Pittsburgh public schools. The scheme classifies textbook passages suitable for critical thinking activities. The proposed questions are intended to provide teachers with suggestions tailored specifically to the textbooks they were using in their classes, so that they could more easily redirect activities to emphasize higher order skills. This excerpt from an analysis of a ninth-grade civics text suggests that students could debate whether the electoral college should be abolished, or they could compare taxes paid by farmers, factory workers, small business owners, and corporate executives. Also, analysis of a fourth-grade text proposed activities in which students would compare how the climates of different countries influenced work and life-styles or debate whether an Oregon town with high unemployment should open the redwood forest to the lumber company. Similar kinds of critical thinking activities have been developed by teachers in our higher order thinking (HOT) project to help teachers infuse reasoning skills into their ongoing curricula.

Our general instructional approach has been to design lessons that directly instruct the problem-solving process. We use instructional methods that extensive research has found to promote learning. The instructional variables include techniques for orienting learners (objective, review), guidance (modeling, explaining, illustrating), practice (assisted and individual), and feedback. We apply these methods in lessons where students are asked to explain the bases for their analyses, comparisons, interpretations, or evaluations. Generally, we ask them to reference their explanations to information being studied in classroom curricula presented in textbooks or literary material. Table 5-7 presents the major lesson components: the goal, planning strategies, gathering information, analysis and interpretation, writing (or explanation), reviewing and revising and transferring.

Students are presented with the objective of the lesson in order to focus their attention on the goal. The teacher introduces the lesson by reviewing

Table 5-6 Example of Classification of Textbook Material for Higher Order Skills

Pages	Topics	Skills	Questions
196–197	Electoral college	Evaluate	What do you think? Should the electoral college be abolished? How could it be improved? Explain.
200	Practical politics	Infer	Check up—Question 2. How is your life affected by practical politics?
201	Political news	Infer	Civics skills. What is the point of view of your newspaper?
206–207	Loopholes	Evaluate	What do you think? Should we keep or close some tax loopholes? Explain.
210	Taxes	Evaluate	Consider and discuss: Would it be better to have just one kind of tax? Explain.
211–214	Tariffs	Evaluate	Consider and discuss: Do you think protective tariffs are a good idea? Explain.
218	Budget	Evaluate	Consider and discuss: Should governments be allowed to go into debt to maintain services? Explain.
218	Budget priorities	Evaluate	What services should be cut? Explain
218	Sales tax	Evaluate	Class project. Debate whether the sales taxes is unfair to people with small incomes.
219	Taxes	Compare	Compare the taxes paid by a farmer, an owner of a small business, a worker, and a corporation executive.

and modeling reasoning strategies required and by discussing students' background knowledge about the lesson concept or topic and strategies for gathering relevant information from the information source. Reading or information gathering strategies vary according to the discourse structure (e.g., a diary entry or encyclopedia article) and data source (e.g., a biased observer). For a lesson on inferring character traits, students might discuss how to draw an inference, the kinds of actions and feelings that would imply one kind of a trait rather than another, and the importance of looking for these behaviors in the story. After reading the material, students may review it with the teacher. Depending on the reading level of the class and the complexity of the material, the class may analyze the passage with the teacher or proceed independently. The analysis/interpretation stage involves identifying appropriate information and its relationship to the requested analysis, comparison, interpretation, or evaluation. Students are then ready to synthesize the analysis to explain their conclusions. Students plan the point they will make, most often in the form of an essay, and write. For younger students, the teacher circulates, as they plan and write, to assist those who need help. Following assessment of the essay by the teacher or peer groups, there is a discussion of strengths and weaknesses of papers and recommendations for how to improve or replace

Table 5-7 Higher Order Thinking (HOT) Lesson Components

Thinking skill objective: Analyze, compare, infer/interpret, evaluate
Lesson objective/purpose

Lesson activities

Set lesson goal

Plan
   Discuss strategy appropriate for the thinking skill
   Review background knowledge and experience about the topic
   Review strategies for getting information from the type of reading material (or
      other source)

Read (gather information)
   Review relevant information

Analyze/interpret

Write (explain)
   Plan
   Draft
   Assess

Review/revise
   The essay
   Efficient use of thinking skill strategy
Discuss transfer of thinking skill to other areas

---

weak reasons. The lesson ends with discussion of the reasoning strategies used to draw the inference, and how the strategies generalize to similar assignments and transfer to inferential assignments in other subject areas.

The planning activities at the beginning of the lesson and the review/revision activities concluding the lesson are intended to help develop students' meta-cognitive skills. By repeatedly critiquing an argument or analyzing a story, students learn the problem type and the concommitant strategies appropriate for completing that kind of assignment well. The teacher's recurring questions, "What strategies are we using here? What information are we looking for? How do we connect it?", help students explicate the reasoning strategies necessary to compare (e.g., What are the relevant dimensions?), analyze, infer, or evaluate. The lessons may proceed inductively or deductively. The teacher may tell students the relevant dimensions or let them induce the dimensions. The order in which guidance occurs is less important than that it occurs at all.

For example, high-school lessons might ask students to read a set of primary documents about the Boston Massacre and write an essay acting as the defense attorney or prosecutor of the British soldiers who were tried for murder of the colonists. In a science class, students might be asked to write a paper comparing two theories about the extinction of the dinosaurs.

Although some educators believe that disciplined reasoning is too demanding for students in the elementary grades, our experience in the HOT project has been that younger students are quite willing and able to engage in challenging tasks. Table 5-8 presents a third-grade lesson in which students who

Table 5-8 A Sample from the Higher Order Thinking (HOT) Project (Grade 3)

Thinking skill objective: Infer/Interpret

Lesson objective
  Students infer a character trait by writing an essay in which they explain whether Jack ("Jack and the Beanstalk") was a curious or a greedy boy.

Materials
  "Jack and the Beanstalk" in *Junior Great Books*, Series 3.
  Planning sheets. (See attached)

Lesson activities

Set the goal
  Tell students that they will be reading the story, "Jack and the Beanstalk," and writing a composition in which they explain whether Jack is a greedy or curious boy.

Plan
  Introduce the lesson by explaining to students the importance and relevance of being able to figure out (infer) character traits by looking for clues that lead or add up to a trait or type. Suggest some previsouly read or well known stories where knowledge of the character trait helps the reader to understand the story. Suggest personal and community situations where knowing how to figure out a character trait is relevant.

(continued)

Table 5-8 (*continued*)

Discuss the strategy appropriate to the thinking skill: identify the possible traits; decide what information about the character is relevant; read to gather information about the character; sort and judge evidence that relates to one of the traits; explain how the evidence supports selection of a trait; recognize plausible alternative interpretations. Model or review the process for a well known character.

Review background knowledge about the story: Ask students to summarize briefly what they remember about the story.

Review strategies for getting information from the story: Ask students what kinds of things people do who are greedy or who are curious. Suggest that students watch for curious or greedy behaviors as they read the story.

Read (gather information)

Ask students to read the story silently.

Review: Ask students to discuss the main events in the story. Write these events, in sequence, on the board.

Analyze/interpret

Write two headings on the board, "Jack was curious." and "Jack was greedy.". Ask students to suggest things that Jack did or felt that they think fit under one heading or the other. Encourage them to speculate about why Jack did each thing.

Write (explain)

Plan

On the board write the assignment, "Write an essay in which you explain whether Jack was a greedy or a curious boy."

Distribute the Planning Sheets and ask students to suggest topic sentences that will tell the reader which trait they have picked. Circulate and help students as they write their topic sentences next to the heading "Topic Sentence" on their Planning Sheet.

Ask students to write two or three supporting sentences next to the heading "Support" on their Planning Sheet. Circulate and help students.

Have students write a summary sentence next to the heading "Conclusion" on their Planning Sheet.

Draft

Now ask students to write their compositions. Circulate and help.

Assess

Read students' compositions and comment on the topic sentences, supporting sentences and conclusion.

Review/revise

Return the compositions. Read some particularly strong reasons and or selected elements. Ask students to suggest alternative explanations. Ask students to suggest ways to strengthen or replace weak reasons. Circulate and help students as they revise their compositions.

Ask students to review and discuss the thinking strategies they used to infer (figure out) a character trait.

Transfer

Discuss other stories and areas of application.

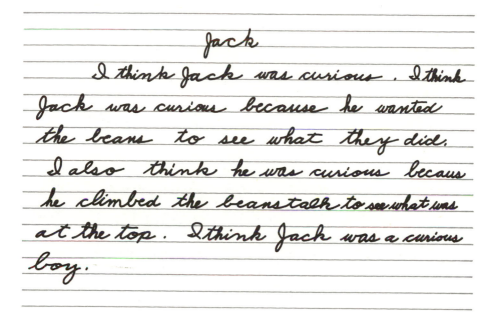

Figure 5-1 Sample student essay, grade 3.

were reading "Jack and the Beanstalk" in the *Junior Great Books* program were asked to explain whether they thought Jack was a greedy or curious boy because he kept going back up the beanstalk. The lesson permitted different interpretations of essentially the same actions. One student felt that Jack was curious (Figure 5-1), while another student disagreed (Figure 5-2). The third-graders were equally flexible in their interpretations of science content. After

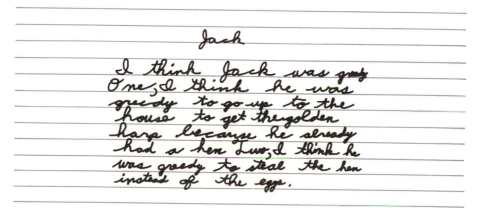

Figure 5-2 Sample student essay, grade 3.

reading a chapter on protective coloration, they completed a review sheet in which they described how the colors of two creatures protected them in the summer and the winter. The writing assignment posed the assumption that glowing pink mice from Mars had landed in the Arctic. Students were to explain how the mice would have to change to survive the Arctic winter and summer. Although most students felt that the mice should turn white in the winter, some suggested brown would be appropriate—if the mice stayed close to the rocks. For summer wear, the students gleefully offered quite an array of colors the mice might assume in order to blend with the grass, trees, and colored flowers.

Second-graders also managed quite well. Given the assignment to agree or disagree that television should be unplugged, students selected one of the two positions, "I agree/I disagree," then gave the names of shows and explained why a show was harmful or helpful. When introduced to the term bias in a lesson where they had to conclude "Who did it?" from witnesses' accounts of a jewel theft, one child defined bias as "our neighbors." Further probing revealed she interpreted the term as people who live "by us." Soon, however, the entire class could identify the testimony of a suspect's spouse as biased.

First-graders did present a challenge. It seemed that their command of handwriting and spelling might present major problems for essay production. It was quite clear in discussion though, that they could offer convincing reasons for clear issues. They were also able to grasp the basics of plot analysis. They practiced summarizing the problem and solution of several stories. The essay shown in Figure 5-3 demonstrates that this student, along with many others was able to capture the bare essence of the plot of "Peter Rabbit."

There are numerous possibilities for designing lessons to promote higher level reasoning skills. The ones we have developed in the HOT Project represent one viable approach. Bear in mind that developing such lessons is time consuming and demanding.

THE NEED FOR A LONG-TERM, SYSTEM-WIDE COMMITMENT

School systems committed to the development of higher order skills are more likely to achieve their goals if they adopt a systematic strategy for instituting a focused project. Simple exhortations to increase higher order skills are not likely to produce results, nor are disparate packaged programs. School systems must make a substantial, long-term organizational commitment if reasoning skills are to become integral components of all courses. Whether the intent is to teach higher order thinking in generalized courses or within existing subjects, improving reasoned interpretations and evaluations of course content is one of the schools' primary goals.

Once a school system has taken stock of the available resources, it can then decide on the most appropriate actions. These may involve developing ad-

Once there were four little rabbits Flopsy, Mopsy, Cotton tail, and Peter. His problem was he never listened to his mother. One day he went to Mr. McGregors garden. He got caught and escaped.

Figure 5-3 Sample student essay, grade 1.

ditional higher order goals, developing assessment tasks to measure goal attainment, indexing appropriate activities, arranging for staff development, or developing new instructional resources.

Instructional resources should include, but not stop at, questioning strategies. Too many studies have shown that teachers with as much as five weeks of in-service classes on questioning skills still did not use higher order questions routinely in classroom discussions.

The most useful resources for materials are likely to be actual lessons and demonstrations. Model representative lessons will be useful; however, there is a danger that teachers will not generate additional ones. A number of school systems that are developing thinking skills are mounting multiyear efforts and involving teams of teachers, administrators, and subject-matter specialists. It is more likely that such collaborative efforts will develop strategies and materials that teachers can and will use.

SUMMARY

I propose that some common, fundamental reasoning skills can be extracted from the morass of concepts of critical thinking and reasoning. These core skills would seem to be a reasonable starting point for developing a coordinated program of instruction.

Some of the current efforts to address higher order skills are developing coherent skill frameworks and exploring a broader range of possible tasks. I suggest that we should design tasks that permit multiple interpretations, require explanations of reasoning strategies, and have analogies in academic, practical, and novel settings.

Finally, I have described an instructional approach that uses writing as a vehicle to help students develop and express their reasoning skills. I believe that with some focus and effort we can teach reasoning skills explicitly and well. However, we need commitment and long-term support to accomplish our goals.

REFERENCES

Boyer, E. L. (1983). *High School: A report on secondary education in America*. New York: Harper & Row.

Bloom, B. S. (Ed.). (1971). *Taxonomy of educational objectives handbook: Cognitive domain*. New York: McGraw-Hill.

Bransford, J. D., & Stein, B. S. (1984). *The IDEAL problem solver*. New York: W. H. Freeman and Company.

Chi, M. T. H, Glaser, R. & Rees, E. (1982). Expertise in problem solving. In R. J. Sternberg (Ed.), *Advances in the psychology of human intelligence* (Vol. 1). Hillsdale, N.J.: Erlbaum.

Dewey, J. (1933). *How we think*. Boston: Health.

Ennis, R. (1962). A concept of critical thinking. *Harvard Educational Review*, 32:81–111.

Ennis, R. H. (1975). An alternative to Piaget's conceptualization of logical competence. *Child Development*, 47:903–919.

Ennis, R. H. (1985). *Large-scale assessment of critical thinking in the fourth grade*. Paper presented at the annual meeting of the American Educational Research Association, Chicago.

Guilford, J. P. (1956). The structure of intellect. *Psychological Bulletin*, 53:267–293.

Kneedler, P. E. (1985). *Assessment of critical thinking in history/social science*. Sacramento: California State Department of Education.

Linn, M. C. (1983) Theoretical and practical significance of formal reasoning. *Journal of Research in Science Teaching*, 21:235–254.

National Assessment of Educational Progress (NAEP) (1981). *Reading, thinking and writing: Results from the 1979–1980 assessment of reading and literature*. Denver: Education Commission of the States.

Newell, A. & Simon, H. A. (1976). Computer science as empirical inquiry. *Communications of the ACM*, 19:113–126.

Smith, B. O. (1953). The improvement of critical thinking. *Progressive Education*, 30:129–134.

Sternberg, R. J. (1985). *Beyond IQ: A triarchic theory of human intelligence*. New York: Cambridge University Press.

6

ROBERT J. SWARTZ

Critical and Creative Thinking Program
University of Massachusetts at Boston

Teaching for Thinking: A Developmental Model for the Infusion of Thinking Skills into Mainstream Instruction

Teachers can adapt and use existing material in K–12 instruction to teach for critical thinking in ways that are as diverse and idiosyncratic as individual teaching styles. Despite the diversity, common elements should appear based on an understanding of what critical thinking is—what skills, competencies, attitudes, dispositions, and activities go into making good critical thinking— and how to help students develop these. While the latter is a matter of the artistry of good teaching the former can be achieved effectively through a new model for curriculum development that makes the classroom teacher the focal point. In this chapter I will present three examples of what creative teachers have done to restructure their classroom instruction, explore the concepts of thinking that lie behind these examples, and describe a process and structure for translating these concepts into an integrated program of thinking-oriented instruction. (The quotations of the three teachers cited in this chapter, are from the texts of their presentations at the March 1985 Connecticut Thinking Skills Conference.)

AN EXAMPLE OF TEACHING FOR CRITICAL THINKING

In reflecting on the way that he has brought critical thinking into his teaching of American history, Kevin O'Reilly, a high-school teacher from the Hamilton-Wenham Regional High School in Wenham, Massachusetts, says:

> One of the key aspects of critical thinking is the evaluation of arguments. Opposing interpretations of history provide students with many arguments to evaluate. Students can be taught to analyze arguments by examining evidence, reasoning, value judgments, and language.

Kevin has thoroughly restructured his presentation of course material to teach students important critical thinking skills in each of these four areas while they learn history. This sometimes involves "warm-up" activities that introduce key critical thinking concepts by utilizing the experience of the students. In focusing them on evidence, Kevin says:

> Before evidence can be evaluated it must be identified. A good way to introduce the abstract concept of evidence is to have a concrete demonstration. For example, have a few students act out a robbery in the hallway. Then have them come back into the classroom and have the class members try to reconstruct what happened by asking questions of the actors and actresses. The statements made in response to the questions are one type of evidence. Other types of evidence are written documents (such as a letter or diary) and objects (such as a wallet). It is important that a distinction be made between information in which a source is given (I call this evidence) and information in which the source is not given (I call this factual information). It is only when the source of the information is given that students can evaluate whether evidence is reliable.

Kevin goes on to describe how he applies this concept to traditional subject matter in American history:

> Students can learn some criteria for evaluating evidence by reading and thinking about conflicting eyewitness accounts of an historical event such as the Battle of Lexington in 1775. First, they read two historical interpretations of the battle that are raw material to stimulate critical thinking.

What Kevin has in mind here are two accounts of the battle, like these from the excellent source book, *What Happened on The Lexington Green?* (Brown, 1970):

> In April 1775, General Gage, the military governor of Massachusetts, sent out a body of troops to take possession of military stores at Concord, a short distance from Boston. At Lexington, a handful of "embattled farmers," who had been tipped off by Paul Revere, barred the way. The "rebels" were ordered to disperse. They stood their ground. The English fired a volley of shots that killed eight

patriots. It was not long before the swift riding Paul Revere spread the news of this new atrocity to the neighboring colonies. The patriots of all of New England, although still a handful, were now ready to fight the English. Even in faraway North Carolina, patriots organized to resist them. (Samuel Steinberg, *The United States: Story of a Free People*, p. 92)

At five o'clock in the morning the local militia of Lexington, seventy strong, formed up on the village green. As the sun rose the head of the British column, with three officers riding in front, came into view. The leading officer, brandishing his sword, shouted, "Disperse, you rebels, immediately!"
    The militia commander ordered his men to disperse. The colonial committees were very anxious not to fire the first shot, and there were strict orders not to provoke open conflict with the British regulars. But in the confusion someone fired. A volley was returned. The ranks of the militia were thinned and there was a general mêlée. Brushing aside the survivors, the British column marched on to Concord. (Winston Churchill, *A History of the English Speaking People*, Vol. 3, pp. 180–181)

The first of these accounts is from a typical American history textbook, the sort of book used to get students to "learn the facts" on which they are frequently tested. Kevin uses this material in a different way. The contrast between Steinberg's account and Churchill's account helps students to stand back from *both* accounts and raise questions. First, clearly the language of these accounts contrasts in ways that betray different points of view about the battle. Samuel Steinberg, for example, speaks about "embattled farmers" and the British committing an "atrocity." Churchill would never charge the British with an atrocity. What does this contrast tell us about these authors and their ability to give us an "objective" account? But the contrast runs deeper. It seems that the *factual* accounts of these authors differ also: One claims that the British fired first, the other implies that a colonist fired first. These passages can be used as raw material to help students look at what is involved in conflicting points of view and stimulate the desire to exercise critical judgment to determine which account is more accurate.

Kevin describes how he develops this activity into a lesson designed to satisfy the latter by specifically helping students use and further understand the concept of evidence and the reliability or unreliability of the sources of information used as evidence:

After discussing the importance of the question of who fired first, the class is asked how the disagreement about the question can be resolved. Students have always been able to suggest something like "look at statements by people at the battle." I make sure they understand that these statements are evidence, by analogy to the scuffle in the hallway, and that like in that case, there remains an issue about the reliability of the evidence.
    Next, students are given a series of conflicting eyewitness accounts of the battle which I just happened to have around my classroom. Each has something definite to say about who fired first.

Here are two such accounts (Brown, 1970) that happen to agree:

> The British troops approached us rapidly in platoons, with a General officer on horse-back at their head. The officer came up to within about two rods of the centre of the company, where I stood—the first platoon being about three rods distant. They there halted. The officer then swung his sword, and said, "Lay down your arms, you damn'd rebels, or you are all dead men—fire." Some guns were fired by the British at us from the first platoon, but no person was killed or hurt, being probably charged only with powder. Just at this time, Captain Parker ordered every man to take care of himself. The company immediately dispersed; and while the company was dispersing and leaping over the wall, the second platoon of the British fired, and killed some of our men. There was not a gun fired by any of Captain Parker's company within my knowledge. (Sylvanus Wood, deposition, p. 36)

> I, John Bateman, belonging to the Fifty-Second Regiment, commanded by Colonel Jones, on Wednesday morning on the nineteenth day of April instant, was in the party marching to Concord, being at Lexington, in the County of Middlesex; being nigh the meeting-house in said Lexington, there was a small party of men gathered together in that place when our Troops marched by, and I testify and declare, that I heard the word of command given to the Troops to fire, and some of said Troops did fire, and I saw one of said small party lay dead on the ground nigh said meeting-house, and I testify that I never heard any of the inhabitants so much as fire one gun on said Troops. (John Bateman, sworn testimony p. 496)

At first, these may seem to be definitive eyewitness accounts. They certainly seem to have it over Samuel Steinberg and Winston Churchill. The detail and tone of Sylvanus Wood's account makes it seem quite credible, and the fact that John Bateman was a British regular claiming that the British fired first is equally convincing. But this impression dissipates rapidly when it is revealed that Sylvanus Wood gave his account in 1826, *51 years after the battle*, and that John Bateman gave his testimony while a captive of the colonists.

Kevin uses a simple structure to help his students think systematically about factors that will help them assess the reliability and unreliability of accounts such as these:

> After each account that I give them there are two columns, one for the strengths of the account, the other for the weaknesses. Students work individually to fill in the sheet. Then, they are put into groups of three or four students to discuss their answers, and to decide as a group who fired first. In order to answer the latter question the students necessarily have to evaluate the various accounts.
>
> As the groups give their reports I list on the chalkboard under the heading "Criteria for the Evaluation of Evidence" their reasons for accepting or rejecting pieces of evidence as more or less reliable. For example, if a student says that we shouldn't believe Major Pitcairn's account because Pitcairn was biased, I discuss what the student means by calling him biased and then list something like, "Does the author have a reason to lie?" Other criteria which students commonly suggest are:

Is it a primary or secondary source?
How close or far away from the incident was the witness?
How long after the event was the report written?
Was this a public or a private statement?
Is this person an expert on what he or she observed?
Is there other evidence supporting what is in this report?

Students list the criteria they give for evaluating evidence in the skills section of their notebook. Another method the teacher could use is to have a student make a poster on the criteria for evaluating evidence, and post it in the classroom. At first the students could use their poster as an aid to evaluating evidence. The teacher and/or the students could develop an acronym to help them remember the main criteria, but with the warning that these should not be taken as hard and fast rules that apply in every case. I have used something like the following:

P—*Primary* or secondary
R—*Reason* to distort?
O—*Other* evidence supporting this statement?
P—*Private* or public?

but always with the addition that there are other relevant factors that sometimes crop up. But eventually, with practice, and a deeper understanding of how to use these criteria, the props should be removed.

We should note an important feature, which some have called the "direct" teaching of critical thinking skills (Beyer, 1985*a,b*), that has been incorporated into this lesson on reliable and unreliable sources of information. While students use these skills in making judgments about the reliability or unreliability of the reports of eyewitnesses, they *also* stand back and explicitly think about and discuss what these skills involve. In particular, they think through what criteria should be used in judging the reliability or unreliability of sources of information. This is practiced with a critical spirit. Kevin does not tell his students what he views as *the* criteria and ask them to learn and use them.

The direct teaching of critical thinking skills, when practiced with this critical spirit, is a crucial aspect of this lesson. It helps students learn about good thinking in ways that can impact on the *transfer* of these skills to other examples in history, across subject areas in high school, and in their own lives. Thus, activities of this sort that now permeate Kevin O'Reilly's American History courses in all of the areas of critical thinking he identified earlier are important not simply because they represent a new way of learning history. They are important because they also form the basis for developing important critical thinking skills that have application throughout the study of history and in other important areas of the experience of the students. Kevin summarizes,

Like any other skill, the critical thinking skill of evaluating evidence can be taught directly and systematically, and can be mastered by students through guided practice and repeated use. Conflicting eyewitness accounts of accounts of an historical event provide an ideal setting for introducing and teaching the skill.

Kevin's collection of materials developed for high school American history (O'Reilly, 1985), of which this lesson represents only a small segment, is based on an approach that brings a focus on critical thinking into school classrooms in sharp contrast with the traditional device of importing prepackaged curricula, developed by professional curriculum developers, and usually involving materials that are to be *added on* to mainstream instruction. Kevin's method involves teachers in developing *their own* critical-thinking-oriented materials based on *their own* exploration of the basic concepts of critical thinking using a technique that restructures traditional content. I call this the *conceptual-infusion* approach to bringing a viable emphasis on thinking skills into mainstream classroom instruction.

LOOKING BENEATH THE SURFACE: CRITICAL THINKING ABOUT POINT-OF-VIEW

Before looking in depth at this approach, it will be instructive to look at another example of it in the work of a second teacher, Mary Anne Wolff, another high-school teacher whose field is social studies and who teaches in the North Reading, Massachusetts, school system. This example, together with Kevin's, demonstrates the versatility and power of this approach, as well as its ability to revitalize the role of the teacher in the educational process.

Among the factors that can influence the viability of eyewitness testimony are a cluster that relate to interest, prior expectations, general beliefs, attitudes, values, and even theories and ideologies. These can nonconsciously or deliberately impact on what we report as eyewitnesses, as Kevin O'Reilly's students have learned, and they can therefore influence the accuracy of our reporting, positively or negatively. When these factors are pervasive and unjustified, they shade into bias and prejudice and influence more than our observations. Mary Anne Wolff engages her students in an in-depth exploration of what goes into point of view and frame of reference that is a natural extension of the kind of investigations Kevin's students engaged in regarding factors that influence the reliability of eyewitnesses.

In thinking critically, it is important to lay bare what lies behind a point of view and subject it to critical scrutiny. Explorations of point of view and frame of reference also impact on some key attitudes and dispositions that must be viewed as necessary underpinnings of any good critical thinking. We must be prepared to consider points of view other than our own and give these a fair hearing in any critical investigation. These broader goals motivate Mary Anne Wolff in developing lessons for her high-school social studies students. (Richard Paul's conception of "dialogical reasoning" is very much like the one behind Mary Anne Wolff's approach: Cf. Paul, 1984; and Chapter 7, this volume). She relies on a conceptual model concerning point of view that teachers can use to help students become skilled at investigating how an author's frame of reference influences his or her choice of subject matter, important ideas, and even the facts an author happens to notice or, at any rate, to consider important. Students can use this model to compare and evaluate contrasting accounts of another society, of a person, or of an event, such as the Battle at Lexington Green. They can use it to become more aware of possible biases in a research study, book, or report. Finally, the model can help students uncover some of their own biases as they discuss or write about some topic.

The model is based on a conception of the relationship between an author's frame of reference and what he or she writes which is illustrated in the following diagram, adapted from Giroux (1978):

Frame of reference	Subject	Set of information	Hypothesis or organizing idea	Evidence

This model links the subject an author chooses to study and the kinds of information he or she considers to be relevant to that author's belief and value system. It is the interests embedded in that system which influence an author to focus on some things and to discount others. Each of us has a "field of vision" which includes many subjects and sorts of information. However, that field is not limitless. It exists within a frame of reference which sets boundaries on what we consider, question, and hypothesize. A frame of reference is a person's most basic beliefs and values. A frame of reference can change, but at any one time for any one author it still functions as a finite lens through which some experiences are filtered and beyond the bounds of which other experiences simply do not register.

In the diagram above "set of information" refers to the types of studies an author considers to be important to his or her field of interest. For example, some anthropologists consider primate studies to be valuable in understanding the forces underlying human social organization, but other anthropologists argue that such studies are largely irrelevant to questions about human behavior.

The set of information used by a social scientist in turn influences the types of hypotheses he or she will develop. For historians these hypotheses are more often called organizing ideas. Some hypotheses or organizing ideas may never be considered by researchers because the set of information they use is not conducive to raising certain possibilities.

Finally, even a researcher's use of evidence will be influenced by his or her frame of reference. While social scientists try to be "objective", the literature is full of episodes in which a researcher refuses to abandon his or her theory and continues to seek confirming evidence long after less interested scholars have given up. This has been true in the natural sciences as well.

Very often people who disagree with each other, not only in research in the social and natural sciences, but on broad social and political issues, seem to talk past each other. Sometimes this betrays a difference in frame of reference of the sort that Mary Anne is concerned about, and when it does, this basic difference rarely comes to the surface.

The lessons that Mary Anne has developed are an important step in helping students develop the attitudes and skills they need to be able to stand back and uncover frame-of-reference differences that must then be understood and critically scrutinized. In these lessons, like in Kevin's, students not only use the model Mary Anne has introduced, they are given an opportunity to reflect on it and consider the breadth of its application. The lessons concern two different points of view about sex roles in a primitive society based on a study of an African tribe often mentioned in school textbooks as a paradigm from which an understanding of some basic features of human nature that play themselves out in modern society can be derived. Mary Anne continues:

A lesson I developed based on this model is about the role of women in one society. It should be apparent how teachers in other fields can apply the same method to their own subject area. The particular society we look at is often used as a touchstone by researchers interested in questions about many aspects of human nature. This is because that society, the !Kung, or the Bushmen of the Kalahari, as they are commonly called, lived until recently in small bands of related people who foraged for their food in much the same way that all humans are thought to have done for 90% of human history. Paleontologist Richard Leaky claims that the !Kung are "Something of a model for what true hunting and gathering is all about." Although not everyone agrees with Leakey, data from studies of the !Kung have been frequently used both to support and to oppose theories about a genetic basis for such behaviors as male dominance, altruism, and mother-infant bonding. The purpose of this series of lessons is to help students examine and evaluate several different pictures of sex roles in this much-studied hunting-gathering society. It is designed to contrast sharply with the usual way that students are exposed to information about societies like the !Kung: through the one or two paragraphs on sex-roles in early societies found in many standard textbooks and which claim to give definitive research findings.

To illustrate the concept "frame-of-reference" to students and to open discussion about the ways an author's frame of reference can influence reports of another culture, students are given excerpts from two contrasting accounts about the relationship between !Kung men and women. Students have been prepared for these readings by a brief explanation of the importance many anthropologists attach to foraging societies, particularly in relation to the issue of sex roles. Students are also informed that they may eventually be asked to write their own description of sex roles in !Kung society, and to relate this description to the issue of whether male dominance is universal.

The two excerpts that Mary Anne gives her students are from Marshall (1976) and Draper (1975):

Excerpt 1
Their preciousness as mates and the magnitude of their contribution do not put women forward into a dominant position or a position of leadership in the society. Men come forward into that position. Women in some ways and to some degree lean upon their men, look to them for protection, depend on them.

!Kung women are encouraged to be gentle and compliant by the fact that in their love of peace the !Kung like quiet, modest women. Overbearing, strident, demanding or nagging women would disturb not only their own husbands but the whole encampment, and group disapproval would be expressed.

Women appear to acquiesce in their role and expect to be followers. In their dealings with us they were notably more circumscribed, less outgoing, than the men. Women were more apprehensive of strangeness and strangers and drew back from new experiences, such as riding in trucks. As informants they held back. Some said explicitly that they feared they would not know the correct answers to my questions. Others made the sweeping statement that men know more than women do. In our frequent conclaves, when we tried to explain our purposes, we asked the !Kung for cooperation and made plans together, the women did not take part. They said we must ask the men: The men must decide. One woman said, as if by way of explanation, "Men can do everything, they can shoot and make fire."

Women bring most of the daily food that sustains the life of the people, but the roots and berries that are the principal plant foods of the Nyae Nyae !Kung are apt to be tasteless, harsh and not very satisfying. People crave meat. Furthermore, there is only drudgery in digging roots, picking berries, and trudging back to the encampment with heavy loads and babies sagging in the pouches of the karosses: there is no splendid excitement and triumph in returning with vegetables. (Marshall, pp. 175–178)

Excerpt 2

A common sight in the late afternoon is clusters of children standing on the edge of camp, scanning the bush with shaded eyes to see if the returning women are visible. When the slow-moving file of women is finally discerned in the distance, the children leap and exclaim. As the women draw closer, the children speculate as to which figure is whose mother and what the women are carrying in their karosses . . . .

A stereotype of the female foraging role in hunting and gathering societies (in contrast with men's work, which is social in character) is that the work is individualized, repetitious, and boring (Service, 1966: 12). Descriptions of the work of gathering leaves the reader with the impression that the job is uninteresting and unchallenging—that anyone who can walk and bend over can collect wild bush food. This stereotype is distinctly inappropriate to !Kung female work, and it promotes a condescending attitude toward what women's work is all about. Successful gathering over the years requires the ability to discriminate among hundreds of edible and inedible species of plants at various stages in their life cycle. This ability requires more than mere brute strength. This stereotype further ignores the role women play in gathering information about the "state of the bush"—presence of temporary water, evidence of recent game movements, etc.

!Kung women impress one as a self-contained people with a high sense of self-esteem. There are exceptions—women who seem forlorn and weary—but for the most part, !Kung women are vivacious and self-confident. Small groups of women forage in the Kalahari at distances of eight to ten miles from home with no thought that they need the protection of the men or of the men's weapons should they encounter any of the several large predators that also inhabit the Kalahari (for instance, hyena, wild dog, leopard, lion and cheetah). (Draper, pp. 82–83)

Longer excerpts have been used successfully with high-school classes in which students' reading abilities ranged from eighth grade to college levels.

Mary Anne continues her description of the way these lessons are organized in the following way:

> To highlight the differences in tone between the two readings, it is better initially to divide the class and have each group read only one of the excerpts. They can switch assignments the next night. For both readings students are directed to take notes on the main points each author makes about the following areas:
>
> The relative influence of !Kung men and women
> The relative prestige of !Kung men and women
> The specific adjectives each author uses to describe !Kung women.
>
> Each student is also asked to write a sentence which he or she thinks summarizes how the author would answer the question of whether there is male dominance in !Kung society. Essentially, this is the student's attempt to identify the author's main hypothesis or organizing idea. After the first assignment students who have read Marshall's article are generally convinced that there is male dominance in !Kung society, while those who have read the Draper article are not so sure. When each half of the class has still read only one article, the author's claims can be put on the board so the class can see the similarities and differences and look for ways to reconcile the two views or to account for the contradictions. Students are generally very enthusiastic about trying to determine what is "really going on."
>
> The lists of ideas and information which students generate from the articles usually include the following claims:
>
> *List 1:* Ideas and information both authors agree upon
> Women gather most vegetable food
> 60–80% of !Kung diet is vegetable food
> Men hunt large game
> Meat is considered the more desirable food by both men and women
> There is no system of offices or rules giving !Kung men power over women
>
> *List 2:* Ideas and information from Marshall
> Women in some ways lean on the men, look to them for protection, and depend on them
> !Kung women are less outgoing than the men
> Some !Kung women say the men know more than the women do
> Returning hunters are greeted with excitement; returning gatherers are not. Gathering is drudgery.
> *Adjectives* the author uses to describe !Kung women: quiet, modest, gentle, compliant.
> *Possible organizing idea or hypothesis:* In !Kung society men are the dominant sex.
>
> *List 3:* Ideas and information from Draper
> There is a relaxed and egalitarian relationship between !Kung men and women in their traditional society

Small groups of !Kung women forage 8–10 miles from home with no thought
that they need protection
Gathering requires great skill and includes collecting information about game.
Women derive self-esteem from their work
Returning gatherers are greeted excitedly by the children
Women retain control over the food they gather
Adjectives the author uses to describe !Kung women: vivacious, self-confident,
autonomous or independent, self-contained
Possible organizing idea or hypothesis: In !Kung society women are not dom-
inated by men

While comparing the three lists on the board students find some apparent contradictions which can be reconciled; for example, !Kung women could be both
'quiet' and 'vivacious' depending on the occasion and whom they are with. On
the other hand, some statements, such as those about returning gatherers, seem
directly contradictory and require more analysis. In addition, the tone of the readings and the sense one gets of the relationships between !Kung men and women
are different and lead to different conceptions of the quality of their lives.

At this point at least one student usually asks, "So whom do we believe?" Some
students express frustration and wonder whether social studies is all "just opinion!" Here is where the frame of reference diagram shown above can be introduced. I point out that both authors probably have some of the "truth" and both
probably have missed or misconstrued other things. After explaining the diagram
I ask students to suggest what each author's frame of reference might be and how
it might influence the author's research and reporting.

Here, as in Kevin O'Reilly's activities, Mary Anne guides her students to
the final stage in these lessons, that of trying to make explicit the system of
beliefs that constitutes the authors' frames of reference. Some of these may be
well founded, others only assumptions, but exposing them is a prerequisite
to evaluating them using a whole array of critical assessment skills. Mary Anne
continues:

One way to help students make inferences about an author's frame of reference
is to help them develop a set of categories that could contribute to such a framework: these might include age, time of fieldwork, specialty within a discipline,
political or professional affiliations, theories the author has developed or been
associated with, and significant life events. Students can also work back from an
author's set of information and subjects of major interest to suggest what some
components of the author's frame of reference might be. For example, in this unit
students looking at background information on Draper in *Toward an Anthropology
of Women* would find her stated interest in new studies indicating that in band
level societies the distinction between male and female roles is substantially less
rigid than previously supposed. She did her fieldwork in the late 1960s. Students
generally suggest that whether or not she herself is a feminist, Draper is probably
interested in feminist interpretations and has likely been influenced by the wom-
en's movement. Similar information can be gathered about Lorna Marshall's suggesting a different background perspective.

At this point I also point out that there are other influences on a researcher's findings in addition to his or her frame of reference. These influences include the length of the study, location and time of the study, limitations of methodology and researcher's skills, and countless other variables that can make a difference between what two authors' investigations of the "same" topic uncover. Draper and Marshall studied two different !Kung groups, which were in varying stages of "modernization" at different times. Students should also consider these factors when evaluating information or accounting for differences in the data.

After students have proposed a frame of reference for Draper and for Marshall and have considered these other influences just mentioned they can suggest what areas each author might have overemphasized, what she might have overlooked, and what alternative interpretations of observed behaviors or statements would be possible.

To close this exercise students can draw up three lists in relation to the issue of male dominance among the !Kung:

1. Things about !Kung men and women we know (tentative).
2. Things about !Kung men and women we would still need to find out to answer our questions about dominance.
3. Terms we need to define more clearly (i.e., dominance).

While it is necessary to provide some closure to the lessons on the !Kung, it is also important not to give students the idea that complex questions about society can be "settled" in several days. By asking students to identify facts that are generally agreed upon, the teacher can counteract the uneasiness that some students will feel at not being given "right" answers. The frame of reference approach should be used to stress the value and difficulty of arriving at a consensus about reality, rather than simply to "unmask" the biases of various authors. Students need to realize that the process of doing research involves reflective self-examination on everyone's part, and that their own biases, not just those of published authors, need to be scrutinized.

EXPLORING CONCEPTS OF GOOD THINKING

The work of Kevin O'Reilly and Mary Anne Wolff is based on a well-founded and systematic concept of critical thinking that breaks it into a wide and interrelated set of dispositions and attitudes, on the one hand, and skills on the other. The conceptual-infusion approach to bringing critical thinking into classroom activities involves teachers in two sorts of conceptual activities that are usually not present in traditional approaches in which teachers are simply trained to use specific pre-developed materials. First, teachers are involved in developing a deep conceptual understanding of specific attitudes and skills, and second, the *relation* between these and other ingredients we want to include in a comprehensive attempt to infuse thinking skills into the curriculum is also considered. Infusion occurs when lessons and units are developed based on these activities.

The list of dispositions and skills in wide circulation today developed by Robert Ennis (see Table 1-1) of the Illinois Thinking Project is one of the most comprehensive attempts to date to give a new taxonomy of critical thinking attitudes and skills. It represents a fine tuning of the concept that goes well beyond the very general categories of thinking skills found in sources like Bloom's taxonomy or expressed simply by terms like "evaluation" and is far more useful to the classroom teacher than earlier attempts. This list—called Goals for a Critical Thinking/Reasoning Curriculum—is based on two decades of research and is elaborated in a number of important and influential articles (see Ennis, 1962, 1981; Chapter 1, this volume). The conception of critical thinking embodied in this list—that of *reasonable and reflective thinking aimed at deciding what to believe and do*—has served as the basis for the well-known Cornell Critical Thinking Test and the same basic conception has been used by the California and Connecticut Departments of Education in the development of their statewide assessments of critical thinking. The central categories of skills that Ennis elaborates, which are crucial in promoting rational belief and action, link critical thinking with the development of human knowledge. These categories include skills involved in *clarifying* ideas and reasoning, determining the *accuracy of basic information* (through observation and communication), and *reasoning and inference* that can extend our beliefs and knowledge (through the use of evidence and deduction).

This list can serve as the basis for the kind of conceptual explorations I referred to above. Enough time must be allowed for the first stage of the conceptual-infusion approach, in which teachers explore what each disposition and skill involves and, in particular, develop the *normative* criteria that are to be employed in critical judgment: criteria that *justify* belief. This necessitates elaborating skill categories like reliable/unreliable sources, causal inference, and prediction to consider what *counts for* reliability, well-supported causal claims, and well-founded predictions (in contrast to speculation about what will happen, or wild guesses). The philosophical spirit must most clearly be brought to bear in these explorations. It is equally important that these explorations must not take place abstractly, but should be tied to examples in practice (e.g., When is an economic or political forecast a good prediction and when is it speculation?). In short, these explorations must first involve teachers in developing their own critical thinking skills to their utmost capacity, as they will later try to develop these skills in their students.

Activities like those of Kevin O'Reilly and Mary Anne Wolff can result from the second stage of the conceptual-infusion approach to the development of thinking-oriented instruction. In this stage, teachers attempt to translate their own understanding of what is involved in critical thinking into classroom practice. The lessons that Kevin described are based on his own exploration of concepts in the Ennis category of *basic support*, which includes judging the credibility of a source and observation. This, of course, is only one of a number of critical thinking skill categories, and Kevin has also developed lessons that are based on a similar exploration of concepts related to *inference*, especially in connection with the use of evidence to support claims that historians make about the causes of slavery, the Civil War, or the Depression.

But while the example of Kevin's lessons on the Battle of Lexington in the Revolutionary War is a high-school-level example in one of a larger number of critical-thinking-skill categories, it can serve as a model for a wide variety of other K–12 lessons in other subject areas. Elementary-school teachers using the same approach have structured and successfully used similar lessons about witnesses to an accident or incidents in early childhood literature (e.g., Do the animals who follow Chicken Little, and indeed does Chicken Little herself, have reliable information? What would make it reliable?). Upper-elementary and middle-school teachers have developed similar lessons in which students involve themselves with great zeal, some on UFOs and one on the research on the Loch Ness Monster. One high-school English teacher developed an engaging lesson on the reliability of witnesses based on the book *Twelve Angry Men*. Although content and grade levels vary, the same basic critical thinking concept is utilized: the concept of the reliability of sources of information, a tremendously important concept to introduce children to in an age suffering from acute information overload.

In exploring this concept, most teachers isolate key criteria that they want to incorporate into their lessons after being exposed to examples like Kevin's and being given some time to think through how they could do similar things with their students. As we have seen, these criteria include, for example,

1. observation conditions (distance, was it in view, good eyesight, etc.),

2. expertise (special training and knowledge of what is being observed),

3. when the incident was reported (on the spot or later?),

4. attitudinal factors (special interest, prejudgements, theories and ideologies, etc.).

This deep conceptual understanding on the part of teachers, which is by no means a difficult and time-consuming activity, motivates a thorough and systematic teaching of critical thinking skills of the sort that Kevin comments on in his concluding remarks.

TEACHING FOR CRITICAL AND CREATIVE THINKING

Comprehensive characterizations of critical thinking skills and attitudes like those of Ennis are not the only bases of teaching for thinking that attempt to isolate skills for students to develop. Consider, for example, the types of skills promoted by advocates of teaching for *creative* thinking. A shorter taxonomy of creative or imaginitive thinking skills based on the work of E. Paul Torrance, and underlying some of the better-known creativity tests, has also had an impact on classroom activities (see Taylor, 1974; Parnes, 1976a,b). The primary skills in this conceptualization are *fluency* of thought (generating ideas in a multitude of different categories), *originality* of thought (coming up with new ideas), and *elaboration* in one's thinking (generating as many details as possible). These skills are typically viewed by their promoters as nonjudgmental, hence, as different in kind from critical thinking skills. Yet they are argued to be necessary ingredients in inventiveness and creativity and of great importance in teaching for thinking. Developing multiple alternatives in solving problems, coming up with novel solutions that work, and in general being open to new ideas seem to involve using the skills that Torrance has isolated. Thinking through what these skills involve and designing skill-oriented lessons based on this understanding has been an equally productive basis for lesson development and a revision in teaching styles that many teachers have engaged in using the conceptual-infusion approach. The technique of brainstorming is used often to promote the development of these skills.

There is danger, though, in separating critical thinking from creative thinking, and separating each into sets of skills, then structuring lessons that involve students in using these skills piecemeal. In developing good thinking skills, students must also develop a sense of *where* they can be used most appropriately and effectively in dealing with problems and issues that call for good clear thinking. How do the two conceptualizations of critical thinking, on the one hand, and creative thinking, on the other, relate to each other? Are they alternatives or do they complement each other? And how do they relate to the various other conceptions of thinking being promoted as a basis for classroom activity—for example, problem solving, decision making, and informal reasoning?

To answer these questions we should stand back from these skills approaches and look holistically at what we want to view as good thinking. What happens in individual classrooms must be based on a sound and thorough exploration of these issues by individual teachers, preferably working together in any given school system. Good goal setting and a well-conceived plan in teaching for thinking will result. This will be based on a conception of good thinking that locates the purpose, and hence the *appropriate use*, of the skills that appear on these lists.

What emerges first is that the lists we have mentioned are *complementary*. Both creative thinking and critical thinking must be emphasized in teaching. In situations where they are best used, the norm—not the exception—is to use them in combination, not in isolation. Seeking an explanation for some event—for example, why a recent plane crash happened—will be furthered if we consider a number of possible explanations (fluency) and sort out the plausible ones (assessment). One must look critically at sources of information, consider specific pieces of evidence and what likely causes they support, and in general move from speculation to hard-nosed reasonable judgment. In deciding on a course of action, our thinking will be more effective if we take the time to consider a number of possibilities and assess which are both more feasible and have the fewest disadvantages. Critical thinking taxonomies typically tend to be far less developed vis-à-vis creative thinking, and taxonomies like Torrance's productive thinking skill list tend to be underdeveloped with regard to critical thinking skills. In combination we have an approach that is more powerful because it is in keeping with the way that people naturally approach good thinking. If we think about creative thinking skills as skills at the *generation* of ideas that stretch our mental abilities to consider a number of alternatives without prejudging any, and think about critical thinking skills as skills that operate on our cognitive attitudes *toward* those ideas, once generated (e.g., belief, disbelief, doubt), the necessity to develop both *in combination* becomes obvious. The development and continual use of one without the development and use of the other can lead to overly narrow or overly fanciful thinking that may not be very effective.

The second thing that emerges is that critical thinking skills and creative thinking skills are not just another set of skills to be taught the way subject-area skills are. Good critical and creative thinking take place in a context of questioning and open inquiry that requires a certain spirit of thought manifested in certain attitudes and dispositions like being open minded and considering points of view other than one's own. These attitudes and dispositions can be cultivated in the classroom. As Mary Anne Wolff clearly demonstrates, the teacher can model these attitudes and dispositions—rather than always giving the right answers—and can create a classroom environment in which open exploration is encouraged. To many teachers this, rather than teaching for specific skills, is the more difficult aspect of teaching for thinking, and it requires continual self-monitoring.

COMBINING DIFFERENT THINKING SKILLS IN TEACHING FOR THINKING

To illustrate the power of integrating and interweaving a number of different components that encourage good thinking, I include here a unit developed for an upper-elementary/middle school classroom in the Norwood, Massachusetts, school system. The teacher is Michelle Commeyras, and the unit was developed as part of her work while a student in the Critical and Creative Thinking Graduate Program at the University of Massachusetts at Boston.

Michelle has taken the historical novel, *The Hessian*, by Howard Fast, and developed a play based on an episode in it. She starts this unit by asking the students to do a dramatic reading of the play. The play is about the trial of Hans Pohl, a Hessian drummer boy who is a survivor from a detachment of Hessians that has just marched through the town of Ridgefield, Connecticut, in the later stages of the Revolutionary War. While passing through, the detachment caught a member of the community named Saul, whom they executed as a spy. Hans, who can barely speak English, is on trial for murdering

Saul. During the trial it is revealed that Raymond Heather, a Quaker, and Dr. Feversham tended to Hans, who came to them after the battle sick and wounded. Neither man reported Hans's whereabouts. Raymond admits that according to his religion he should not lie but reveals that he concealed Hans because he has a duty to care for the sick and wounded. Because of this, his testimony of his son's description of the incident is challenged.

During the trial the prosecutor accuses Hans of being one of the four people who pulled the rope into a tree in order to hang Saul. Hans denies this. While testifying about this he reveals that Saul was caught following the detachment with a slate on which he had written some marks apparently to record the number of Hessians. This led the commander to think that Saul was a spy. While Saul was being questioned by the officers who understood English far worse than Hans did, Hans recognized something strange about Saul that led him to wonder whether or not he was a bit crazy. In fact, another member of the community testifies that Saul was an imbecile with a mental age of a boy. However, Hans does not challenge his superiors for fear of being punished. The play ends with adjournment to consider the verdict, but with no verdict yet declared.

In the typical classroom, a novel like *The Hessian* and even the play that Michelle has constructed might be used for building vocabulary skills and plot recall. However, it is rich in possibilities for integrating thinking-skill-oriented instruction. Leaving the play open-ended is an important structural device that is bound to stimulate students to think about what the verdict should be. Issues about individual and collective responsibility and blame and punishment are familiar and nagging issues that arise in a variety of contexts and there is no substitute for good thinking in dealing with them. Locating Hans's actions in the complexities of cause and effect that lead to Saul's death and then considering whether they justify holding him responsible raises sophisticated questions that call for thinking skills that are within the grasp of these students. Michelle's own exploration of these concepts and of models of *reasoning and inference* that turn on the relevance and strength of evidence lies behind the way she presents these issues to students.

Michelle describes an activity that she introduces prior to asking the students to think through these questions. Her directions are to "ask the students to identify the issues relating to responsibility that are in the play." Students come up with the following examples:

> Raymond Heather is a Quaker. His religion tells him it is right to tend the sick and wounded that come to him for shelter. His religion also tells him it is wrong to tell a lie. Was it wrong for Raymond to lie in order to conceal Hans, whose life was at stake?

> Dr. Feversham is a physician. He feels it is his duty to care for the sick whether they be friend or foe. Was it his responsibility to report the whereabouts of Hans Pohl?

> Who is responsible for the murder of Saul Clamberham?

> Hans recognized that there was something strange about Saul. Did he have a
> responsibility to talk to his superiors about Saul's appearing strange or crazy?

This activity clearly prompts the need to help students to clarify the concept
of responsibility. The sense in which someone is responsible for a murder
(Was it really a murder?) and in which a person has a responsibility to do
something are related, but different. It is important to help students use clarification skills to understand that there is an ambiguity here.

Each of the issues the students raise calls for the kind of guided thinking
that Kevin O'Reilly mentions, and each can involve the interweaving of a
variety of thinking skills. Michelle feels that discussion of each can be enhanced
through an excursion into establishing what the facts of the case are. To do
this she feels it is important to introduce students to the distinction, so often
misinterpreted in critical thinking curricula, between fact and opinion. She
treats this as marking a contrast between items that are *acceptable as fact* based
on good reasoning, and unsupported *opinions*. This part of the activity begins
by having the students brainstorm what they think the facts might be while
withholding judgment for the time being. But it does not stop there.

> For example, if the student says that one of the facts is that the teacher testified
> that Saul was slow witted you would ask the students to think about whether or
> not the teacher is a reliable source. Judging the credibility of the source gets
> students thinking about criteria like expertise, reputation, or conflict of interest.

The facts of the case are relevant to each of the initial issues the students
raise about this incident. Michelle structures discussion of each of these issues.
Here are her directions about how she will blend in relevant thinking skills to
an assessment of the last issue—whether Hans had a responsibility to talk to
his superiors about Saul's appearing strange or crazy. This is a value-oriented
issue, and her emphasis reveals how important she feels it is to superimpose
both a critical- and creative-thinking-skill framework on consideration of issues of this sort. The skills she interweaves are of great importance in real-
life decision-making contexts.

The first stage of this activity focuses students on relevant facts, the second
on values and value principles. Michelle briefly describes these two stages:

> *Predicting and verifying the consequences of Hans' intervening on behalf of Saul*
> The rationale for predicting and verifying consequences is that it focuses on
> cause and effect relationships. Students consider all the alternatives while
> keeping in mind the original questions. Verification requires comparing and
> contrasting information and gets students thinking about chance, likelihood,
> necessity, or the impossibility of causal relationships.
> *Strategy:* Have students list proposed consequences on the blackboard. Then
> have them discuss the probability of these consequences by rating them from
> most to least likely and explaining why. For example, if they listed these two
> possible consequences: (1) The Hessians might decide that Saul isn't a spy,

and (2) Hans might get kicked out of the unit, we would consider, given the evidence in the text, how likely each is, and compare the two in connection with Hans' thinking.

List the reasons for or against Hans' intervention on behalf of Saul
   The rationale for listing the reasons for and against Hans' intervention is that it encourages looking at many possible reasons before coming to a conclusion. Both stated and unstated reasons can be identified through this process. It also provides opportunities for generalizing about values or principles, and considering these critically.
   Strategy: List the students' reasons on the blackboard under the heading *for* and *against*. Have the students vote on which reason is best in each category. Ask the students to be advocates for their choices. In this activity students can be directed to prioritize the values and value principles that underlie the reasons, and to argue for these priorities. Finally, ask the students to make a decision on the original question. *Did* Hans have a responsibility to talk to his superiors about Saul Clamberham's appearing strange or crazy? Why?

In fleshing out this lesson in the classroom, Michelle blends the use of brainstorming techniques to stimulate nonjudgmental generation of ideas about possible consequences of Hans's actions with critical assessment of their likelihood.★ The use of causal inference clearly provides an opportunity to stand back and help students reflect on some general principles of good prediction, as she suggests in her commentary. In the second stage, she moves this discussion into a broader context of practical reasoning structures in which pro and con arguments are considered, each of which turns on the use of factual information about Hans's actions, their consequences, and implicit value premises. Students are invited to think through their priorities: Is saving Saul's life more important than Hans's not being punished or being kicked out of the unit?

One natural extension of this unit involves Michelle's helping students identify some of the issues concerning the basic patterns of moral decision making that emerge in this discussion. Questions like "Are the consequences of Hans's actions *for himself* the only important factors to consider in deciding what he should do?", "Should we do things that lead to the best consequences for everyone affected?", and "Are *consequences* the only factors we should take into account in deciding what to do?" help students consider basic moral perspectives without prejudgment. Michelle's own explorations of moral reasoning

---

★ Based on a similar exploration of the concepts of cause, effect, responsibility, and criteria for using evidence in supporting causal claims, a high-school English teacher from the Groton, Massachusetts, school system recently developed a similar unit using Shakespeare's *Romeo and Juliet*. Students were asked to brainstorm possible causal connections leading to the tragedy after being introduced to the concept of causality and an analysis of its structure. Raising questions about the justification for holding anyone in particular responsible for the tragedy brought her students to explore critically these same deep issues about human action and responsibility.

and moral philosophy lies behind bringing these issues to students: They are typically raised to help students think through broad issues concerning egoism and utilitarian and nonutilitarian approaches to moral decision making (see Davis & Hall, 1975; Wright, Daniels, & Coombs, 1980).

This unit represents a forceful example of how teacher initiative·and an understanding of how critical and creative thinking skills interweave can lead to a transformation of materials like the Fast novel into structured thinking-skills-oriented lessons about issues that touch many basic human concerns. It shows the power of combining a focus on holistic problems with a systematic thinking-skills approach that helps students develop a sense of the context for the use of these skills. Michelle's prompting of a systematic and sequenced *reasoning strategy* through appropriate questioning about whether Hans should have revealed his suspicions about Saul accomplishes this. It provides students with a *framework for thinking* that is as important as the specific thinking skills that are employed. This is something that teaching for thinking must also incorporate if we are to avoid the dangers of fragmentation to which thinking-skills approaches give rise.

CONCLUSION

In this chapter I have discussed the work of three teachers who have restructured material they customarily use in their teaching to teach for thinking. These teachers have not opted to purchase new curriculum materials or programs designed for teaching thinking. Rather, they have used an approach I call the *conceptual-infusion* approach. This involves focusing their attention on and thinking through what the ingredients in good thinking are—the skills, competencies, attitudes, dispositions, and activities of the good thinker—and then developing lessons to enhance the development of these through the restructuring of what they already teach. Critical thinking has been my focus. I have discussed ways of teaching for specific critical thinking skills, helping students to uncover and assess the basic beliefs incorporated in points of view, structuring classroom activities to promote good thinking attitudes, and helping students to think through holistic issues that blend the use of both critical and creative thinking skills through the employment of broad thinking strategies. The power and versatility of this approach to bringing teaching for thinking into the classroom should be evident from this discussion.

The lessons I have included in this chapter serve as examples and models on which I encourge teachers to reflect in developing their *own* materials. I am arguing for a process, not a product. The challenge is to adapt, enhance, embellish, and improve the models contained herein to your own teaching context in content-appropriate and grade-appropriate ways. This *can* be done given time and the right in-service support structure. The results are bound to be exciting to both students and teachers.

When teachers become immersed in teaching for thinking, their best abilities emerge. I urge administrators at the district and school level to provide the structures, time, and support to make this happen.

REFERENCES

Bateman, J. Sworn statement quoted in P. Force (Ed.), *American archives* (1839, 4th series, Vol. 2). Washington D.C.: Clarke and Force.

Beyer, B. (1985a). Critical thinking: What is it? *Social Education*, 22:270–276.

Beyer, B. (1985b). Teaching critical thinking: A direct approach. *Social Education.* 22:297–303.

Brown, S. (1970). *What happened on Lexington Green? An inquiry into the nature and methods of history.* Menlo Park, Calif.: Addison-Wesley.

Churchill, W. S. (1957). *A history of the English speaking peoples: The age of revolution* (Vol. 3). New. York: Dodd, Mead.

Davis, S., & Hall, T. (1975). *Moral education in theory and practice.* Prometheus.

Draper, P. (1975). !Kung women: Contrasts in sexual egalitarianism in foraging and sedentary contexts. In R. Reiter (Ed.), *Toward an anthropology of women.* New York: Monthly Review Press.

Ennis, R. H. (1962). A concept of critical thinking. *Harvard Education Review*, 32: 81–111.

Ennis, R. H. (1981). Rational thinking and educational practice. In J. Soltis (Ed.), *Philosophy and education* (Vol. 1): Chicago: National Society for the Study of Education.

Giroux, H. (1978). Writing and critical thinking in social studies, *Curriculum Inquiry*, 8:291–310.

O'Reilly, K. (1985). *Critical thinking in American history.* (4 vols.). Beverly, Mass.: Critical Thinking Press.

Marshall, L. (1976). *The !Kung of Nyae Nyae.* Cambridge: Harvard University Press.

Parnes, S. (1976a). *Creative actionbook.* New York: Scribner.

Parnes, S. (1976b). *Guide to creative action.* New York: Scribner.

Paul, R. (1984). Critical thinking: Fundamental for education in a free society, *Educational Leadership*, Sept. 1984.

Steinberg, S. (1963). *The United States: Story of a free people.* Boston: Allyn & Bacon.

Taylor, C. (1974). *Implode: Igniting creative potential.* Salt Lake City: Utah School District.

Wood, S. Deposition quoted in E. Ripley, *A history of the fight at Concord* (1832). Concord, Mass.: Herman Atill.

Wright, I., Daniels, L., & Coombs, J. (Eds.) (1980). An introduction to *Values reasoning series.* Association for Values Education and Research. Toronto: Ontario Institute for Studies in Education.

7

RICHARD W. PAUL

Center for Critical Thinking
and Moral Critique
Sonoma State University

Dialogical Thinking: Critical Thought Essential to the Acquisition of Rational Knowledge and Passions

When psychologists concerned with cognitive psychology and problem solving want to test their theories, they choose different kinds of problems from those generally chosen by philosophers concerned with critical thinking and rationality.

Cognitive psychologists like to analyze and generalize about problems that are defined, explored, and settled in a fundamentally self-contained way. They prefer atomic problems, especially ones having to do with technology, math, science, and engineering. Mathematical and verbal puzzles are a favorite. They choose problems that can be represented and settled in a definitive way within one frame of reference, for example:

1. A man once offended a fortune teller by laughing at her predictions and saying that fortune telling was all nonsense. He offended her so much, in fact, that she cast a spell on him which turned him into both a compulsive

gambler and, in addition, a consistent loser. That was pretty mean. We would expect the spell would shortly have turned him into a miserable, impoverished wreck. Instead, he soon married a wealthy businesswoman who took him to the casino every day, gave him money, and smiled happily as he lost it at the roulette table. They lived happily ever after. Why was the man's wife so happy to see him lose?

2. You are visiting a strange country in which there are just two kinds of people—truth tellers and liars. Truth tellers *always* tell the truth and liars *always* lie. You hail the first two people you meet and say, "Are you truth tellers or liars?" The first mumbles something you can't hear. The second says, "He says he is a truth teller. He is a truth teller and so am I." Can you trust the directions that these two may give you?

3. Ten full crates of walnuts weigh 410 pounds, whereas an empty crate weighs 10 pounds. How much do the walnuts alone weigh?

4. In how many days of the week does the third letter of the day's name immediately follow the first letter of the day's name in the alphabet?

I call these problems (adapted from Hayes, 1940) and the means by which they are solved *monological*: This implies that they are settled within one frame of reference with a definite set of logical moves. When the right set of moves is generated, the problem is settled. The answer or solution proposed can be shown by standards implicit in the frame of reference to be the "right" answer or solution.

Philosophers concerned with critical thinking and rationality are drawn to a very different kind of problem. They tend to choose nonatomic problems, problems that are inextricably joined to other problems and form clusters, with some conceptual messiness about them and very often important values lurking in the background. When the problems have an empirical dimension, that dimension tends to have a controversial scope. It is often arguable how many facts ought to be considered and interpreted and how their significance ought to be determined. When they have a conceptual dimension, there tend to be arguably different ways to pin the concepts down.

The result is that the problem's precise identification and definition depend upon some arguable choice among alternative frames of reference. I call these questions multilogical. More than one kind of incompatible logic can be advanced for their settlement. Indeed, more than one frame of reference can be used to argue their construal.

Now, because more than one frame of reference is contending for their construal and settlement, we must somehow "test" the frames of reference themselves. The only way to test whole frames of reference without begging the question is by setting the frames of reference dialectically against each other so that the logical strength of one can be tested against the logical strength of the contending others by appealing to standards not peculiar to either.

If we are not familiar with how to make the case for the logical strength of an answer proposed from a contending frame of reference, we can get a proponent to make the case for it. Then we listen to the case made from a competing frame of reference. Most especially, we try to determine how successful each constructed logic is in answering the objections framed from the opposing point of view. A trial by jury with opposing arguments of prosecution and defense is a good illustration of this traditional approach to multilogical issues.

However, if we do not have informed proponents of opposing points of view available, we have to reconstruct the arguments ourselves. We must enter into the opposing points of view on our own and frame the dialogical exchange ourselves. I contend that this required skill of empathy and reciprocity is essential to the development of the rational mind. Only such activity forces us outside our own frame of reference, which, given the primary nature of the human mind, tends to become an inflexible mind set. Unless we counter this tendency early on, it begins a process that becomes progressively harder to reverse.

Even though the lives of children are deeply involved in multilogical questions, and how the children come to respond to these questions has a profound influence on how they later define and deal with the central issues they will face as adults, children rarely are given a real opportunity in school to reflect upon questions in mutually supportive dialogical settings. I have in mind questions *like* the following although not necessarily any of these *precisely*):

Who am I? What am I like? What are the other people around me like? What are people of different backgrounds, religions, and nations like? How much am I like others? How much am I unlike them? What kind of a world do I live in? When should I trust? When should I distrust? What should I accept? What should I question? How should I understand my past, the past of parents, my ethnic group, my religion, my nation? Who are my friends? Who are my enemies? What is a friend? How am I like and unlike my enemy? What is most important to me? How should I live my life? What responsibilities do I have to others? What responsibilities do they have to me? What responsibilities do I have to my friends? Do I have any responsibilities to people I don't like? To people who don't like me? To my enemies? Do my parents love me? Do I love them? What is love? What is hate? What is indifference? Does it matter if others do not approve of me? When does it matter? When should I ignore what others think? What rights do I have? What rights should I give to others? What should I do if others do not respect my rights? Should I get what I want? Should I question what I want? Should I take what I want if I am strong enough or smart enough to get away with it? Who comes out ahead in this world, the strong or the good person? Is it worthwhile to be good? Are authorities good or just strong?

Questions like these are in the background of most of the satisfactions and frustrations of childhood. The deepest orientation of the person to self and life is determined by how the individual *responds* to them.

BACKGROUND PRINCIPLES

Before proceeding with my argument for the necessity of dialogical thinking to the development of rational knowledge and passions, I would like to introduce some background principles, including:

1. A reasonable person solves problems or comes to decisions about what to do or believe in accordance with, that is, by adjusting his or her thinking to, the nature of the issue being faced. Different questions require different modes of thinking. If a question's settlement presupposes the gathering of some empirical data, a reasonable person uses his or her thinking to facilitate that gathering. If that gathering requires an examination of sources or cases representing more than one point of view, the person looks at multiple sources and listens to the case for more than one point of view. If there are reasonable doubts that can be raised as to the accuracy, relevance, completeness, or implications of these data, they are raised. If there are values or purposes implicit in the problem-solving activity that a reasonable person would clarify or question, he or she clarifies or questions them.

2. People have both a primary and a secondary nature. Our primary nature is spontaneous, egocentric, and strongly prone to irrational belief formation. It is the basis for our instinctual thought. People need no training to believe what they want to believe, what serves their immediate interests, what preserves their sense of personal comfort and righteousness, what minimizes their sense of inconsistency, and what presupposes their own correctness. People need no special training to believe what those around them believe, what their parents and friends believe, what is taught to them by religious and school authorities, what is often repeated by the media, and what is commonly believed in the nation in which they are raised. People need no training to think that those who disagree with them are wrong and most probably prejudiced. People need no training to assume that their own most fundamental beliefs are self-evidently true or easily justified by evidence. People naturally and spontaneously identify with their own beliefs and experience most disagreement as personal attack, adopting as a result a defensiveness that minimizes their capacity to empathize with or enter into points of view other than their own.

   On the other hand, people need extensive and systematic practice to develop their secondary nature, their implicit capacity to function as rational persons. They need extensive and systematic practice to recognize the tendencies they have to form irrational beliefs. They need extensive practice to develop a dislike of inconsistency, a love of clarity, a passion to seek reasons and evidence and to be fair to points of view other than their own. People need extensive practice to recognize that they indeed have a point of view, that they live *inferentially*, that they do not have a direct pipeline to reality, that it is perfectly possible to have an overwhelming inner sense of the correctness of one's views and still be wrong.

3. Instruction that does not further the development of human rationality, though it may properly be called training, is not education. The cultivation of the educated mind and person presupposes the cultivation of rational skills and passions. Insofar as schooling furthers, utilizes, or reinforces irrational belief formation, it violates its responsibility to *educate*. A society of uneducated persons is incompatible with a democratic mode of government.

Unfortunately, the rule rather than the exception in schooling today is that students are in countless ways encouraged to believe that there are more or less authoritative answers readily available for most of the important questions and decisions we face, or at least, authoritative frames of reference through which such answers can be pursued. Students are led to believe that they are surrounded by experts whose command of technical and nontechnical knowledge enables them to settle definitively the important issues they face socially and personally. Students tend to ego-identify with the monological answers of their parents, teachers, or peers. They have no real experience with dialogical thinking.

MOST IMPORTANT ISSUES OF EVERYDAY LIFE ARE MULTILOGICAL AND HUMAN

We do not live in a disembodied world of objects and physical laws. Instead, we live in a humanly contrived and constructed world. And there is more than one way to contrive and construct the world. Not only our social relations but our inner cognitive and affective lives are inferential in nature. We do not deal with the world-in-itself but with the world-as-we-define-it in relation to our interests, perspective, and point of view. We shape our interests and point of view in the light of our sense of what significant others think, and, as a result, live in a world that is exceedingly narrow, static, and closed. For purposes of self-protection, we assume our view to be moral and objective. For the most part, our viewpoints are in fact amoral and subjective. Goffman (1959) explains this tendency as follows:

> In their capacity as performers, individuals will be concerned with maintaining the impression that they are living up to the many standards by which they and their products are judged. Because these standards are so numerous and so pervasive, the individuals who are performers dwell more than we might think in a moral world. But, *qua* performers, individuals are concerned not with the moral issue of realizing these standards, but with the amoral issue of engineering a convincing impression that these standards are being realized. Our activity, then, is largely concerned with moral matters, but as performers we do not have a moral concern with them. (p. 19)

This is not, as Whitehead (1929) shrewdly points out, how we *describe* ourselves, but "It does not matter what men say in words, so long as their activities are controlled by settled instincts. The words may ultimately destroy the instincts. But until this has occurred, words do not count" (p. 12).

As young children we begin to internalize images and concepts of what we and others are like, of what, for example, Americans are like—of what atheists, Christians, communists, parents, children, businesspeople, farmers, liberals, conservatives, left-wingers, right-wingers, salespeople, foreigners, patriots, Palestinians, Kiwanis Club members, cheerleaders, politicians, Nazis, ballet dancers, terrorists, union leaders, guerillas, freedom fighters, doctors, Marines, scientists, mathematicians, contractors, waitresses, are *like*. We then ego-identify with our conceptions, we assume them to be accurate, and spontaneously use them as guides in our day-to-day decision making.

Unwittingly, we begin as children—and unless we get extensive dialogical practice—we continue as adults to use egocentric and self-serving theories of people and the world. We organize our experience and make judgments from the perspective of assumptions and theories we would not admit, if questioned, to having. Studies in social perception demonstrate this property in detail. Toch and Smith (1968) summarize it as follows:

> The process of reaching a value-judgment, the unconscious weighing that man's brain is able to make of numerous cues during a fraction of a second, is by no means a random and chaotic procedure. The weighing process, resulting in a perception, goes on for a purpose, whether that purpose is seeking food, adjusting one's footsteps to a curbing, picking up a book, reading or underlining certain passages in a book, joining some gang or group, or accepting or rejecting some political ideology. (p. 6)

> We see people as instant wholes. A "theory" is commonly viewed as something used exclusively by scientists. The discussion, however, emphasizes that everyone has, and inevitably uses, theories about people. These theories guide the wholes they perceive and the parts that they fit into the wholes. (p. 10)

> We all use theories in dealing with people: We invent concepts, assume relationships between them, and make predictions from our assumptions. Our theories are not, however, useful in the scientific sense, for they are implicit rather than explicit. That is, we are only dimly aware of our theories. As a result, we rarely make any real effort to test them. Yet they rule our impressions and our judgments. (p. 13)

People from different ethnic groups, religions, social classes, and cultural allegiances tend to form different but equally egocentric belief systems and use them equally unmindfully. These different construals of the world represent alternative settlements of the same basic set of issues that all people face in everyday life. We must all decide who we are as individuals and members of a community. We must construct a history, a place in time. We must envision an emergent future. We must define and decide who our friends and enemies are. We must invest our time, energy, and resources in some everyday projects and not others. We must decide what is *ours* and *why it is* ours. We must decide what is just and unjust and what grievances and grudges we have. We must decide to whom to give and from whom to withhold credibility. We must decide what is possible and impossible—what to fear and what to hope for. All of these decisions determine our fundamental life-style and, ultimately, our destiny. They all presuppose the settlement of multilogical issues. Yet, few of us realize the process by which we internalize and construct a logic, a point of view, an organized way of experiencing, reasoning, and judging. Most of us, unfortunately, think of the world in terms of a monological definition of reality. How we see things seems simply *the correct way* to see them. How others see them seems simply wrong or prejudiced.

This can be illustrated by the flagrant differences between the colonial and British perceptions of the so-called Boston Massacre. The accounts at the time testify to the way in which people automatically presuppose the correctness of their ethnocentric perceptions:

1. A colonial onlooker, standing 20 yards from the colonists, gave sworn testimony to the justices of the peace on April 23, 1775, that the British fired the first shot.

2. A colonial Tory (a sympathizer with the British) wrote an account on May 4, 1775, to General Gage (the British commander in Boston), in which he said that the colonists fired the first shot.

3. A young British lieutenant wrote in his diary on April 19, 1775 that the colonists fired one or two shots, then the British returned the fire without any orders.

4. The commander of the colonial militia, John Parker, in an official deposition on April 25, 1775, stated that he ordered the militia to disperse and not to fire, but the British fired on them without any provocation.

5. The *London Gazette* stated on June 10, 1775, to its British readers that the colonists fired on the British troops first.

Most teachers, I suspect, simply assume the account that favors their nation is correct and then teach it as fact to be committed to memory. In this way, students are encouraged to think monologically about historical events.

As a result, the essential multilogical character of history is never grasped by most students (or their teachers). By not grasping that all history is history-from-a-point-of-view, the students do not recognize appropriate logical parallels, such as, for example, that all news is news-from-a-point-of-view. The result is that students do not learn how to read history or the news critically.

INERT KNOWLEDGE AND ACTIVATED IGNORANCE

John Bransford (see Chapter 9) reminds us of the problem (originally suggested by Whitehead, 1929) of inert knowledge—knowledge that we in some sense *have* but do not use when logically relevant, knowledge that just sits there in our minds, as it were, without activating force. Typically, this inability to put knowledge to work is viewed as an inability to *transfer*. In light of the above, I suggest instead that the problem is in large part derived from the fact that we already have *activated* beliefs that are firmly entrenched in instinctual ego-centric thinking. The young child does not come to school with an empty head ready to be filled with new ideas and knowledge. The egocentric mind abhors a vacuum. The capacity to suspend judgment pending evidence is a higher order, secondary-nature, skill. The problem of inert knowledge, I am suggesting, is equivalent to the problem of activated ignorance. Children do not *transfer* the knowledge they learn in school to new settings because they already have activated ideas and beliefs in place to use in those settings. The child's own emerging egocentric conceptions of children, teachers, parents, fun, work, and play are much more activated and real than any alternative conceptions fostered by classroom instruction or textbooks. Only by bringing out the child's own ideas in dialogical/dialectical settings can the child begin to reconstruct and progressively transcend these conceptions. As long as school learning is simply superimposed on top of the child's own activated ignorance, that ignorance will continue to rule in the life-world of the child and his or her scholastic learning will remain largely inert. Perhaps this is part of the reason why so many adults, including those in high positions, often seem to act or talk like egocentric children.

There are, therefore, at least two fundamental justifications for giving children extensive dialogical practice in school: (1) that practice is essential for all of those issues that the child must face which are intrinsically multi-logical and (2) that practice is essential for the child to come to discover, reconstruct, and ultimately transcend the ideas and beliefs that he or she is uncritically and unconsciously internalizing. A case can be made for the value of dialogical reasoning even when dealing with monological issues, as will be shown by the work of Jack Easley on math and science education. But first, let me be more explicit about the nature of dialogical thinking.

DIALOGICAL THINKING IN EARLY SCHOOL YEARS

Children begin developing an egocentric identity, point of view, and frame of reference through which they experience, think about, and judge the world. Many of their beliefs are taken from the beliefs of those around them. Nevertheless, from their earliest days, they come up against opposing points of view, differing interpretations of events, contradictory judgments, and incompatible lines of reasoning. First, their parents and peers and then their teachers and other authorities often disagree with them and thwart their egocentric desires.

But little is usually done to provide children with a way of entering into thoughts and feelings other than their own. Of course, they *hear* what others say, but children are not taught to experience the inner logic of alternative points of view. That children are capable of developing in this direction is demonstrated in their play: "You can be the mommy. I'll be the daddy. And my sister can be the baby." But schools do not, by and large, take advantage of this tendency and use it to construct exercises wherein students present reasons and evidence for alternative conclusions.

Children often utilize their capacity to think up reasons for and against an idea or decision only when they are already egocentrically for or against it. Of course, they must often bow to the superior power or authority of a parent, teacher, or older peer. But they typically do not do this by entering into the point of view of the other and rationally assenting. As a result, they do not grasp that they themselves have a point of view. Rather, they tend to make absolute moral judgments about themselves or others. They frequently develop hostile feelings (often repressed) toward themselves or toward those who force them, rightly or wrongly, to accept their point of view. They are not given an opportunity to work out their own thoughts and discover ways of judging *reasons* without judging the *worth* of the person advancing them.

Children need assignments in multilogical issues. They need to discover opposing points of view in nonthreatening situations. They need to put their ideas into words, advance conclusions, and justify them. They need to discover their own assumptions as well as the assumptions of others. They need to discover their own inconsistencies as well as the inconsistencies of others. They do this best when they learn how to role-play the thinking of others, advance conclusions other than their own, and construct reasons to support them.

Children need to do this for the multilogical issues—the conflicting points of view, interpretations, and conclusions—that they inevitably face in their everyday life. But perhaps we should go further. All or most of what we come to learn rationally requires dialogical exchanges and opportunities to judge between conflicting points of view. The work of Jack Easley on math and science education suggests this thesis.

SHOULD DIALOGICAL INSTRUCTION BE USED FOR MONOLOGICAL ISSUES?

In a series of articles on mathematics and science education, Jack Easley (1983a, b; 1984a) argues that children should learn how to solve virtually all problems—even the most monological and formalistic ones—dialogically or dialectically. He argues that field and cognitive studies indicate that primary school teachers (1) cannot *transmit* knowledge, (2) should therefore leave most discussion of math and science content to pupils, (3) should choose and present appropriately challenging problems and tasks to the pupils, (4) should train group leaders who facilitate dialogical exchanges, and (5) should serve, fundamentally, as moderators of class communication. Most important, children should work in small but heterogeneous groups, trying to convince, and coming to understand, each other. Through arguing children discover their own views as well as their weaknesses and also discover contrasts between their views and the views of others. Here are some of the ways Easley (1984b) formulates these points:

> Primary teachers in the U.S., at least, should leave most discussion of mathematics and physical science content to their pupils. (a) Cognitive research shows that young children develop and test alternative rational explanations which authoritative exposition can't displace. (b) The conflicts that arise between presentations by teachers and texts and the pupil's unexamined math-science concepts generate severe anxieties about mathematics and science in most children.

> Only by reflection on the alternative schemes in the light of conflicts with standard schemes can revisions be produced.

> Those few students who do truly master mathematical or scientific subjects do so through a long process of doubting and challenging authority which few teachers are willing to take the time to do, even in pre-service training.

> Teachers of regular primary grade classes should train group leaders on a regular basis to provide appropriate challenges for every member of their group.

> Primary children should strive first to develop expression in some form by working in heterogeneous groups, trying to convince each other by clear speaking and writing.

> They should also learn to say in advance what kind of contribution to the dialogue they are trying to make: an objection, an alternative view, a supporting point, etc.

> I became convinced that teachers should be accepted by school reformers as the persons who are effectively in charge of instruction and who can change only as their perceptions of the classroom context are opened up through dialogues which respect the perceptions they have built from their own experience.

> In Kitamaeno School, use of peer group dialogues helped children recognize alternative schemes and deal with them. Organizing children into small working groups around pre-selected, appropriately challenging tasks required group leaders with confidence and some training in what to do when things went wrong.

> The teachers' role was to present, often very dramatically, the challenging problem they had selected for the lesson, and almost totally abstaining from demonstrating or explaining how to solve it and to serve as master of ceremonies to see that every child had ample opportunity to be heard and took the responsibility to express ideas and to listen critically to those of others.

> As children discover they have different solutions, different methods, different

frameworks, and they try to convince each other, or at least to understand each other, they revise their understanding in many small but important ways.

As you can see, Easley is arguing that irrespective of whether we adults have at our disposal a precise and thoroughly defensible monological system for settling certain types of problems, children need to work their way to that mono-logic through dia-logic. Because students have alternative beliefs and frames of reference even in the area of scientific and mathematical concepts, they need to confront them or they will remain implicit, unchallenged, and unreconstructed. If we do not provide an environment in which children can discover their own *activated* ideas, they may become and remain invincibly ignorant when it comes to putting knowledge into action. Their biases, stereotypes, distortions, illusions, and misconceptions will not dissolve without the purging power of dialogical exchange. They will simply superimpose adult beliefs on top of unreconstructed but still highly activated infantile ones.

Students leave school not only with unreconstructed mathematical and physical ideas but with unreconstructed personal, social, moral, historical, economic, and political views. Students leave school not knowing what they *really*, that is *deeply*, believe. Students leave school with a great deal of inert knowledge and even more activated ignorance. Therefore, students do not understand how to read, write, think, listen, or speak in such a way as to organize and express what they believe. Students do not know how they are responding to the mass media and to what extent it is reinforcing their subconscious egocentric or sociocentric views. They do not grasp how to read a newspaper or a book critically or how to listen to a lecture critically. They have no *rational* passions. They feel deeply only about egocentric concerns, justifying getting what they want and avoiding what they do not want. If dialogical thinking enables students to reconstruct mathematical and scientific ideas, it is most certainly called for in dealing with personal, social, moral, historical, economical, and political ones.

DIALOGICAL THINKING AS A STRATEGY FOR BREAKING DOWN EGOCENTRIC IDENTIFICATIONS AND MIND SETS

Children need to experience dialogical thinking because such thinking is essential for rationally approaching the most significant and pervasive everyday human problems, and because without it we will not develop the intellectual tools essential for confronting our own instinctual egocentric thought. Until we discover our own egocentric thinking, we will not be able to monitor or work through it. Indeed, to hold beliefs egocentrically is to hold them in nontestable ways. As Piaget (1976) puts it:

Many adults are still egocentric in their ways of thinking. Such people interpose between themselves and reality an imaginary or mystical world, and they reduce everything to this individual point of view. Unadapted to ordinary conditions, they seem to be immersed in an inner life that is all the more intense. Does this make them conscious of themselves? Does egocentrism point the way to a truer introspection? On the contrary, it can easily be seen that there is a way of living in oneself that develops a great wealth of inexpressible feelings, of personal images and schemas, while at the same time it impoverishes analysis and consciousness of self. (p. 209)

Like egocentric children, egocentric adults assimilate everything they hear or experience to their own point of view. They learn how to affect reciprocity—to create the appearance of entering into points of view other than their own. But when there is conflict, they "enter" them only to negate or refute. They never genuinely leave their own mind set.

I am reminded of a distinction drawn by the great American sociologist, C. Wright Mills (1962), which sheds light on how people relate to the belief systems they come to accept. Mills argued that there were three types of believers—vulgar, sophisticated, and critical. Vulgar believers can only operate with slogans and stereotypes within a point of view that they egocentrically identify. If they become "Marxists," they use slogans like "Power to the people!", "Smash the state!", "Down with the capitalist pigs!". They use these slogans to badger their would-be opponents. They are not interested in reading books on capitalism or by capitalists, but consider them only as the enemy.

In contrast, sophisticated Marxists are interested in reading books on capitalism, or by capitalists. But they are interested only in refuting them. They stand on their heads if necessary to show that Marxism is in all senses and respects superior to capitalism. They might be intellectually creative, but all of their creativity is used to further one and only one point of view.

Only critical believers would, in Mills's sense, be willing to enter sympathetically into opposing points of view, for only they recognize weaknesses in their own point of view. If they become Marxists, it is as a result of reading Marx as Marx read others—sympathetically and critically. They are capable of learning from criticism and are not egocentrically attached to their point of view. They understand it is something to be developed continually and refined by a fuller and richer consideration of the available evidence and reasoning through exposure to the best thinking in alternative points of view.

If Mills is right, we have vulgar, sophisticated, and critical capitalists; vulgar, sophisticated, and critical Christians; vulgar, sophisticated, and critical Americans, Frenchmen, and Russians. Given their fundamental mode of thinking and their shared capacity to enter into points of view other than their own and to learn from criticism, critical Marxists, capitalists, Christians, Muslims, Americans, Frenchmen, and Russians share more in common with each other than they do with their vulgar or sophisticated counterparts.

A fundamental problem of schooling today in all societies is a marked tendency to produce vulgar and sophisticated but not critical believers. This problem is in large part due to the fact that dialogical thinking is not emphasized. Most instruction is monological, with various *authoritative* perspectives being nurtured and inculcated. When the inculcated perspective is incompatible with the child's own egocentric beliefs, the academically learned perspective is simply superimposed as a facade or veneer. This facade or veneer may itself be egocentrically defended, but the defense is merely *verbal*, because the primary and more primitive system is maintained in behavior. Hence, people can vehemently defend Christianity and yet behave continually in a most un-Christian fashion, apparently and self-righteously oblivious of their contradictions. Or they can defend democracy with passion and abandon, and yet act so as to undermine all possibility of its being practiced. This is the case for any system of beliefs, whether scientific, religious, social, political, or personal. Wherever we find people, we find blatant contradictions between word and deed. Whenever we find people, we find a great deal of defensive self-delusion.

TEACHING CRITICAL THINKING IN THE STRONG SENSE: SCHOOL AS PURGATORY

I would like to use a religious metaphor to characterize the problem of education. For a Catholic, there are three possible divine dispensations as a result of the manner in which one lives. In addition to heaven or hell, one may be sent to purgatory, a place in which one must work one's way back to God. The assumption is that one can die with one's thoughts and will still somewhat resistant to God. One then must go through a process of purging one's sinful tendencies. This process involves some pain and struggle, but issues ultimately in a purification of heart and will, a rooting out of one's sinful tendencies, and a reconstruction of one's inner thoughts.

This concept is apt for understanding what schooling should be like if it is to result in that very rare breed—the educated, rational person. If we want persons who believe critically, who are neither vulgar nor sophisticated in their beliefs, then we waste our time by trying to make school heaven—all fun and games, all pleasant and satisfying, all positive reinforcement. Of course, I take it for granted that we will get nowhere by going to the other extreme and making it hell. The challenge is to foster a process whereby students progressively and over a long period of time rid themselves of their egocentric and sociocentric beliefs and attachments. As things now stand, it does not appear that schooling does more than make people's instinctual egocentrism a bit more sophisticated, at least with respect to issues that are alive, issues that *matter*, that we care about, that affect whether we get or do not get what we (often egocentrically) want.

However, this is not to say that schools that foster dialogical or dialectical thinking would be hotbeds of strident argument, closed-minded debate, or personal trauma. Our present experience of argument, debate, and controversy only occurs in the context of unreconstituted egocentric attachment. People typically argue for egocentric purposes and with egocentric ends in view. They argue to score points, *defeat* the other person, make their point of view *look* good. They experience it as *battle*, not as a mutual or cooperative search for a fuller grasp of what is so.

Yet I know from some years of working with students that they can learn to reason dialogically in mutually supportive ways, that they can learn to experience the dialogical process as leading to discovery, not victory. The first rule to guarantee this end is to ensure that, as soon as possible, they learn to argue for and against each and every important point of view and each basic belief or conclusion that they are to take seriously. The second rule is to raise issues that they care about and engage their egocentric thoughts and beliefs. Then the dialogical thinking that is nurtured helps develop critical thinking skills in the strong sense.

Teaching critical thinking in the strong sense is teaching it so that students explicate, understand, and critique their own deepest prejudices, biases, and misconceptions, thereby allowing students to discover and contest their own egocentric and sociocentric tendencies. My key assumption is that only if we come experientially to contest our inevitable egocentric and sociocentric habits of thought can we hope to think in a genuinely rational fashion. Only dialogical thinking about basic issues that genuinely matter to the individual will provide the kind of practice and skill essential to strong-sense critical thinking. I grant that every student needs to develop the particular skills that Robert Ennis and others have delineated (see Table 1-1), but I am arguing that *how* these skills are nurtured is crucial.

Students need to develop all critical thinking skills in dialogical settings if they are to extend ethically rational development, that is, genuine fair-mindedness. If simply taught as atomic skills separate from the empathic practice of entering into points of view that students are fearful of or hostile to, they will simply become additional means for rationalizing prejudices and preconceptions, of convincing people that their point of view is *the* correct one. They will be transformed from vulgar to sophisticated but not to critical thinkers.

FACT, OPINION, AND REASONED JUDGMENT

Unfortunately, many programs designed to enhance critical thinking fail to give students insight into the nature of multilogical issues and the need for dialogical thinking. Inadvertently, they foster the view that all questions are reducible either to matters of fact (where science, math, engineering, and technical learning are dominant) or matters of opinion (where personal taste, culture, religion, preference, and faith are dominant). This problem occurs when students are encouraged to divide all beliefs into facts and opinions. In neither case, then, is there any real place for dialogical thinking. In the first case, it is unnecessary, because scientific, mathematical, and technological procedures and methods presuppose relatively agreed–upon frames of reference and modes of issue settlement. In the second case, it is useless, because presumably there is no room for reasoning in matters of pure taste: De gustibus non est disputandem. Schools under the sway of this view take as their first and foremost responsibility teaching students *the facts*, and then secondarily, passing on the shared values and beliefs of the culture.

Unfortunately, a taxonomy that divides all beliefs into either facts or opinions leaves out the most important category: *reasoned judgment*. Most important issues are not simply matters of fact, nor are they essentially matters of faith, taste, or preference. They are matters that call for our reasoned judgment. They are matters that can be understood from different points of view through different frames of reference. We can, and many different people do, approach them with different assumptions, ideas and concepts, priorities, and ends in view. When analytically applied to these perspectives in dialectical contexts, the tools of critical thinking enable us to grasp genuine weaknesses. The dialectical experience enables us to gain this perspective.

For example, it is exceedingly difficult to judge the case made by a prosecutor in a trial *until* we have heard the arguments for the defense. Only by stepping out of the perspective of the prosecutor and actually organizing the evidence in language designed to make the strongest case for the defense can we begin to grasp the true strength and weakness of the prosecutor's case. This approach is the only proper way to deal with the important issues we face in our lives, and I am amazed that we and our textbooks refuse to recognize it. The most basic issues simply do not reduce to unadulterated fact or arbitrary opinion. True, they often have a factual dimension. But characteristically, some of what is apparently empirically true is also arguable. And we are often faced with the problem of deciding which facts are *most* important, which should be made central, and which should be deemed peripheral or even irrelevant. Then, typically, there are possibilities for alternative arguable interpretations and implications. Make your own list of the ten most important issues and see if this is not true (but beware the tendency to see your own answers to these issues as self-evident facts!).

THE CULTIVATION OF RATIONAL PASSIONS

If we are to grasp the problem of teaching critical thinking skills in a strong sense, we must challenge the reason-versus-emotion stereotype, which fosters the view that a rational person is cold, unfeeling, and generally without passion, whereas an irrational person is passionate but unintellectual. A false dichotomy is set up between reason and passion, and we are forced to choose between the two as incompatible opposites. Therefore, we must choose between following our reason or our emotions, because by definition, we cannot follow both.

But this point of view is profoundly misleading. All action requires the marshaling of energy. All action presupposes a driving force. We must *care* about something to do something about it. Emotions, feelings, and passions of some kind or other are at the root of all human behavior. What we should want to free ourselves from is not emotion, feeling, or passion per se, but irrational emotions, irrational feelings, and irrational passions. A highly developed intellect can be used for good or ill either at the service of rational or irrational passions. Only the development of rational passions can prevent our intelligence from becoming the tool of our egocentric emotions and the point of view embedded in them. A passionate drive for *clarity*, accuracy, and fair-mindedness, a fervor for getting to the bottom of things, to the deepest root issues, for listening sympathetically to opposition points of view, a compelling drive to seek out evidence, an intense aversion to contradiction, sloppy thinking, inconsistent application of standards, a devotion to truth as against self-interest—these are essential commitments of the rational person. They enable us to assent rationally to a belief even when it is ridiculed by others, to question what is passionately believed and socially sanctioned, to conquer the fear of abandoning a long and deeply held belief. There is nothing passive, bland, or complacent about such a person.

Emotions and beliefs are always inseparably wedded together. When we describe ourselves as driven by irrational emotions, we are also driven by the irrational beliefs that structure and support them. When we conquer an irrational emotion through the use of our reason, we do it through the utilization of our rational passions. To put this another way and link it more explicitly with the earlier sections of this chapter, our primary egocentric nature is a complex mixture of belief, values, drives, and assumptions. It is an integrated cognitive and affective system. It generates a total frame of reference through which we can come to perceive, think, and judge. When we develop our secondary nature, we develop a countervailing system, equally complex and complete. We may of course experience intense internal struggles between these incompatible modes of being. Both systems can become highly *intellectualized* so that intelligence per se is not what distinguishes them. It is quite possible to find highly intelligent but essentially irrational persons, as well as basically rational ones of limited intelligence. In this way, a highly intelligent but sophisticated (i.e., sophistic) thinker can create the illusion of defending a more rational point of view than that defended by a thinker who is basically rational but not as clever.

Therefore, as educators we should embrace the nurturing of rational passions as an essential dimension in the development of the *thinking* of our students. I regret that there is no time to develop some of the ways of doing this. Suffice it to say that it is essential for teachers to model rational passions. This, of course, presupposes that teachers genuinely have them. It will do no good for a teacher to pretend. This is not a matter of *technique*. This is an important reason why successful critical thinking instruction cannot be achieved as the result of a few weekend in-service workshops.

CRITICAL AND CREATIVE THINKING

Just as it is misleading to talk of developing a student's capacity to think critically without facing the problem of cultivating the student's rational passions—the necessary driving force behind the rational use of all critical thinking skills—so too is it misleading to talk of developing a student's ability to think critically as something separate from the student's ability to think creatively. Creativity is essential to all rational dialogical thinking, because dialogical thinking is a series of reciprocal creative acts wherein we move up and back in our minds from categorically different imagined roles. We must first of all imagine ourselves in a given frame of reference. Then we must imaginatively construct some reasons to support it. Next we must step outside the framework of those acts and imagine ourselves responding to those reasons from an opposing point of view. Then we must imagine ourselves back in the first point of view to create a response to the opposition we just created. Next we must change roles again and create a further response. And so on. The imagination and its creative powers are continually called forth. Each act must be constructed to fit the unique move that preceded it. In dialogical exchange, we cannot predict in advance what another, or indeed what we, will say. Yet what we say, to be rational, must be responsive to the logic of what was just said by the other.

Students, of course, should not begin by playing both sides of a dialogue simultaneously. But we should continually nurture them toward the ability to frame dialogical exchanges, first brief, then extended ones. Their creative imagination will be continually challenged to develop through this process.

CONCLUSION

People become educated, as opposed to trained, insofar as they achieve a grasp of critical principles and an ability and passion to choose, organize, and shape their own ideas and living beliefs by means of them. Education is not a mere piling up of more and more bits and pieces of information. It is a process of autonomously deciding what is and what is not true and false. It calls for self-motivated action on our own mental nature and a participation in the forming of our own character. It is a process in which we learn to open our mind, correct and refine it, and enable it to learn rationally, thereby empowering it to analyze, digest, master and rule its own knowledge, gain command over its own faculties, and achieve flexibility, fairmindedness, and critical exactness.

This process cannot be accomplished when learning is viewed monologically. The process of gaining knowledge is at its roots dialogical. Our minds are never empty of beliefs and never without a point of view. They cannot function framelessly. Since our instinctive intellectual drives are inevitably egocentric initially and then typically ethnocentric, we must learn to bring our implicit ideas and reasonings into open dialogical conflict with opposing ones

> Baby Bear had the smallest bowl.
> "Why do I have the smallest bowl?" he said.
> "Because you are the smallest bear." said his mother.
> "Is that fair?" said Baby Bear.
>
> • *Did Baby Bear need as much as the big bears? Why?*
> • *Could he eat as much as the big bears? Why?*
> • *Did he deserve as much as the big bears? Why?*
> • *Do you think it is fair for Baby Bear to have a smaller bowl? Why?*
> • *What problems have you seen like the one in this story?*

Figure 7-1

in order to decide rationally, as best we can, upon their merit as candidates for mindful belief. Our implicit everyday theories of ourselves, our friends and neighbors, our nation and religion, our enemies and antagonists, and our hopes, fears, and premonitions must become overtly known to us that we might learn continually to reassess them as we enter empathically into belief systems more or less alien to our own.

Children begin by engaging in mere collective monologue, but early on they also begin the process of responding to the points of view of others. Their play suggests that they enjoy taking on the role of others and acting as if they were someone else. This initial drive must not be allowed to wither away but must be cultivated, expanded, and reshaped. Whether we begin with empathy into the thinking and predicaments of characters in children's stories (Figure 7-1), lead children into reflective philosophical discussions (Figure 7-2), or provide challenging ethical questions and dilemmas for them to think about (Figure 7-3), we must lead students to the point that they begin to get comfortable dealing with dialogical issues rationally (Figure 7-4). Progressively, the issues that students deal with should get more and more complex (Figure 7-5).★

More and more students should have assignments that challenge their ability to identify and analyze frames of reference and points of view—the frames of reference in their texts, various subject areas, TV programs, news broadcasts and daily papers, the language of their peers and teachers, political speeches

---

★ Figures 7-1, 7-3, and 7-5 are adapted from *Justice*, a series produced by Law in a Free Society, 5115 Douglas Fir Drive, Calabasas, CA 91302. Figure 7-2 is from "Pixie: Looking for Meaning," by Matthew Lipman and A. M. Sharp, in *Philosophy for Children*, 1984, Institute for the Advancement of Philosophy for Children, Montclair State College, Montclair, N.J. Figure 7-4 is from *Thinking Critically*, by John Chaffee, 1985, Houghton Mifflin, Boston.

DISCUSSION PLAN: Friends

---

1. Can people talk together a lot and still not be friends?
2. Can people hardly ever talk together and still be friends?
3. Are there some people who always fight with their friends?
4. Are there some people who never fight with their friends?
5. Are there some people who have no friends?
6. Are there people who have friends, even though they have hardly anything else?
7. Do you trust your friends more than anyone else?
8. Are there some people whom you trust more than your friend?
9. Is it possible to be afraid of a friend?
10. What is the difference between friends and family?
11. Are there animals you could be friends with, and other animals you could never be friends with?

Figure 7-2

and personal discussions, and everyday decisions and ways of living. And they should do this not to discover that everything is relative and arbitrary or a matter of opinion, but that all beliefs and points of view are subject to rational analysis and assessment. As they achieve increasing success in this process, their rational passions will develop by degrees and their egocentric defensiveness will concomitantly decrease.

WHAT DID SARA LEARN?

Making Things Right

The children had damaged the wall. Sara thought they should *make things right.* One way was for them to put a new coat of paint on the wall.

The children's parents might have to pay to have new paint put on the wall. Sara thought that might be another way to *make things right.*

- *What would be fair? Why?*
- *What problems like this have you seen?*
- *What does MAKING THINGS RIGHT have to do with being fair?*

Figure 7-3

◆ • ◆   For each of the following issues, identify reasons that support each side of the issue.

Issue

Students' grades should be based not only on how much they learn, but also on how hard they try.

Students' grades should be based only on how much they learn.

Supporting Reasons

1. This policy will encourage students who learn slowly.

2. _____

   _____

3. _____

   _____

Supporting Reasons

1. Teachers don't always know how hard a student is trying.

2. _____

   _____

3. _____

   _____

Issue

The best way to deal with crime is to give long prison sentences.

Long prison sentences will not reduce crime.

Supporting Reasons

1. _____

   _____

2. _____

   _____

3. _____

   _____

Supporting Reasons

1. _____

   _____

2. _____

   _____

3. _____

   _____

Figure 7-4

> "If a man destroy the eye of another, they shall destroy his eye."
> Hammurabi, about 1950 B.C.
>
> Convicted of theft, Mustafa was taken into the public square where, before a fascinated crowd, the executioner chopped off his right hand with a sword.
>
> The court ordered Sarah to pay $5,500 for damages to Paul's car and $8,376 in medical bills for injuries to Paul after she crashed into his car while he was stopped for a red light.
>
> Three members of a teen-aged gang beat and robbed a 60-year-old woman standing at a bus stop. The woman was hospitalized for two months and permanently crippled by the beating. The boys were arrested and placed in Juvenile Hall for six months where they were given psychological counseling, released, and placed on probation for one year.
>
> Each of the above situations involves an issue of *corrective justice*. Corrective justice refers to the fairness of responses to wrongs or injuries.
>
> *What Do You Think?*
>
> 1. *What is fair or unfair about each of the above responses to wrongs or injuries?*
>
> 2. *What values and interests, other than fairness, might be important to take into account in deciding what might be a proper response to a wrong or injury?*

Figure 7-5

The students will not become progressively more unruly and hard to handle. On the contrary, they will become more and more amenable to *reason* and the power of evidence. They will, of course, eventually question us and our point of view, but they will do so rationally and hence help us to develop as well. Ideally, the process will come to pervade the school climate and be reflected in the deepest structures of school life. By this means, schools can perhaps begin to become leading institutions in society, paradigms of rationality, by helping an irrational society to become what it itself has said is its own highest goal: a free society of free and autonomous persons.

REFERENCES

Easley, J. (1983a). A Japanese approach to arithmetic. *For the Learning of Mathematics*, 3 (3).

Easley, J. (1983b). What's there to talk about in arithmetic? *Problem Solving* (Newsletter, The Franklin Institute Press) 5.

Easley, J. (1984a). Is there educative power in students' alternative frameworks? *Problem Solving* (Newsletter, The Franklin Institute Press), 6.

Easley, J. (1984b). A teacher educator's perspective on students' and teachers' schemes: Or teaching by listening. Unpublished paper, presented at the Conference on Thinking, Harvard Graduate School of Education.

Goffman, E. (1959). *The presentation of self in everyday life*. Garden City, N.J.: Doubleday.

Hayes, J. (1940). *The complete problem solver*, Philadelphia: The Franklin Institute Press.

Mills, C. W. (1962). *The Marxists*. New York: Dell.

Piaget, J. (1976). *Judgment and reasoning in the child*. Totowa, N.J.: Littlefield, Adams.

Toch, H., & Smith, H. C. (Eds.). (1968). *Social perception*. New York: Van Nostrand.

Whitehead, A. (1929). *The aims of education and other essays*. New York: Dutton.

Part III

PROGRAMMATIC APPROACHES TO THE TEACHING OF THINKING SKILLS

MATTHEW LIPMAN

Institute for the Advancement of Philosophy for Children
Montclair State College

Some Thoughts on the Foundations of Reflective Education

Pixie (Lipman, 1981) is a novel for children in grades K–4. It is a part of the newest genre of children's literature, philosophy for children. Pixie's class is going on a zoo trip. They each have an assignment: to select a "mystery creature," look for it in the zoo, and then write a story about it. Pixie looks in vain for her secret creature in the zoo. She breaks down and cries. Only then do we discover that her mystery creature was a *mammal*. Her classmates explain to her that mammals are not animals, but are a *class* of animals. They explain to her that the class of ducks cannot fly and the class of redheads is not redheaded. They also discuss the difference between class relationships and family relationships. The novel spends a good deal of time on the topic of relationships. But in any event, this is how it begins:

Now it's *my* turn. I had to wait *so long* for the others to tell their stories!

I'll start by telling you my name. My name is Pixie. Pixie's not my real name. My real name my father and mother gave me. Pixie's the name I gave myself.

How old am I? The same age you are. (p. 1)

After the children—the live children, that is—have read the first episode (or have had it read to them), they are asked to describe what in it they found interesting. Those who can do so may formulate questions. Others may merely point to a sentence or a word. For example, someone may point to the phrase "*my* turn" in the first sentence. Another person may say, "real name." And someone else may ask, "How can Pixie be the same age we are, if we're not all of the same age?"

These comments then become the basis of class discussion, starting with the question of what it means to take turns. It would not be unusual for a kindergartner to suggest that taking turns is a form of *sharing*. (Finding the genus—in effect, generalizing—from a single instance is a shrewd move.) Here the teacher might intervene with the question, "Can anyone tell me some other kinds of sharing?" One quickly hears about the sharing of rooms, beds, and sandwiches. One may even hear, as a kindergarten teacher did recently, "My parents share *me*." By exploring the many meanings of the word *share* and by offering differently nuanced examples, the students gradually clarify the concept of *sharing*. They willingly move from instantiation to concept-formation, because it helps them understand better the story they've just read.

They may move on to discussions of *names* and even to what it is to be *real*. Here the teacher may offer an assignment (once the students have begun to distinguish between things that are really real and things that only seem to be real). The children are to bring some object to class the next day and put it in one of four boxes. The boxes are labeled "things that seem real and are;" "things that seem real but aren't;" "things that don't seem real but are;" and "things that don't seem real and aren't." It is an exercise in elementary logic (and metaphysics), just as the previous discussion on sharing was an application of logic to an area of ethics.

Now there's a clamor about the problem of Pixie's age. Can Pixie actually be as old as we are? How can one person be many different ages? How can one be many or many, one? But someone in the class may suggest a way of resolving the mystery: Pixie may not be talking to us. She may be talking to a group of children her own age. This interpretation, of course, requires a drastic shift in one's frame of reference to realize that Pixie may be talking to someone else rather than to us; to understand it may require an almost Copernican shift of perspective. Many children, of course, do not understand this interpretation or actively reject it, with the result that they continue to think of Pixie as having many ages or as being ageless, so that, as one fourth-grader put it, "she has birthdays every day of the year."

The *Pixie* program is one of six programs that has been developed by the Institute for the Advancement of Philosophy for Children. Each program consists of a children's novel, usually about 100 pages in length, and a 400-page instructional manual crammed with exercises and discussion plans keyed to the concepts and skills in the novels. Two programs, *Pixie* and *Kio and Gus* (Lipman, 1982b), are for K–4. *Harry Stottlemeier's Discovery* (Lipman, 1982a) is for grades 5–6 and plays a pivotal role in the entire series, because it introduces children to the principles of logic. The remaining three novels apply the reasoning skills developed earlier to specific academic areas. *Lisa* (Lipman, 1983), which is used in grades 7–8, deals with ethical reasoning and moral practice. Thinking and writing are blended in the early high-school program called *Suki* (Lipman, 1978). And a reflective approach to social studies is to be found in the *Mark* (Lipman, 1980) program, suitable for later secondary school.

TRANSFORMING THE CLASSROOM

One of the governing ideas in a democracy, an idea that regulates both curriculum development and teacher preparation, is that reasonableness is perhaps the single most important characteristic of the educated person. Democracies are inclined to this view because they have found it difficult to function when their citizens are inclined to be unreasonable. At the same time, many educators have found this view appealing because it is conducive to the development of autonomous, rational beings. According to such educators, educated people are not merely well learned, they think well.

To shift priorities in education from learning to thinking in effect requires a redefinition of the function of the classroom. The classroom as presently constituted is a receptacle for students who are themselves receptacles of information. It must be transformed into an association of thinking children or, more properly, into a community of inquiry, as shown in Figure 8-1.

The Philosophy for Children program can, of course, be viewed as merely another curriculum innovation aimed at improving children's thinking skills. However, from another perspective, it is a prototype of the new era in education that is just beginning. When it is thought of in this fashion, it invites being unpacked into its components, their sources, and their modes of functioning in the program as a whole.

Disciplinary and Methodological Sources

Formal and Informal Logics

The first novel to be written in the program was *Harry Stottlemeier's Discovery*, which draws upon the class logic of Aristotle (especially in the areas of conversion, contradiction, and categorical syllogisms). This logic is supplemented by the logic of relations (transitivity and symmetry) and modern propositional logic (conditional syllogisms). These deductive logics are reinforced by excursions into induction and informal logic.

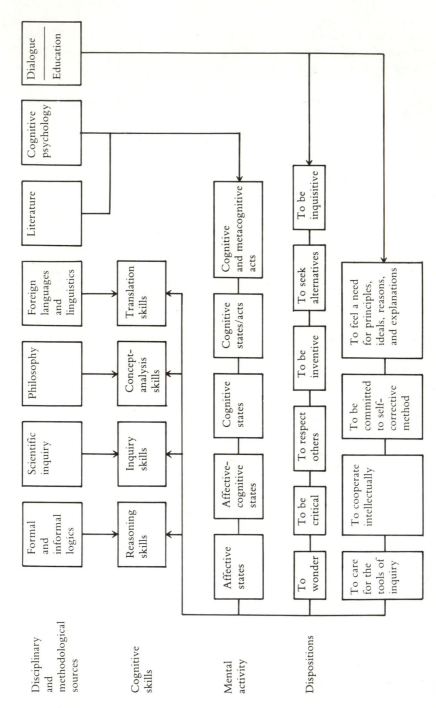

Figure 8-1 Transforming the classroom into a community of inquiry.

Scientific Inquiry

Chapter One of *Harry* represents a paradigm of the process of inquiry, much in the way Dewey (1933) constructs such a paradigm to show the continuity between everyday problem solving and scientific method. The stages of the process in the *Harry* chapter are: feeling difficulty, doubting what one has taken for granted, defining the problem, forming a hypothesis, inferring possible consequences, discovering a counterinstance, revising and broadening the hypothesis to explain the counterinstance, and applying the revised hypothesis to a life situation.

Philosophy

Although it is true that Philosophy for Children in its entirety is derived from the academic discipline of philosophy (minus, of course, the names and dates of philosophers and their schools), certain aspects of traditional philosophy are highlighted in the children's version. One such aspect, already mentioned, is logic. Another is the predilection philosophers have for fastening upon the problematic aspects of any discipline or form of knowledge while seeking to analyze and clarify the concepts to be found therein. Conceptual analysis is, of course, characteristic of virtually all schools of philosophy, even though modern Anglo-British philosophy has tended to favor it almost exclusively. In any event, philosophical analysis provides a regimen much needed by children who are perplexed by muddled and contestable concepts and need a set of tools for getting at their meanings. Needless to say, unpacking meanings draws upon the critical and interpretive functions of philosophy as much as it derives from its analytical functions.

Foreign Languages and Linguistics

It is possible to construe every academic discipline, from algebra to zoology, as a symbol system or language. Once this assumption is made, it is possible to reinterpret the problem of transfer and recognize that translation is the bridge that enables us to transfer our meaning-acquisition operations from one linguistic context to another. Ordinarily, there is no ready transfer from one discipline to another, just as there is no ready translation from one language to another—say, from Greek to English. But if students are equipped with translation skills, they can learn to carry meanings over from one language to another. Likewise, if students are provided with interdisciplinary, bridge-building skills, they can establish continuities among the disciplines.

Literature

Normally, children are equipped with textbooks and readers. The readers contain stories that are supposed to invite reading. Therefore, they are easy to read and are wholly innocent of any cognitive content that might make them burdensome. Anything perplexing or problematical has been removed.

Such stories can be read with the same passive fascination that one accords to television cartoons. They may make for literacy, but it is a literacy devoid of intellectual stimulation. The disjunction between reading and thinking is firmly established at the earliest possible moment in the child's life. In reflective education (of which Philosophy for Children is an example), children are encouraged to read and write thoughtfully, just as they are encouraged to recognize the crucial role thinking plays in whatever we make or say or do.

Instead of a dichotomy between secondary texts bulging with unappetizing, unpalatable, and undigestible information, on the one hand, and vapid, vacuous reading materials on the other, it is possible to construct a literary genre in which the stories to be read reveal to children how thinking can be conducted so that the materials to be learned can be discovered by the children themselves. (If cognitive psychologists have emphasized anything, it is that contextualized information, i.e., information presented in story form, is more readily learned than decontextualized information.) Moreover, such presentations disclose the model of the child as thinker to children. It is not surprising that without such a model children in the past have had a hard time taking their own thinking processes seriously and have discounted the value of their own thoughts, which might otherwise have seemed so precious to them.

Not only, then, does the literary vehicle provide a model of thinking children, but it serves to awaken (if awakening is needed) the mental life of the child. This awakening is of vital importance, for if thinking is not taking place, it can hardly be improved. The sharpening of thinking skills is not likely to be effective among children who are in a state of mental torpor. Something is needed to arouse their wonder, curiosity, and inquisitiveness and give them practice in performing the cognitive acts that are prerequisites of the acquisition of cognitive skills.

Thus, to read a Sherlock Holmes mystery is to have our wonder, curiosity, and inquisitiveness aroused; we find ourselves engaging in such mental acts as supposing, assuming, guessing, and judging. When Holmes examines a footprint and tells Watson what sort of person it was who made such a footprint, we are impelled to reenact Holmes's thought processes, for only by going through his reasoning can we explain his conclusions to ourselves. If Holmes tells us that the man who made that footprint must have weighed 200 pounds, we cannot help asking ourselves what such a footprint must look like to be able to infer from it the weight of the man who made it.

When children discuss what they have just read, they in effect reconstruct the thinking that went into the writing; even though such discussions may not disclose the writer's intentions, they disclose his or her meanings. This combination of thinking, reading, and meaning is also useful when the same children must engage in writing and discover that it too is inseparable from thinking and meaning.

Cognitive Psychology

Cognitive psychology and the philosophy of mind have analyzed mental activity into a continuum of affective states, affective-cognitive states, cognitive states, cognitive states/acts, and cognitive (as well as metacognitive) acts. It is generally taken for granted that mental states cannot be conveyed by teaching; whether the same is true in the case of mental acts is more controversial.

Dialogical Practice and Educational Theory

From the time of Socrates, dialogue has been recognized as an important way of structuring educational interactions. Socratic dialogue, in which the teacher helps the learner bring to light what he or she apparently already knows and in which both teacher and student explore and discover together, has been a particularly interesting dialogical procedure. Nevertheless, Deweyan educational theory is no less important in this regard, because Dewey stresses the educational value of students' reflecting upon—discussing, analyzing, and interpreting—their own experience (1944). From this it follows that in the absence of such experience, classroom discussions will be impoverished. All the more reason, then, to begin each class session with an experience in which aesthetic, scientific, cognitive, and affective strands are deliberately knotted together followed by urging the students to unravel these strands and examine them individually and in relation to one another. Such discussions are far from being idle chatter. They are the work of intelligence and the process by means of which cognitive skills are most effectively sharpened.

Cognitive Skills

Reasoning Skills

Virtually any taxonomic approach to cognitive skills is bound to be problematical, and efforts to simplify matters tend to be arbitrary. On the whole, it is advisable to avoid hierarchical approaches—one of the more obvious difficulties with Bloom's taxonomy (1956). Another danger results from being too selective. This danger is also illustrated by Bloom, who virtually ignores the skills needed for deductive reasoning.

Now there are a great many kinds of thinking: Anything we do intentionally or deliberately involves thinking. However, when the criteria that thinking must conform to are established—such as the logical criteria that enable us to distinguish valid from invalid reasoning—then the thinking that takes place is called *reasoning*. This argument may seem to suggest that all reasoning is governed by rules, but such an interpretation may be overly restrictive. When we reason deductively, our reasoning is governed by rules, but we are still reasoning when, after we discover that our deductions are invalid or our premises are shaky, we go back and review our premises and the format of our inferences. Indeed, we are still reasoning when we reason inventively. In such cases, we are not actively *guided* by rules, although it may be found subsequently that the way we thought can be *expressed* by rules.

Obviously, there can be many kinds of reasoning: mathematical, symbolic, geometrical, linguistic, and so on. From the point of view of those who measure intelligence, all of these kinds of reasoning are potentially of equal worth, and no one could be said to lack intelligence who had one but not the others. For all that psychologists tell us about "body language," "tacit knowledge," "symbolic intelligence," and the like, it is not to these that thinking skill improvement must be primarily addressed, but to reading, writing, speaking and listening—in English.

The distinction is often made between elementary and higher order cognitive skills, although the grounds for such a distinction are seldom disclosed. For our purposes, such a distinction is useful. We can think of elementary cognitive skills as those involving a single reasoning step, whereas the higher order skills involve the making of several such steps. (The distinction is particularly useful in testing, since it is more difficult to pinpoint weaknesses in multiple-step items than in single-step items.)

There is thus a broad sense in which anything that is a skill involves reasoning. There is a narrower sense in which all elementary and higher order cognitive skills may be called reasoning skills. And there is a still narrower sense in which reasoning proper involves the use of single-step cognitive skills, so that they alone are called *reasoning skills*, whereas inquiry skills, concept-analysis skills, and translation skills are all higher order cognitive skills. (It is not unusual for terms to have genus-species ambiguity. Think of terms like *society* and *art*, for example.) Therefore, if, *thinking* is too vague a term for general usage, *reasoning* tends to have too many closely associated and hard-to-distinguish meanings. Under the circumstances, those who speak of reasoning at any length find it difficult to avoid being equivocal.

Still, we can find paradigms that provide relatively clear-cut cases against which we can measure the cases that blend into one another. Thus, examples of single-step reasoning moves might be found in such logical operations as conversion, contradiction, and symmetry, whereas multiple-step reasoning might be exemplified by working out a contraposition or by constructing an analogy based on a counterfactual conditional.

Certainly, we can look at cognitive skills as forming a continuum ranging from the simple to the complex, depending upon the number of operations involved. Thus, very elementary mental acts such as guessing and surmising are necessary for hypothesis construction; hypothesis construction permits one to engage in reasoning with conditional syllogisms; and such reasoning, in turn, plays an important role in problem solving and other aspects of inquiry.

Inquiry Skills

Scientific inquiry compels the mobilization of internally diversified clusters of skills, as has just been noted. If we were to examine explanation, description, evaluation, verification, falsification, observation, or any other inquiry skills, we would find them to be composed of teams of skills in disciplined cooperation. Reluctance to decompose inquiry skills into their components does not make for effective pedagogy in science education, for the lack of proficiency in a complex skill is often the fault of a malfunctioning   it skill. If we cannot decompose complex skills into component fur   nediation, where indicated, may become difficult to achieve.

Concept-analysis Skills

The simplest skills are often the most fundamental. The best examples are making connections and making distinctions. Without competence in these two areas, one's hopes for more general cognitive competence must be dim indeed. On the other hand, once one is able to make reliable distinctions and connections, one can begin to group, classify, and define.

Students are often eager to explore the boundaries of a concept—the edges of its meaning. This exploration can be done by assembling roughly synonymous terms to constitute the central meaning of the concept, while also assembling the antonyms to establish the outer boundaries. One is then left with an intervening twilight zone or no-man's land inhabited by fuzzy terms and blurry meanings. However, it is precisely these ambiguous cases, rather than those that are clear-cut, that are the most interesting to examine and most likely to give rise to classroom discussion.

Translation Skills

It is often said, and with good reason, that proficient readers are those who comprehend what a passage states, implies, and assumes, who can interpret the passage both sympathetically and critically, and who can apply its meanings to relevant life situations. Fostering the skills of application and critical interpretation is best achieved through discussion of the passage in the context of a classroom community of inquiry. In such a community and through such dialogue students can develop appreciation for the variety of possible interpretations, points of view, and perspectives and try out relevant applications under the watchful eyes of their peers.

On the other hand, there are the difficult cognitive skills that must be used to come to grips with what a passage states, implies, and assumes. Obviously, these skills include finding assumptions and using inferential skills. But more is involved if one is to get at what the passage actually *states*. To grasp what a difficult expository passage means is to translate it into language one is more comfortable with—to paraphrase it into a more colloquial, but still nearly synonymous, version. Now translation is in a sense the counterpart of inference: Inference preserves truth regardless of meaning, whereas translation preserves meaning regardless of truth. The two work together, as do the left hand and the right hand. The reasoning skills most directly involved in translation are analogical reasoning (indispensable for comparing the original passage with inexact paraphrases of it) and logical standardization (valuable for showing how rules can be constructed to govern translation from general linguistic usages into the specialized locutions of classical logic).

Mental Activity

Here we have a continuum that ranges from affective states with only a germ of cognitive activity to cognitive acts with only a mild affective tinge. These affective states may be rudely appetitive (craving, desiring), accompany weak or strong preferences (liking, disliking, loving, hating, fearing, dreading), anticipate action (intending, willing, determining), or be related to one's understanding or lack of understanding of the world (wondering, believing, admiring, respecting, hoping, expecting). Some of these affective states may pass over into combinations of states and acts, becoming more heavily weighted on the cognitive rather than the affective side (doubting, knowing, understanding).

When we come to cognitive acts, we can distinguish between those that are verbalized from those that are not. Verbal acts are, of course, legion, and can be exemplified by telling, uttering, hinting, claiming, saying, insisting, and asserting. Unverbalized cognitive acts (sometimes just called mental acts) include supposing, assuming, surmising, remembering, judging, deciding, comparing, and associating. A special subcategory of unverbalized cognitive acts are metacognitive acts, in which we think about thinking (our own or anyone else's). Metacognitive acts are important to cultivate, because they provide an impulse to self-correction that is essential to a community of inquiry.

Dispositions

Attitudes and dispositions are an individual's responses to the quality of the social interaction prevalent in the group situation. One either internalizes the quality or develops negative attitudes toward it. In a classroom in which there is intellectual cooperation and intellectual criticism, the lively demanding of reasons for opinions and explanations for puzzling events, and the quest for meanings and the exploration of alternatives, children are motivated to wonder, inquire, be critical, be inventive, and care for and love the tools and procedures of inquiry. They acquire—or perhaps reacquire—a need for principles, ideals, reasons, and explanations. Without such dispositions, children lack the readiness for sustained cognitive practice, yet it is only through such practice that the readiness is created.

REFERENCES

Bloom, B. S. (1956). *Taxonomy of educational objectives, Handbook I: Cognitive domain.* New York: McKay.

Dewey, J. (1944). *Democracy and education.* New York: Macmillan.

Dewey, J. (1971). *Experience and education.* New York: Collier.

Dewey, J. (1933). *How we think.* New York: Heath.

Dewey, J. (1955). *The child and the curriculum.* New York: Macmillan.

Lipman, M. (1982a). *Kio and Gus.* Upper Montclair, N.J.: First Mountain Foundation.

Lipman, M. (1982b). *Harry Stottlemeier's discovery*. Upper Montclair, N.J.: First Mountain Foundation.

Lipman, M. (1983). *Lisa*. Upper Montclair, N.J.: First Mountain Foundation.

Lipman, M. (1980). *Mark*. Upper Montclair, N.J.: First Mountain Foundation.

Lipman, M. (1981). *Pixie*. Upper Montclair, N.J.: First Mountain Foundation.

Lipman, M. (1978). *Suki*. Upper Montclair, N.J.: First Mountain Foundation.

9

JOHN D. BRANSFORD

ROBERT D. SHERWOOD

TOM STURDEVANT
Learning Technology Center
Peabody College
Vanderbilt University

Teaching Thinking and Problem Solving

"*There are no simple solutions; only intelligent choices.*" The preceding quotation is relevant to educators in several ways. First, it emphasizes the need to help students become independent thinkers and problem solvers. Second, it reminds us that there is no simple procedure for achieving such a goal. We need to make intelligent choices each step of the way.

In this chapter, we discuss some of the research literature that is relevant to teaching thinking. In particular we:

1. provide descriptions of hypothetical ideal thinkers and problem solvers,

2. discuss the problem of *teaching* thinking and problem solving, and

3. explore the issue of evaluating programs so that they can be revised and improved.

THE IDEAL PROBLEM SOLVER

During the past ten years, there has been a great deal of research on the processes that underlie effective thinking and problem solving (Hayes, 1981; Newell & Simon, 1972). Our discussion of the issue will follow Bransford and Stein's *The IDEAL Problem Solver* (1984). Bransford and Stein emphasize five components of thinking that are applicable to a wide variety of situations. These include the ability to *identify* problems, *define* and represent them with precision, *explore* possible strategies, *act* on these strategies, and *look* at the effects. The first letter of each of these components forms the word IDEAL.

I = Identification of Problems

The ability to *identify* the existence of problems is one of the most important characteristics of successful problem solvers. In business, it can mean the difference between failure and success. In his book, *Getting Things Done*, Bliss (1976) notes that leaders of a company in Great Britain discovered that they were requesting a great deal of unnecessary paper work from their employees. Employees had to fill out cards for each item that was sold to keep track of inventory, and they were required to complete daily time cards indicating the number of hours worked. Within one year after the problem of excessive paper work had been discovered, 26 million cards and sheets of paper were eliminated. Obviously, a solution would never have been generated if the problem had not been identified in the first place.

Problem identification is also important in academic settings. Assume that young students are working with a computer-simulated problem of a farmer who wants to fence a small lot. The farmer measures the lot by counting the number of steps necessary to walk around it and then goes to a hardware store and orders 80 "feet" of fence. Ideally, even the young problem solver will notice that this measurement process will probably lead to error if the farmer wants to buy exactly the right amount of fencing.

As another example of problem identification, assume that an IDEAL problem solver is reading a text and confronts a statement such as "The notes were sour because the seam split." Unlike a less effective learner, who may simply be going through the motions of reading while actually daydreaming, the effective learner will realize that a problem exists (i.e., the statement does not make sense). If the problem is not identified, possible strategies such as rereading and asking questions of clarification will not be tried.

Whimbey (1975) provides an example of the importance of problem identification for reading comprehension. He presented the following passage to college students who were poor readers:

If a serious literary critic were to write a favorable, full-length review of How Could I Tell Mother She Frightened My Boyfriends Away, Grace Plumbuster's new story, his startled readers would assume that he had gone mad, or that Grace Plumbuster was his editor's wife.

When he came to the paragraph, Whimbey had to stop and reread it several times in order to comprehend its meaning. In contrast, many poor readers simply continued to read without realizing the existence of a comprehension problem that needed to be solved.

D = Definition of Problems

Once a problem has been identified, it must be *defined* precisely. People can agree that a problem exists, yet differ on how they define it, and their definitions of problems can have important effects on the types of solutions that are tried. For example, a number of educators have identified a problem with many school systems, namely, that they are not helping students become effective thinkers. Although we may all agree that such a problem exists, there are many different ways to define it. The problem may be due to poor teachers and hence might be solved by increasing admissions standards in college, paying teachers more money, and so forth. Others might define the problem as due to poor curriculum materials, and still others might define it as being caused by a lack of knowledge about what we mean by thinking. Of course, each of these definitions has some degree of truth. The important point is that different definitions of a problem lead to different solution strategies. For example, the strategy of increasing teachers' pay is different from the strategy of encouraging more research on the teaching of thinking. Similarly, a strategy such as creating special science and mathematics schools for high-achieving students reflects a definition of the problem that emphasizes the need to educate a few thousand highly trained people rather than the need to increase everyone's problem-solving skills.

Differences in problem definition can have strong effects on people's abilities to think and solve problems. The history of science contains many examples of scientists who were more successful than their predecessors because they defined problems in more fruitful ways. Copernicus (Sagan, 1980) provides an interesting illustration. He eventually solved a problem that others before him had failed to solve: how to account for the movement of the planets in the heavens. Astronomers had collected data indicating where various planets were at particular points in time (e.g., during different months). Nevertheless, no one had been able to come up with a theory of their orbits that predicted where and explained why they should appear.

After years of study, Copernicus finally created a theory that predicted the movements of the planets. To do so, he had to make a radical assumption. Prior to Copernicus, everyone had taken it for granted that the sun and other planets revolve around the earth—and indeed, it looks that way to the naked eye. Copernicus argued that if one made this assumption, one could not accurately predict the movement of the planets. His theory began with an alternate assumption, namely, that the earth and other planets in our solar system revolve around the sun. Note that Copernicus's predecessors had implicitly defined their problem as "Why do the planets move as they do, given that the earth is the center of the universe?" Copernicus eventually defined the problem differently and only then was able to achieve success.

We have already defined a problem as, "Why are school systems not helping students become effective thinkers?" This definition of the problem involves the assumption that the school system is solely responsible for poor training in thinking—an assumption that may render the problem impossible or at least much more difficult to solve. An alternative approach to developing thinking and problem-solving skills is to assume that society as a whole guides thinking and enlist the support of a number of different factions in our society, rather than focusing only on schools. For example, parents could be encouraged to emphasize thinking and problem solving, businesses could provide information about the importance of problem solving in the workplace, cultural heroes and heroines such as sports figures and movie stars could support the effort, and so forth. By defining problems too narrowly, we place unnecessary limits on the strategies for solution.

Problem definition is closely related to the representation of problems. If you represent a problem by writing, "What is $\frac{2}{5}$ of $\frac{1}{2}$?," you will probably multiply the fractions. However, if you represent the problem as "What is $\frac{1}{2}$ of $\frac{2}{5}$?," a much simpler strategy for solution will come to mind.

The units of measurement that we employ also reflect different definitions of problems. If you are in the business of transporting large groups of people, you will face questions about fuel efficiency. For this type of business, the problem of fuel efficiency will probably be defined in terms of *passenger miles per gallon* (where buses are more efficient than cars) rather than *miles per gallon* (where cars are more efficient than buses). Thus, a particular unit of measurement may or may not be appropriate, depending on the problem one is trying to solve.

Different manufacturers often adopt particular units of measurement that influence how people think about various products. Thus, one manufacturer of computers might argue that its product is the most efficient in terms of cost per kilobyte of memory. A second manufacturer might emphasize the importance of cost relative to the amount of quality software available, and a third might emphasize cost relative to the ease of learning about the system. It seems clear that these different ways of thinking about computers can have strong effects on the decisions that potential purchasers eventually make.

E = Exploration of Strategies

It is clear that the ability to identify and define problems provides no guarantee of a successful solution. Therefore, IDEAL problem solvers *explore* a variety of strategies that can help them succeed. Several examples of successful strategies are provided below.

Breaking Problems into Manageable Subproblems

One general strategy that is characteristic of effective problem solvers is to break complex problems into subproblems that are more manageable. People who fail to do this frequently conclude that complex problems are impossible to solve. A mother who was enrolled in one of our problem-solving courses supplied the following example. Her child decided that she could not learn to spell the word "Tennessee" because it was too complex. The mother helped her child break the problem into simpler subproblems by focusing on the spelling of "ten," "nes," and "see."

Earlier in this chapter, we used the following passage to illustrate the importance of identifying comprehension problems (Whimbey, 1975):

If a serious literary critic were to write a favorable, full-length review of How Could I Tell Mother She Frightened My Boyfriends Away, Grace Plumbuster's new story, his startled readers would assume that he had gone mad, or that Grace Plumbuster was his editor's wife.

A reader could identify a comprehension problem, define the problem as being due to processing difficulties (as opposed to insufficient information in the passage, for example), and yet still fail to comprehend the passage. Without strategies that attempt to break the overall passage into comprehensible subunits, it is doubtful that anyone could understand what the author intended to say.

The Use of Special Cases

Another general strategy is to solve a problem by first looking at a special case. As an illustration, assume that a manager of a health club focuses on a subproblem such as the following (adapted from Bransford & Stein, 1984):

A racquetball tournament will be held at the Managers' Club. One hundred and six people have entered the open single elimination tournament (after losing once, the player is eliminated). If the manager needs a score card for each match, how many cards will she need if each player shows up?

This is not an easy problem. One way to solve it is to program a hypothetical tournament on a computer. To do so, however, you may first need to imagine a special case where only two people are enrolled in the tournament. You would then require only one scorecard. If three people were enrolled, you would need two scorecards; if four were enrolled, there would be a need for three scorecards, and so forth. It is possible to derive a general rule to determine the number of matches that will be played in such tournaments by examining a few simple cases (number of matches = number of players − 1). This general rule can then be used to solve the problem for a tournament involving 106 players (the answer is 105).

Working Backward

A third general strategy involves working backward on a problem. The following example is adapted from Bransford and Stein (1984):

It is 4:00 P.M. and you have just received notification that you are expected for an important company meeting in Chicago at 8:00 A.M. the next morning. There are two flights open. One is a dinner flight that leaves at 6:00 P.M. and arrives in Chicago at 6:00 A.M. the next day. The other flight departs at 7:30 P.M. and arrives in Chicago at 7:30 A.M. the next day. When you arrive in Chicago you will need to wait 20 minutes for your luggage and it will take 20 minutes by taxi to get to your meeting. Which flight should you take?

To solve this problem, an effective strategy is to begin with your goal, which is to be at a meeting in Chicago at 8:00 in the morning, and work backward. If you do this, you will see that you need to take the earlier flight.

Working backward is also useful for many other problems. On tests of reading comprehension, students are usually presented with passages to read and are then required to answer questions about them. An effective strategy on these tests is to work backward by *first* reading the questions and then reading the passages with the questions in mind.

Additional Strategies

There are many additional strategies that are used by effective problem solvers, such as using images and mnemonics to remember information, looking for implicit assumptions in one's definitions of problems, searching for inconsistencies in arguments, and so forth. In *The IDEAL Problem Solver*, Bransford and Stein (1984) argue that the most important strategy for improving problem solving is to learn about new concepts, theories, and procedures that can then function as tools which enable one to perform activities that otherwise would be difficult and perhaps even impossible. However, an understanding of how concepts and principles can function as conceptual tools is quite different from the mere memorization of factual content. The issue of developing conceptual tools is discussed in more detail in the section on teaching thinking and problem-solving skills.

A and L = Acting on Ideas and Looking at the Effects

The fourth and fifth components of the IDEAL problem-solving framework are to *act* on the basis of a strategy and *look* at the effects. If people simply think about possible strategies without actively attempting to apply them, they deprive themselves of information that can help identify unforeseen problems caused by old modes of thought.

Imagine that a group of students is studying for an essay test. All students may identify and define their problem and select study strategies. Nevertheless, successful students will also act on the basis of a study strategy and look at the effects before actually taking the test. For example, successful students may select a study strategy and then pretest its effectiveness by attempting to recall the information while writing practice essays. Failures in such endeavors provide new opportunities for learning. In contrast, the student who fails to act and look has no idea that new problems exist that need to be solved.

Attempts to conduct scientific experiments represent excellent examples of the importance of the act and look components of the IDEAL framework. Students often believe that the ideal experiment is one that confirms existing hypotheses. In contrast, researchers realize that experiments are often valuable because they make apparent the existence of problems that previously were unrecognized. Without active attempts to experiment, problems with existing methods and theories would often fail to be noticed, and the ability to learn would be impaired.

The IDEAL Cycle and Creativity

Note that the preceding discussion emphasizes the importance of problem-solving cycles. After acting and looking, one may identify the existence of a new problem, define it, explore strategies, act on the basis of these new strategies, and look at the effects. This cycle may be repeated until no new problems are identified. In this case, one can exit the IDEAL cycle.

The IDEAL cycle can be illustrated by the example of students who complete a mathematical word problem and come up with the answer that someone works 36 hours per day. Effective problem solvers will *identify* the existence of a problem with this answer; namely, that it cannot be correct. The problem may then be *defined* as being due to an error in calculation, which will prompt an *exploration* of strategies such as checking one's calculations. The effective problem solver will then *act* on the strategy and *look* at the effects. If the answer still looks incorrect (e.g., it still comes out as 36 hours per day), this again signals the existence of a problem and the IDEAL cycle will be reentered. This time the problem may be redefined as a result of misreading the word problem rather than an error in calculation, and this change in problem definition should prompt the exploration of new sets of strategies (e.g., carefully reread the entire problem). The effective problem solver will then act on a strategy and look at the effects. If the answer now seems reasonable, the problem solver can exit the IDEAL cycle.

Different ways of entering the IDEAL cycle can result in strategies that vary in creativity. The creative person who reenters the IDEAL cycle will often redefine a problem in a way that suggests simpler and more workable strategies. Consider an example from Adams's book, *Conceptual Blockbusting* (1979). Adams notes that a group of engineers was trying to design an improved method for mechanically picking tomatoes that would be less likely to bruise the tomatoes. Their implicit definition of the problem was: "How can we design a mechanical picker that will not bruise tomatoes?" Given this definition of the problem, suggestions for strategies included ideas such as putting more padding on the picking arms, slowing the speed of the picking arm, and so forth. A different definition of the problem, and one that is quite creative, is "How can we keep tomatoes from getting bruised while they are being picked mechanically?" This definition of the problem led to solutions such as developing a new strain of tomatoes that had slightly stronger skins and that grew further out on the tomato vine.

In his book, *New Think*, de Bono (1967) distinguishes between vertical thinking (proceeding systematically from a single concept or definition) and lateral thinking (seeking alternate ways of defining or interpreting a problem). He states:

> Logic is the tool that is used to dig holes deeper and bigger, to make them al-
> together better holes. But if the hole is in the wrong place, then no amount of
> improvement is going to put it in the right place. No matter how obvious this
> may seem to every digger, it is still easier to go on digging in the same place than
> to start all over again in a new place. Vertical thinking is digging the same hole
> deeper; lateral thinking is trying again elsewhere.

This comment suggests that an important aspect of creative problem solving is to ask ourselves whether we are making implicit assumptions about the nature of a problem that limit our ability to find solutions.

A friend of ours was able to redefine a problem creatively that involved the purchase of software for his three-year-old daughter. He first evaluated the degree to which various programs were appropriate for his daughter to use by herself and concluded that, in most instances, they were not. For example, one program projected patterns that, over time, gradually produced the image of an animal such as a sheep or a dog. The person using the computer was supposed to hit the escape key as soon as he or she could identify the figure. The next step was to type in the name of the figure (e.g., dog); the computer would show a clear image of the figure if the answer was correct. Our friend's daughter became very good at this program and had no trouble finding the escape key and pressing it. Nevertheless, she did not yet know how to spell and hence could not work the program without adult supervision.

If our friend had restricted the definition of his problem to "find available software that my daughter can use by herself," he would have had to reject the program involving the recognition of animals. He eventually redefined the problem as, "How can I create contexts that make existing programs suitable for use by my daughter?" This redefinition led to the strategy of finding pictures of various animals and printing their names under them. The girl was than taught how to refer to this sheet to determine the correct spelling of animal names. She was readily able to use the sheet and, in a short amount of time, learned to spell the names of a number of animals without having to refer to the sheet. Overall, our friend's redefinition of the problem led to the creation of an exciting context within which learning occurred.

TEACHING THINKING AND PROBLEM SOLVING

Our goal in the preceding section was to describe some characteristics of ideal thinkers and problem solvers. These descriptions are useful for clarifying desired end states, but they provide little information about how to get there. In this section, we explore some of the research literature that is relevant to issues of *teaching* thinking and problem solving.

Access and the Problem of Inert Knowledge

At first glance, the problem of teaching thinking and problem solving is straightforward: Provide students with information about effective thinking and problem solving and make sure this information is learned. The short-comings of this approach involve the problem of access. The fact that people can remember information provides no guarantee that it will be utilized when it is needed.

As a simple illustration of the preceding argument, consider the problem of comprehending statements such as, "The haystack was important because the cloth ripped" and "The notes were sour because the seam split" (Bransford & McCarvell, 1974). Most people have difficulty comprehending these state-ments, but not because they lack the knowledge necessary to do so. Instead, the problem is that they fail to activate relevant knowledge that they have already acquired. When given prompts that provide them with access to rel-evant information (i.e., parachute and bagpipes, respectively), they can com-prehend the preceding statements.

The statements about the haystack and the notes are trick sentences, of course. An important component of the art of creating trick sentences and problems involves the ability to phrase things in a way that will cause otherwise competent people to fail to access information that they already know. We know of no educators who are so devious that all of their lectures and tests are composed of trick questions. Nevertheless, there appear to be many in-stances where students fail to access information that they have learned.

Many years ago, Alfred Whitehead (1929) warned about the dangers of *inert knowledge*—knowledge that is accessed only in a restricted set of contexts even though it is applicable to a wide variety of domains. He also argued that traditional educational practice tended to produce knowledge that remained inert. A study conducted by Gick and Holyoak (1980) provides an informative illustration of the problem of inert knowledge. They had college students memorize a story about a military campaign that contained information such as the following:

A general wishes to capture a fortress located in the center of a country. There are many roads radiating outward from the fortress. All have been mined so that while small groups of men can pass over the roads safely, a large force will detonate the mines. A full-scale direct attack is therefore impossible. The general's solution is to divide his army into small groups, send each group to the head of a different road, and have the groups converge simultaneously on the fortress.

After the students had successfully recalled the military problem and its solution, they were given Duncker's radiation problem (1945) to solve.

Suppose you are a doctor faced with a patient who had a malignant tumor in his stomach. It is impossible to operate on the patient, but unless the tumor is destroyed the patient will die. There is a kind of ray that may be used to destroy the tumor. If the rays reach the tumor all at once and with sufficiently high intensity, the tumor will be destroyed. At lower intensities the rays are harmless to healthy tissue, but they will not affect the tumor either. What type of procedure might be used to destroy the tumor with the rays, and at the same time avoid destroying the healthy tissue?

This problem can be solved in much the same way as the general solved the military problem. In the radiation problem, many sources of less intense radiations could pass safely through the healthy tissue and converge on the tumor in sufficient intensity to destroy it.

Because subjects in the Gick and Holyoak study memorized the military problem, they presumably had knowledge that could be applied to the radiation problem. In fact, 90 percent of the students were able to use information from the military story to help solve the radiation problem, *given that they received the hint that the prior story was useful.* However, when no hint was given, only 20 percent of the subjects spontaneously used the military story. For those students who were not given a hint, the information they memorized in the context of the military story remained inert.

Studies conducted by Perfetto, Bransford, and Franks (1983) provide additional evidence that relevant knowledge can remain inert even though it is potentially useful. They presented college students with a series of insight problems such as the following:

1. Uriah Fuller, the famous Israeli superpsychic, can tell you the score of any baseball game *before* the game starts. What is his secret?

2. A man living in a small town in the U.S. married twenty different women in the same town. All are still living and he has never divorced one of them. Yet, he has broken no law. Can you explain?

Most college students have difficulty answering these questions unless provided with hints or clues. Prior to solving the problems, some students were given clues that were obviously relevant to each problem's solution. These students first received statements such as, "Before it starts the score of any game is 0 to 0," and "A minister marries several people each week." The students were then presented with the problems and explicitly prompted to use the clue information (which was now stored in memory) to solve them: Their problem-solving performance was excellent. Other students were first presented with the clues and then given the problems but they were not *explicitly* prompted to use the clues for problem solution. Their problem-solving performance was very poor; in fact, it was no better than that of baseline students who never received any clues.

The Perfetto et al. results represent an especially strong demonstration of access failure (i.e., of inert knowledge) because the clues were constructed to be obviously relevant to problem solution. Indeed, the authors noted that before conducting the experiment, they had expected even the uninformed students to access the correct answers spontaneously because of the obvious relationship between the problems and the clues.

Most instructors have experienced situations where students fail to utilize relevant concepts and procedures. In classes on problem solving, for example, we frequently find situations where students are capable of analyzing faulty arguments when explicitly prompted, yet they fail to do so spontaneously. Thus, they may fail to recognize that an argument is based on a faulty analogy, or they may commit an error such as assuming that correlation implies causation, despite knowing better. In short, students are frequently able to think *about* various concepts and procedures but they do not necessarily think *with* them. A challenge for educators is to help students transform facts and procedures that they can describe and think about into useful conceptual tools.

The Development of Conceptual Tools

A number of theorists argue that it is particularly important for people to understand how concepts and procedures can function as *tools* that enable them to solve a variety of problems. Bacon (1620) emphasized this idea long ago when he discussed the importance of "mental helps": "The unassisted hand and the understanding left to itself possess but little power. Effects are produced by means of instruments and helps, which the understanding requires no less than the hand."

The idea of powerful sets of helps or tools for enhancing problem solving is very important. Based on our experiences, few students view their courses from this perspective. For example, we have asked a number of college students majoring in education or arts and science to explain why logarithms are useful. In what ways do they make it easier to solve various problems? Despite remembering something about logarithms, the vast majority of the students were surprised when told that logarithms represent an important invention that greatly simplifies problem solving. They had never been helped to understand logarithms in the way illustrated by the following quotation from the English mathematician Henry Briggs (1624; quoted in Jacobs, 1982):

> Logarithms are numbers invented for the more easy working of questions in arithmetic and geometry. By them all troublesome multiplications are avoided and performed only by addition. . . . In a word, all questions not only in arithmetic and geometry but in astronomy also are thereby most plainly and easily answered.

We have encountered many additional examples of situations where students have memorized facts and theories with very little appreciation of how they make it possible to solve otherwise perplexing problems. For example, many young children feel that it would be easier if there were only one unit of measurement such as inches, rather than multiple units such as feet, yards, and miles. With one unit of measurement, there is less that needs to be learned. The children are correct, to some extent, but they fail to appreciate how different units of measurement provide tools that greatly simplify problem solving. It would be extremely cumbersome to measure the distance between Connecticut and Tennessee in terms of inches. Frequently, we fail to help students appreciate how knowledge functions as a conceptual tool.

As a simple illustration of the power of concepts as tools, consider the drawings in Figure 9-1. By prompting people to activate concepts they have already learned, one can help them conceptualize these drawings in a new manner. The first can be viewed as a bear climbing up the opposite side of a tree and the second as the Eiffel Tower viewed from the inside of an armored car. Note how one understands the drawings differently when they are viewed from these perspectives. The philosopher N. R. Hanson (1970) argues that the creation of new scientific theories fulfills an analogous function: It enables people to conceptualize events in new and previously unappreciated ways.

Access Revisited

In the preceding discussion, we first introduced perplexing situations and then introduced concepts (e.g., bagpipes, bears climbing trees) that rendered them less perplexing. What happens when students are told about concepts and principles, yet are not helped to understand their function? We argue that they are less likely to access relevant concepts and procedures because they do not understand the kinds of problems that these discoveries were designed to solve. As an illustration, consider once again the example about logarithms. Assume that students are without a calculator or computer and must multiply a number of pairs of large numbers. Unless they had previously learned that logarithms enable one to substitute simple additions for difficult multiplications, it is highly unlikely that they would think of using them in this situation.

In our earlier discussion of experiments by Perfetto et al., we noted that college students did not spontaneously access relevant information even though it had just been presented. For example, students were unable to explain how someone could accurately predict the score of any game before it began despite

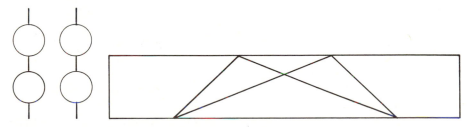

Figure 9-1 Some perceptual patterns.

the fact that, just a few minutes earlier, they had learned that "Before it begins, the score of a game is 0 to 0." This information had remained inert.

Imagine a slight change in the learning situation. In this new situation, Adams, Perfetto, Yearwood, Kasserman, Bransford, and Frankes (in preparation) presented students with statements in the following manner: "It is easy to guess the score of any game before it begins (pause); the score is 0 to 0." This mode of presentation should help students identify and define a problem; as the pause begins, it is not clear why it should be easy to guess the score of any game. After the pause, the answer, "the score is 0 to 0," becomes a tool for solving a problem rather than a mere fact. Initial data from studies at Vanderbilt suggest that, given this latter learning situation, students are much more likely to access relevant knowledge spontaneously when they are given problems to solve. This increase in access is presumably due to the advantages of understanding the kinds of problems that various types of information can help one solve. In a similar manner, studies in which new strategies have been taught report much more transfer when students are helped to understand why and how these strategies can be used (Brown, Bransford, Ferrara, & Campione, 1983).

Teaching Thinking across the Curriculum

Our approach to teaching thinking emphasizes the importance of helping students analyze their own problem-solving processes and understand how inventions and discoveries enable them to solve important problems. For example, we want to help them understand how the invention of writing systems, number systems, procedures for logical analyses, and theories, make it possible for them do things that otherwise might be difficult or impossible. However, it is not sufficient simply to supply students with such information. They need to experience its usefulness. Furthermore, they need to learn to identify and define situations where various types of knowledge can and should be used (Bransford & Stein, 1984).

Students rarely receive the opportunity to practice problem identification and problem definition. For example, assume that we present students with a sample argument and ask them to analyze it for logical consistency. We have identified and defined the problem for them rather than asking them to do so for themselves spontaneously. Similarly, we can ask students to define various concepts, but this request provides no guarantee that the students will spontaneously use the concepts later.

Recently, we have been experimenting with an approach to teaching thinking that helps students appreciate the functions of concepts and procedures while permitting practice at problem identification. It certainly is not the only way to teach thinking, but it seems promising and might serve as a model for other approaches.

The approach that we are developing involves analyses of movies—preferably ones that are displayed on video discs. Video disc technology enables us, for the first time, to exercise control over an existing motion picture: to stop it, back it up, go forward in slow motion or one frame at a time, or even search and find specific scenes almost instantaneously. Until now, there was only one way to view a movie—on the filmmaker's terms. In fact, much of the magic of movies is derived from the filmmaker's ability to draw us into a new reality and sweep us along with a compelling inertia. Now, with the push of a button, that inertia can be interrupted and the magic dispelled by the viewer who says: "Wait a minute, I want to see that stunt in slow motion," or asks: "I wonder what kind of spiders they used in that scene; let's take another look."

We are currently using movies rather than educational films that contain lectures. By eliminating the lectures, we create more opportunity for students to discover questions and issues on their own. As an illustration, consider the movie, *Raiders of the Lost Ark*, an action-packed adventure film directed by Steven Spielberg. When we began to examine a film like *Raiders*, we quickly discovered that there were several distinct perspectives that could be brought to the movie. The first is that of the viewer seeing a movie for the first time. The viewer is there to be entertained, to be transported to a fantasy world of exotic times and places, in this case to South America, Nepal, and Egypt during the rise of Nazi Germany. For an hour or two, the moviemaker's fantasy becomes the viewer's reality. And a roomful of snakes is really something to worry about.

A second perspective occurs when the viewer's own sense of the real world interfaces with the fantasy of the movie and the critical thinker in us comes out. We notice things that do not make sense. We grimace at dialogue that we think is not believable. Or we just ask questions about the movie: I wonder if there really was an Ark of the Covenant? Are cobras found in Egypt? I thought they were from Asia. Even a first-time viewer may adopt this mind set, particularly if the movie is bad. A viewer who looks at a film over and over is sure to begin asking these kinds of questions.

A third perspective occurs when we become curious about the making of the movie. We become interested in the reality behind the fantasy and in the nature of the problems that the film's actors and directors solved. Did Indiana Jones really whip the gun out of the traitor's hand? How did they do that? That cobra looked real, but was it? How come it didn't bite the actors?

With these last two perspectives in particular we begin to recognize many educational opportunities that a movie like *Raiders of the Lost Ark* provides for problem solving and critical thinking that are virtually invisible when we see the film the first time. These problems cover a wide assortment of subject areas: math, history, chemistry, physics, anthropology, psychology, geography, theatre arts, music. Also, they are not presented in isolation but in the context of the movie or moviemaking and are often interrelated and interconnected. And they are always presented in a multisensory way; we can see and hear and sometimes almost feel their nature—thanks to the magic of the filmmaking art and craft.

Take for example, the opening three minutes of *Raiders*, a scene set in the steamy jungles of South America. As we listen to the singing of exotic birds and watch the sun's rays penetrating the dense foliage, we follow Indiana Jones and his guides and porters and witness their encounter first with a statue of some ancient idol, then with a poisoned dart fired by some unseen tribal enemy. If we imagine ourselves as students watching this scene over and over again, we notice that what we see expands, and we are filled with observations and questions.

1. Who are these guides? They are Caucasian and unkempt. They speak with an accent. (Answer: They are of Spanish descent.)

2. Who are these porters wearing knit hats and brightly colored serapes even in the hot jungle? They have dark Indian features. Where do they come from? (Answer: They are highland Indians, maybe of Inca descent.)

3. Why is it that in one scene an Indian leads the mule, and in the next, one of the guides does? (Answer: There is a discontinuity.)

4. Is there hot tropical jungle in Peru? I thought it was a high country in the Andes. (Answer: It has both as well as an arid seacoast.)

5. What culture worshiped idols such as this? Incan? Some other? Why did it frighten the Indians? Or was that just to make the movie scary?

6. Is this an authentic statue or something fabricated for the movie? In either case, how was it made?

7. What kind of people use poisoned darts? What is the poison? What can be discovered by tasting it? How deadly is it? Do they hunt with darts? How does a blowgun work? How is it made?

8. The guide tastes the poison and says: "Three days old . . . still fresh . . . they are following us." Does this make sense? (Answer: Not really. If they were following, they wouldn't have arrived there yet . . . to shoot the dart.)

Other segments of *Raiders* provide many additional opportunities to discover and solve problems. For example, at one point, Indiana Jones needs to replace a golden idol with a bag of sand so that a trap will not be set into motion. We had watched the movie a number of times before it occurred to us to ask whether it was reasonable that a solid gold idol would weigh about the same as a small bag of sand.

Once a problem such as this one is identified, it provides an excellent context for learning new information. For example, all college students with whom we have worked know that one could determine the weight of an idol by putting it on a scale. However, many did not know how to determine the weight of the idol if a scale was unavailable. Similarly, many could not explain how to estimate the weights of a gold versus lead idol, especially if the two were shaped very differently and hence probably had different volumes. When concepts such as density and the Archimedes principle of measuring volume by water displacement are introduced in such contexts, they become especially meaningful for students. Many students noted that they had studied these concepts before but had never understood how they could be used to solve interesting problems.

According to our calculations, a solid gold idol the size of the one in *Raiders* would weight approximately 40 pounds, yet the actors are carrying and throwing it with no difficulty. Given such apparent inconsistencies, a number of aspects of reasoning can be discussed. For example, "If the idol were solid gold, it would be very heavy to carry. It clearly is not especially heavy to carry, however, hence it must not be solid gold." Is this argument valid? Why? A number of other aspects of just the first 14 minutes of *Raiders* provide a host of additional opportunities to identify and define problems and analyze and discuss them. For example, at one point, Indiana Jones jumps across a pit. How can one estimate the width of the pit, and could a man actually jump that far (for example, what is the world record in the running broad jump?)? In addition, if one were to perform experiments to determine information about jumping, how would one proceed? Such problems provide a context for discussing experimentation, averages, variability in performance, and so forth.

At another point in the adventure, Indiana and his cohort use torches to light their way. Why did they not use flashlights? At the beginning of the film, the date is given as 1936. Was electricity available at this time? Were there batteries at this time, and how portable were they? What guidelines exist for making reasonable inferences about questions such as these?

Overall, video disc technology—and to a large extent, videotape technology—gives us the ability to study a motion picture in much the same fashion that a scientist studies phenomena in the laboratory. The more we look, the more we perceive and understand, and the more we want to know. In short, we can learn from movies, even though they are not designed to teach. Maybe that's why they are so effective. There is no discursive educational setup that says: "You are the student, now listen carefully to what I'm going to teach you." Both teacher and student can learn.

As noted earlier, a major advantage of movies is that they provide opportunities to identify and define problems. We find that activities such as these play an important role in transfer. For example, members of our research team now view most films—as well as many segments of everyday life—from a problem-solving perspective. Our knowledge about thinking and problem solving is therefore much less inert than it otherwise would have been, hence, we continue to learn. However, it is important to note that an integral part of this learning process involves efforts to analyze and systematize our general processes and strategies (Brown, Bransford, Ferrara, & Campione, 1983). Without an emphasis on reflection, analysis, and systematization, powerful transfer probably will not occur. By the same token, students need help to reflect upon the processes they use to identify and solve problems. And they need an explicit appreciation of how new knowledge can provide problem-solving tools.

SOME ISSUES INVOLVING EVALUATION

According to the IDEAL framework, evaluation is an important component of educational practice. When designing a thinking skills program, we identify and define a problem to be solved (e.g., poor thinking) and explore possible strategies. We then act on these strategies by actually implementing a program. However, if we stop here and do not look carefully at the results, we may fail to identify problems with our original ways of thinking. Through the careful evaluation of programs, ideas have a chance to evolve.

In this chapter, we have emphasized the issue of helping students learn to think with important concepts and procedures rather than merely to think about them when explicitly prompted to do so. The emphasis presents some constraints on the problem of evaluating thinking skills programs.

Figure 9-2 illustrates a matrix for evaluating a thinking skills program. It compares the "actual" success of a program with its measured success. We can never know the actual success of a program, as it is not observable. What we can observe is the measured success, whether the measure is simple observation, reports from students and parents, or formal test scores. Ideally, the measured success of a program provides an accurate reflection of its actual success. This point is illustrated by the cells in Figure 9-2 (A1, B2, C3, D4). Thus, if a program actually does a poor job of developing thinking skills, we want our measurements to show this (cell A1), and if the actual success is great, we want the measurements to reflect this (cell D4).

The potential dangers of receiving misleading information are reflected in the upper right and lower left corners of Figure 9-2 (i.e., in cells A3, A4, B4, C1, D1, and D2). In these cases, the measured success of our programs is at odds with their actual success. Instances that fall in the top right corner reflect the fact that the measurements look good despite the fact that the program is

		Measured			
		Poor 1	OK 2	Good 3	Great 4
	Poor A				
Actual	OK B				
	Good C				
	Great D				

Figure 9-2 Actual versus measured success of thinking skills programs.

actually poor. Instances that fall in the bottom left reflect cases where the program is good despite the fact that the measurements suggest a lack of success. We briefly consider these two categories of error in more detail.

Successful Programs that Test Poorly

There are a number of reasons why successful programs can look poor after formal evaluations. The most basic one is that the evaluation tests fail to reflect what was learned. One reason may be that different students make gains in different areas. For example, some may apply their newly aquired thinking skills to the problem of learning to comprehend what they read, others to learning about mathematics, others to organizing their time, and so forth. If students develop along different paths, tests that assess change on only a few dimensions will often fail to show any gains.

A second important reason why tests may fail to reveal gains is that they generally measure individual rather than group efforts. Some of the most powerful approaches to problem solving involve the use of skills that are necessary for working cooperatively with others. If tests fail to assess changes in such abilities, we may erroneously conclude that a program is not good.

Poor Programs that Test Well

At first glance, it may be difficult to imagine programs that look successful but really are not. On second glance, however, it becomes easy to see how such situations could arise. For example, imagine a thinking skills program that is composed of a number of components such as bridging to everyday examples of principles and teaching students how to work as a group and evaluate their own contributions to the discussion. The program might also include some drill and practice exercises on reasoning problems.

Now assume that we hire an outside evaluator to assess the program. The evaluator creates a paper-and-pencil test of reasoning that is administered to experimental and control groups. The experimental group performs only slightly (not statistically significantly) better than the control group, so a decision is made to revise the program. In the revised program, much more time is devoted to paper-and-pencil reasoning exercises; hence, there is less time for improving class discussions, identifying and analyzing instances of everyday reasoning, and so forth.

Given these revisions, the experimental students will probably perform much better than controls on the evaluation tests. Nevertheless, the actual value of the program for students may well have declined rather than been improved. A major reason for this claim is that the ability to solve specific types of formal reasoning problems may remain inert (to use Whitehead's term) and have little influence on activities outside the test-taking situation. We believe that it is extremely important to focus explicitly on the goal of improving everyday thinking and problem solving rather than merely on increasing students' scores on tests.

CONCLUSION

The goal of providing students with tools that they spontaneously think with rather than only think about when explicitly prompted is challenging. We believe that improvements in thinking and problem solving represent lifelong processes; hence, it is especially important that students spontaneously use various tools that can be evaluated and refined. An emphasis on problem identification seems to be one way to help students learn to use and refine their knowledge. It helps them learn to find important problems, and by doing so, it provides a framework for understanding the value or significance of concepts and principles. In our work, we are placing increased emphasis on the design of learning environments that encourage students to identify problems on their own.

REFERENCES

Adams, J. L. (1979). *Conceptual blockbusting* (2nd ed.). New York: Norton.

Adams, L., Perfetto, G., Yearwood, A., Kasserman, J., Bransford, J., & Franks, J. (In preparation). Facilitating access. Nashville, Tenn.: Vanderbilt University.

Bacon, F. (1620). *Novum organum.* First book, Aphorism 2.

Bliss, E. C. (1976). *Getting things done.* New York; Bantam.

Bransford, J. D., & McCarrell, N. S. (1974). A sketch of a cognitive approach to comprehension. In W. Weimer & D. Palermo (Eds.), *Cognition and the symbolic processes.* Hillsdale, N.J.: Erlbaum.

Bransford, J. D., & Stein, B. S. (1984). *The IDEAL problem solver.* New York: W. H. Freeman and Company.

Briggs, H. (1624). *Arithmetica logarithmica.*

Brown, A. L., Bransford, J. D., Ferrara, R. A., & Campione, J. C. (1983). Learning, remembering and understanding. In J. H. Flavell & E. M. Markman (Eds.), *Carmichael's manual of child psychology* (Vol. 1). New York: Wiley.

de Bono, E. (1967). *New think.* New York: Basic Books.

Duncker, K. (1945). On problem solving. *Psychological monographs,* 58(5), no. 270.

Gick, M. L. & Holyoak, K. J. (1980). Analogical problem solving. *Cognitive Psychology,* 12:306–355.

Hanson, N. R. (1970). A picture theory of theory meaning. In R. G. Colodny (Ed.), *The nature and function of scientific theories.* Pittsburgh: University of Pittsburgh Press.

Hayes, J. R. (1981). *The complete problem solver.* Philadelphia: The Franklin Institute Press.

Jacobs, H. R. (1982). *Mathematics: A human endeavor.* New York: W. H. Freeman and Company.

Newell, A. & Simon, H. (1972). *Human problem solving.* Englewood Cliffs, N.J.: Prentice-Hall.

Perfetto, G. A., Bransford, J. D., & Franks, J. J. (1983). Constraints on access in a problem solving context. *Memory and Cognition,* 11:24–31.

Sagan, C. (1980). *Broca's brain*. New York: Ballantine.

Whimbey, A. (1975). *Intelligence can be taught*. New York; Dutton.

Whitehead, A. (1929). *The aims of education and other essays*. New York: Macmillan.

The first section of this chapter draws heavily on a chapter by J. Bransford, B. Stein, V. Delclos, and J. Littlefield entitled "Computers and Problem Solving", in C. Kinzer, R. Sherwood, and J. Bransford, (Eds.), 1986, *Computer Strategies for Education: Foundations and Content Area Applications*, Columbus, Ohio: Charles E. Merrill & Co. We thank Beverly Conner and Lynda Berry for their excellent editorial help. A number of our colleagues in Peabody's Learning Technology Center are involved in the video disc project that is described in this chapter. They include Otto Bassler, Wil Clouse, Laura Goin, Charles Kinzer, Ted Hasselbring, Jim Hogge, David Markham, Susan Williams, and Ken Williamson.

10

ROBERT J. STERNBERG
Department of Psychology
Yale University

Teaching Intelligence: The Application of Cognitive Psychology to the Improvement of Intellectual Skills

If one's goal is to improve performance on IQ tests, Scholastic Aptitude Tests, and other tests with similar names, then one should do what people in the test preparation courses and most of the thinking skills training programs do— train to the existing tests. Despite the fact that some instructors in the standard courses do so implicitly and do not admit to what they are doing, if one's goal is to improve people's scores on a particular test, by all means one should train to that test. If one's goal is instead to improve intellectual skills rather than test scores, then training to intelligence tests is the wrong thing to do. Instruction that trains one to get higher scores on existing tests is incomplete and sometimes even incorrect (Wagner & Sternberg, 1984). Why?

WHY INTELLIGENCE IS MORE THAN WHAT IQ TESTS MEASURE

Let us consider why conceptions of intelligence must go beyond IQ tests. I would like to start out with a cross-cultural example. One of the things that psychologists do when they try to understand intelligence in other cultures is to bring our tests and give them to the people to see how their intelligence compares to ours. The typical finding is that people in other cultures are not as intelligent as people in North America. One kind of task that is brought into other cultures is the so-called sorting task. One gives people either pictures or words and the people are asked to sort them. The typical finding is that intellectually more advanced people sort taxonomically. In other words, they might have categories like *animal* at the top, then *bird* and *fish* below that, then kinds of birds and kinds of fish below that. In our culture, taxonomic sorting is considered an intelligent strategy. For example, Piaget's theory states that as a child passes from preoperational to concrete-operational thinking, the child becomes better able to think taxonomically. If one looks at IQ tests, such as the Stanford-Binet and the Wechsler, examinees get more credit for definitions that are taxonomic. If one is asked to define a car, and one says that it is a vehicle of conveyance, one gets more points than if one says it is something that uses gas. So clearly, the smart thing to do in our culture is to sort taxonomically.

When the Kpelle, a Nigerian tribe, were asked to sort, they did not sort taxonomically, but rather they sorted functionally—according to what things did. For example, *animal* might be sorted with *eat*. Typically, cross-cultural psychologists would cite this sorting pattern as yet one more example of how the people in another culture are not as intelligent as the North Americans who have tested them. The psychologists who did this study, Cole, Gay, Glick, and Sharp (1971), went beyond what a cross-cultural psychologist might typically do and suggested to the Kpelle that they might think about another way to sort. The Kpelle still did not sort taxonomically. Finally, in desperation, the experimenters requested that the Kpelle sort the items in a way that they thought an unintelligent person would. The Kpelle then had no trouble at all sorting taxonomically. The point is that they were smart enough to sort taxonomically, but that their conception of the intelligent way to sort was not the same as the test makers' conception. Therefore, a problem is that of whether the so-called demand characteristics are the same for everyone taking a given test. People may not agree as to what is intelligent. But one might say that cross-cultural examples are exotic and strange and tell us little about intelligence within our own culture.

Consider a second disquieting example, one within our own culture. Seymour Sarason, now a psychologist at Yale, went to his first job, which was giving an IQ test to children who were in a school for the retarded. When he got there, he found himself out of business, so to speak, because the students had just successfully executed an escape. Eventually, they were rounded up and brought back to the school, where Sarason gave them the Porteus Maze test, a test of intelligence. Sarason found that the students generally were not even able to complete the first problem on the test. Given that these students, in their escape, were temporarily able to outwit the people who were teaching them, it seems that this test must be missing some intellectual skills that the students had. But, one could say, the retarded are different.

So, the last example I want to give is one that I am sure is familiar to all of us. At Yale, as elsewhere, we require all of our entering students to take the Scholastic Aptitude Test. Occasionally, we get students with very high scores, but when they arrive, we cannot help but wonder who they had take the tests for them. Their poor, indeed, unintelligent performance utterly belies their high test scores. At the same time, we get people who perform splendidly, but whose test scores are lower, even at the bottom of the range of acceptability. One can call people of these various kinds underachievers or overachievers or look for sources of their puzzling performance outside of their measured intelligence. But to me, there is another message: There is more to intelligence than the tests measure. Hence, a program to teach intellectual skills must go beyond the conventional notions of intelligence that have motivated most programs. Programs that teach to the tests may actually make students less intelligent, in some respects.

Training Intelligence as the Tests Measure It: Ten Misguided Strategies

Training to intelligence tests will often lead to any or all of the ten unfortunate strategies listed below. These strategies follow from implications of conventional intelligence tests for training of intellectual skills, not from modern intellectual skills training programs, such as Feuerstein's (1980) Instrumental Enrichment.

1. Work as Quickly as You Can

Intelligence tests are usually timed so that they can be completed only if one works quite rapidly. Therefore, when one takes a course to prepare for one of these tests, one is urged to learn to work as quickly as possible. But, in fact, one should not always work as quickly as one can. Consider some pertinent research findings.

One construct in contemporary accounts of intelligence is that of executive processes, which are used to plan what one is going to do, monitor what one is doing as it is being done, and then evaluate how well one's task was done. If one wants to emphasize executive functioning, certain implications follow. One might predict that people who are intelligent would spend more time planning, monitoring, and evaluating what they do, but less time actually doing it. In other words, a view emphasizing executive processes holds that it is not the total amount of time spent on a task that is important, but rather how one allocates one's time. In everyday life, one often has a specific set of tasks to do, and the intelligent thing is to know how much time to spend on each task rather than just to perform every task quickly.

To test the above prediction, we have done a laboratory study involving very complicated kinds of analogies (Sternberg, 1981). The idea was to make it so that no one strategy would work for all of the problems. Instead, examinees would have to keep switching strategies. From these problems, we isolated two executive processes, which we called *global planning* and *local planning*. Global planning is the kind of planning one does when one has a set of subtasks to be done and needs to organize one's time to complete them all. Local planning is the specific planning one does on each of the subtasks. Once one has structured a task as a whole, one still must plan for the subtasks. The critical finding was that, on the average, better reasoners tend to spend relatively more time in global planning than do poorer reasoners, but relatively less time in local planning. If one looks at the overall time spent in problem solving, one finds that, on the average, better reasoners spend less time in problem solving. But the overall reduction in solution time must be viewed in light of the fact that good reasoners spend more time structuring what they are going to do so that they can then operate on that structure efficiently. In other words, better reasoners do not always work as quickly as they can, but rather they know when to work faster and when to work slower. So it is not true that one should always work as quickly as one can, but rather that one should budget one's time in the most effective way.

2. Read Everything Carefully

If one prepares for an IQ test or the Scholastic Aptitude Test, one is taught to read everything very carefully. Especially in a reading comprehension test, it is essential to read all of the passages with great care to assure oneself of being able to answer all of the questions. If one's aim is to train intelligent thinking, this advice is wrong. Any teacher who has papers to read and also wants to read up on what's being done in his or her field clearly has too much to read in the time available. Administrators often have even more to read than do schoolteachers. For students, too, one of the hardest things to cope with is having too much reading for the time available. So clearly, in the real world, as opposed to on an IQ test, one just cannot read everything carefully. One learns how to budget, or allocate, one's time in reading. One has to learn how to read wisely.

The way we measure time allocation in reading is through a reading task emphasizing allocation of time (Wagner & Sternberg, in press). Rather than just giving people a straight reading comprehension test, we give them four passages (from newspapers, magazines, textbooks—the kinds of things they read everyday) and tell the examinees to read one passage for gist, one for main ideas, another for detail, and another for inference and application. The situation in this reading is close to what we normally encounter. One does not read a magazine the same way one reads a physics textbook. Examinees are told they have a certain amount of time to read the material and that they can allocate their time any way they want. They can read the passages in any order they wish, and they can spend any amount of time they want on each passage.

The critical finding is this: If one looks at time allocation and the relative amount of time spent on the more difficult reading tasks (reading for detail and reading for analysis and application) and one then compares that amount of time to the amount of time spent on the easier reading tasks (reading for gist and reading for main ideas), one finds that better readers tend to spend relatively more time on the passages being read for the difficult purposes and relatively less time on the passages being read for the easier purposes. Poor readers allocate their time essentially uniformly. They do not discriminate in their reading time as a function of reading purpose. Their time distribution curve is essentially flat.

So there is more to reading comprehension than the speed and comprehension measures of typical reading comprehension tests, because one cannot and does not read everything carefully. The particularly important skill is to know what to read carefully and what not to read carefully. Teaching children to read as carefully as possible in *all* their reading is unrealistic and counterproductive.

3. Memorize a Lot of New Vocabulary

Standard intellectual training for particular tests encourages children to memorize large numbers of vocabulary words. Everyone knows that the SATs, ACTs, and many of the tests that students take in high school have some difficult vocabulary words. The idea behind the memorization of vocabulary words is that by learning these words, the student will, first of all, improve his or her score on vocabulary tests and also will have added some new and useful words to his or her vocabulary for use in schoolwork. There are two problems with this memorization strategy.

The first problem is one of which anyone who has had foreign language instruction is aware: One soon forgets many of the words that one memorizes. Everyone who has crammed for an exam knows that within a few days it is very hard to remember much of what was memorized. So just memorizing vocabulary words does not tend to be a good strategy for students, because by the time they get to the test, much less to their reading and their later lives, they will not remember the words. Many of us have come upon a word that we do not know in the course of our reading, looked up the word in a dictionary, and then seen the word a few days later and not remembered what it means. Again, rote memorization is often ineffective.

The other problem is that the chances of any one memorized word, or for that matter a significant number of words, being on a test are fairly small. There are hundreds of thousands of words in our language and at least thousands of words can appear on vocabulary tests. So this strategy turns out to be a very local one, both in terms of improving vocabulary for tests and improving vocabulary for one's life in general.

An alternative teaching strategy is to teach thinking skills and, in particular, learning-to-learn skills. Consider this fact: If one wants a single test that best predicts overall intelligence, that test turns out to be vocabulary. Is the reason for this that people who are very intelligent have memorized lots and lots of unusual words? Probably not. These people must be good at something else. What they are good at is learning words in context. The basis of individual differences in verbal comprehension is the ability to acquire meanings of words encountered in natural contexts. Some people will figure out the meaning of a word the first or second time they see it, some the tenth. The people who are able to learn more effectively from context will ultimately have better vocabularies (Sternberg & Powell, 1983). So the implication for training intellectual skills is that teaching people how to learn from context puts them in a position to be able to increase their vocabularies. When the teacher is not there—and most of the time the teacher won't be there—the children will still be able to learn on their own. It is not enough just to say: "Here is a word in context; learn the word." What one needs to do is to teach the children fairly specific skills, including the kinds of cues that people use to learn words in context. Consider the following brief passage:

Two ill-dressed people, one a middle-aged woman, and the other a tense young man, sat around the fire. The common meal was almost ready. The mother, Tanith, peered at her son through the *oam* of the bubbling stew.

The task is to figure out the meaning of *oam*. What kinds of clues in the passage are helpful for figuring out this meaning? Children are taught to ask themselves questions like: What does it do? Where does it come from? What class is it a member of? Are there any synonyms? One also has to teach people the mental processes to apply to these clues. One process, for example, is selective encoding: figuring out what clues in the text are relevant for learning the meaning of the unknown word. We try to teach people how to find the information in the passage that is relevant for decontextualization (Sternberg, in press). In the long run, it is more effective to teach people to teach themselves than it is to teach them a small set of words that they will probably forget anyway. So the better strategy is to teach children decontextualization skills, rather than to encourage sheer rote memorization.

4. Learn the Best Strategy for Solving Each Problem

Most intellectual-skills training programs teach specific, supposedly optional, single strategies for solving problems of a given type. Such training is process oriented—teaching students what processes to use when. The problem is that there are so-called aptitude-strategy interactions. Many kinds of problems can be solved in multiple ways, and which way is the best depends on the aptitude pattern of the individual child or adult.

Consider spatial visualization problems. In such problems, one is presented with abstract figures to rotate mentally or perhaps unfolded geometric figures that need to be folded mentally. One of the surprising things about these tests is that scores on them are sometimes surprisingly highly correlated with scores on verbal ability tests. Why do such correlations appear? The reason appears to be that there are some clever students who are able to figure out how to do these problems wholly, or partly, by generating a verbal description of a target figure and another figure and then by comparing these verbal descriptions. Thus, it may be more useful to train students to formulate—for themselves—strategies that suit their pattern of abilities than to train them in specific strategies that may not match their individual patterns of abilities.

One of the kinds of problems we have studied, which is sometimes found on ability tests, is the so-called linear syllogism. An example of a linear syllogism is: "John is taller than Sam. Sam is taller than Pete. Who is tallest?" A harder example is: "Mary is not as short as Bill. Sam is not as tall as Bill. Who is shortest?" Our data showed that some people solve problems spatially, by setting up a mental array depicting the people in the problem, some people solve the problems verbally, and some solve them using a combination of verbal and spatial strategies (Sternberg & Weil, 1980). There is no one best strategy for solving these problems. What strategy is best depends on the person's particular pattern of aptitude. So one must consider the individual in order to understand the best way to solve the problems. One should train intelligent strategy selection, rather than a fixed and possibly suboptimal strategy.

5. Get Lots of Practice on Various Tests and Testlike Items

Most intellectual-skills training programs take items off existing IQ tests, or items that are similar to those on IQ tests, and train performance on them. Some such programs just give practice without any real training. But training or giving practice on IQ test items is not enough, because there is so much more to intelligence than what IQ tests measure.

Consider what might make a person act intelligently in everyday life. We studied business executives and academic psychologists to address this question (Wagner & Sternberg, 1985). The idea was to look at performance in two quite different, but intellectually interesting, fields of endeavor. We interviewed people in these two fields and asked them: "What is it one needs to be really successful in your field?" One thing became clear. None of the people who were very successful in their fields indicated that what they had learned in school was terribly important to what they were doing or how they were succeeding in their job. Much of what they had learned just did not seem to be very relevant and was information that they just could not use. Then what was important? The interviewees said that what really counted was what they picked up on the job: tricks of the trade, knacks, or what we call tacit knowledge. Such knowledge was learned in context (just like vocabulary, as discussed earlier). For example, although a teacher may learn things in a lecture hall about disciplining children, what is learned in an actual classroom really seems to count.

We were interested in finding ways to measure tacit knowledge. We asked the business executives various kinds of questions. In one, we gave them a case study of a business executive, and then said, "Here are the things a business executive has to get done in the next month or so, but he doesn't have time to do them all. Indicate on a nine-point scale how important it is to complete each of these things in that period of time." Thus, the executive had to set priorities for what needed to be done. (Recall the importance of priority setting from the earlier discussion of executive processes in reasoning and reading.) Another item said: "You are giving advice to a junior executive on how to succeed in your firm. Here are some things you might say to that junior executive. Rate each of these in terms of how important it is for success." We asked the academic psychologists questions like: "Here are factors that influence the reputation of a scientist. How important is each of these factors in influencing a scientist's reputation?" Or, "Here are things that influence to which journal you should submit an article. Rate the importance of each."

We gave the test for business executives to high-level executives in the top 15 of the Fortune 500 companies, executives in companies that were not in the Fortune 500, graduate students in business, and undergraduates. We used a similar approach for the academic psychologists' questionnaire. The question was whether we could predict the success of business executives or academic psychologists in a way that IQ tests would not. The kinds of criteria we used for the business executives were merit raises, performance ratings, the reputation of the company, and so on. For the academic psychologists, we used criteria like citation rates for published articles, numbers of publications, prestige of the institution with which the psychologist was affiliated, and so on. These criteria are not perfect but they were the best we had. The critical finding was that performance on the tacit-knowledge tests correlated about 0.4 with real-world criteria. This level of correlation is moderate, but quite good as correlations with real-world criteria go. The correlation of scores on the tacit-knowledge tests with IQ, however, was essentially zero. Clearly, there is something involved in performing intelligently in the real world that is not correlated with traditional IQ. So, it may make sense to give some practice and training for IQ tests, but we have to go beyond that and try to verbalize and make explicit the practical know-how one needs to perform intelligently not only on tests, but also beyond the tests, whether in the classroom or in the working world.

Another reason not to teach to IQ tests stems from the problem of transfer. You can teach people how to solve certain kinds of problems and then find that even small changes in the content of the problem will result in failure of the students to apply what they were taught: They don't transfer the training. If one is only teaching at the level of IQ test items, even if one is able to effect some improvement in the scores on the tests, it is unclear that one will find any transfer at all beyond those tests. Thus, even if one wants just to train the more academic kinds of skills, the best way to train those skills is in real-life contexts that will make it clear to the students how to use the skills in their everyday lives.

6. Use All of the Information in the Problem

Students often are told to make sure they use all of the information they are given, because they may get a problem wrong simply because there is some information in there that they didn't exploit. This advice is often wrong.

Consider, for a moment, arithmetical insight problems, such as:

If you have black socks and brown socks in a drawer, mixed in a ratio of 4 to 5, how many socks will you have to take out of the drawer to make sure of having a pair of socks the same color?

The critical feature of this problem and others like it is that students who get the problem wrong tend to focus immediately on all the information, and in particular, on the information that the ratio is four to five. It turns out that this information is irrelevant and even misleading. Not only does one not need the information to solve the problem, but the information leads one astray.

In most of the problems people really confront in the world, there is a lot of information that is as likely to lead them astray as it is to lead them to solution. The difficulty people face is deciding what information is relevant for their purposes (as in learning meanings of words from context). We gave insight problems such as these to gifted and average children (Davidson & Sternberg, 1984). Half of the children had to figure out the insight in each mathematical problem on their own. We supplied the insight to the other half of the children. We predicted that only the average children would benefit from being given the insight, because the gifted children would be able to generate the insight on their own. Indeed, the critical finding was that when we gave the children the insights, the average children benefited but the gifted children did not. In training experiments, usually the smart get smarter: Brighter students benefit more from instruction, because the more intellectual resources they have, the more able they are to use the new information. In the case of insight information, we found the reverse, because the gifted children had the insights spontaneously and thus did not learn anything when the insights were given to them. These children knew that one does not always use all of the information in a problem. Very often the problem itself is to figure out what information is relevant and thus needs to be used. We need to train children how to encode selectively, not to attempt fully to encode everything in sight.

7. Find Your Answer in the Answer Options and Move on

Students in test preparation courses may be taught that as soon as they see the answer to a problem, they should choose it and move on to the next problem. After all, if one is in a hurry, one cannot carefully consider each option. In our research, we have examined the sources of errors in the reasoning of children of different ages. The critical finding was that one of the primary sources of error is not looking at and adequately considering all the answer options (Sternberg & Nigro, 1980). Children do not adequately consider what all the possibilities are. Constructors of standardized tests either explicitly or implicitly know this, and often construct test items in which the incorrect options are close to the correct answer, but not quite correct. The incorrectness of these options becomes evident only when they are compared to the fully correct option. So it is critical to look at all the answer options and evaluate them before selecting one of them.

8. Try to Psyche Out the Test Constructor

A part of many test preparation courses is learning how to psyche out the person who wrote the test. What kinds of answers would the test constructor look for? Teaching students to second-guess the test constructor makes perfect sense if one's sole intention is for the students to get good scores. The problem is that very often we train the students so well in second-guessing ourselves as well as the test constructors that the training does indeed generalize and becomes part of their style. Then, when they become more advanced, they become specialists in psyching out what they think the professor or teacher wants; but they are no longer as creative or good at finding problems as they are good at solving the problems that we explicitly set for them. An important part of intelligence, though, is the ability to think in nonentrenched, or novel, ways—to go beyond just what it is that the teacher or the standardized tests ask for (Sternberg, 1981, 1985). Thus, students need to be encouraged to think in novel ways that are not identical to our own.

One of the ways we measure people's ability to think in novel ways is through a conceptual-projection task (Sternberg, 1982). Consider, for a moment, the case of emeralds. Everyone knows that emeralds are green and sapphires are blue. But consider the possibility that emeralds are really grue and sapphires are really bleen (grue, meaning green until the year 2000 and blue thereafter, and bleen meaning blue until the year 2000 and green thereafter). In another kind of problem, we tell students: On the planet Kyron, there are four kinds of people: people who are born young and die old, people who are born old and die young, people who are born young and die young, and people who are born old and die old. Or, in another example of this task, we tell the students that on Kyron, there are four kinds of substances—substances that are liquid north and south of the equator, substances that are solid north and south of the equator, substances that are liquid north and solid south of the equator, and substances that are solid north and liquid south of the equator. We give the students these otherworldly kinds of problems and devise an elaborate scenario about the conceptual systems. Later, we ask the students to solve reasoning problems based on these novel scenarios. The critical finding is that in terms of inductive ability—the ability to go beyond the information given—the information-processing skills most critical to intelligence deal with novel kinds of stimuli. Thinking in new ways was found to be an important part of intelligence. The standard kinds of skills—read the problem, read the answers, compare things—don't very well measure intellectual ability. Therefore, in a complete intellectual-skills training program we need to go beyond teaching students to psyche out test constructors (and ourselves) and encourage and teach them to think in novel ways.

9. Intelligence Is the Same Thing for Everyone

The implication of current testing practices is that intelligence is the same thing for everyone. I argue that this implication is incorrect (Sternberg, 1984). Consider whatever occupation you are in and the people you know who are extremely intelligent, in a practical sense, in your own field. Then ask yourself what it is that makes these people so successful at what they do. I think you will find that these people do not all have high IQs. People succeed for very different reasons. Of course, real-world success is just one (flawed) criterion for practical intelligence, just as academic success is a flawed criterion for assessing the validity of conventional IQ tests. In all research such as this, it is important to keep in mind that the criteria are often just as flawed as the predictors.

For example, in my own field, one finds some people who are really successful because they are always six months ahead of the field. They know where things are going and get there a little bit before others. Other people are very clever at designing experiments that yield counterintuitive findings. The experiments always come out the opposite of the way everyone predicted. The IQs of these people may or may not reflect their particular talents. Some people do very well on the kinds of knowledge-based and analytical skills measured by conventional intelligence tests. They are very good as problem solvers. There is one academic psychologist who is generally considered just a so-so researcher, but apparently tops out on standardized tests. He is an excellent problem solver, but has trouble finding important problems to solve. If someone gives this researcher a problem, he will solve it, and solve it very well, but he needs to have problems handed to him.

Often, people are not as good at analytical skills, but are very good at finding important problems and thinking in novel ways. They specialize in coming up with ideas of their own. Such people may capitalize upon a kind of intelligence that is different in kind from the analytical skills used by the high-IQ types.

Then, there are some people who are very good at self-promotion. They may specialize in getting along with people or in making their names known. People with these kinds of skills are all intelligent, but in different ways. What they have in common is one or two unusually well-developed skills that they make the most of. They find out the things in which they excel and make them central in their work and their lives in general. One way that they compensate for their weaknesses is by letting other people do their work in areas in which they are not strong. But if all these types of people have anything in common, it is the ability to capitalize on what they are good at and compensate for whatever they are not good at. Intelligence is a different thing for each of them, but each makes the most of his or her own particular brand of intelligence.

10. Intelligence Is What IQ Tests Measure

Whether psychologists and educators admit it or not, they very often think and act as though intelligence is whatever IQ tests measure. You can find explicit expressions of this belief in the writings of many psychologists. Whereas others will not admit it, they secretly believe it nevertheless. What I am arguing for is that there is more to intelligence than what IQ tests measure. You need not believe me: You can ask experts; you can ask people on the street. We have asked both (Sternberg, Conway, Ketron, & Bernstein, 1981). We found that both the experts and the laypersons tend to cite the typical IQ-like skills of problem solving and verbal facility, but they also included social-competence skills that I have been describing throughout this chapter. This is true even of the people who create the theories of intelligence that do not have social competence in them! Skills such as social competencies or problem finding are difficult to measure and test, but they are just as important to a full theory of intelligence as are skills that are easier to measure and teach. The time has come, in our intellectual-skills training programs, to go beyond what IQ tests measure. In the next section, I present an outline of a training program that attempts to do so.

A TRIARCHIC PROGRAM FOR TRAINING INTELLECTUAL SKILLS

In an age in which the ability to function effectively in an ever-changing environment is perhaps more important than ever before, many people question whether the ability to function effectively in complex and changing contexts—intelligence—can be taught. The answer is a resounding yes! Why resounding? Because in asking this question, we forget a fact that may seem startling, but is incontrovertible: We teach intelligence to children from the day they are born.

When an infant is born, we almost immediately attempt to establish communication with the infant: We respond to the infant's cries; we shape both the verbal and nonverbal responses of the baby so as to encourage certain behaviors and discourage others; we talk to the infant, and as the baby learns to talk, we respond with gestures, verbal elaborations, and smiles (or frowns). As time goes on, we teach appropriate and adaptive responses and attempt to discourage inappropriate and maladaptive ones. By the time the child starts school, he or she has been subjected to a complex, differentiated program of intellectual-skills training the like of which will never be repeated in school or anyplace else. In part because the informal training programs of parents, siblings, friends, and others differ widely for different children, these children will be differentially prepared for the challenges they will meet both in school and in other aspects of their everyday lives.

In school, a formal training program of the educational system supplements the informal training program of the parents. For a variety of reasons, the formal training programs found in school often do not maximize youngsters' development of intellectual skills. The goal of the triarchic training program is to build upon the programs of the schools to help each child reach his or her highest level of intellectual-skill development. Although there may be individual differences in these highest levels, so much improvement is possible that we are probably best off concerning ourselves with helping each child's intellectual performance, rather than with worrying about some unknowable maximum level of accomplishment. Indeed, excessive concern with assessment of maximum potentials—as is sometimes found in devotees of intelligence and ability tests—may create self-fulfilling prophecies that hinder rather than help our efforts to develop abilities.

I propose a program for developing intellectual skills in secondary- and college-level students. This program consists of two basic elements: text that contains narrative material and exercises for the student to complete; and a supplement that contains material the teacher can use to maximize the effectiveness of the program. Each of these elements of the program will be described in turn. A summary of the main aspects of the program that will be a useful reference guide in reading this part of the chapter is presented in Table 10-1. Before describing the program, I will briefly described the theory that motivated it.

A Triarchic View of Intelligence

My view of intelligence has three parts and is motivated by the belief that a conception of intelligence should be able to do three things. First, it should be able to relate intelligence to the internal world of the individual—to what goes on inside a person's head when he or she thinks and behaves intelligently. That is what standard psychometric accounts have tried to measure. In other words, they have asked the question: What is it inside the head that makes a person intelligent? The difference in my focus from the psychometric views is that I, and some others, see psychometric views as static. When one says that a person is better on a reasoning test because he or she has a higher score on a reasoning factor, it does not seem to go much beyond saying that the score is higher because it is higher. So what we ask is: What are the underlying mental processes that contribute to individual differences in intelligence?

A theory of intelligence must say more. In part, intelligence develops as a function of an individual's interactions with the environment, and, in fact, the environment helps shape intelligence. So a theory of intelligence must also deal with the relation between intelligence and the external world. How does intelligence function in a real-world environment?

Finally, an account of intelligence must relate it to the experience of the individual. Experience mediates the relationship between intelligence, on the one hand, and the internal and external worlds of the individual, on the other. According to my account, intelligence is best measured when a task is either

Table 10-1 Main Elements of a Triarchic Program for Training Intellectual Skills

The Student's Text

Part I: Background
  Chapter 1: Some Historical Background on Views of Intelligence
  Chapter 2: The Triarchic Theory of Human Intelligence

Part II: The Internal World of the Individual: Components of Human Intelligence
  Chapter 3: Metacomponents (executive processes used to plan, monitor, and evaluate problem-solving performance)
  Chapter 4: Performance Components (nonexecutive processes used to execute the instructions of metacomponents)
  Chapter 5: Knowledge-Acquisition Components (nonexecutive processes used to learn how to solve the problems controlled by metacomponents and solved by performance components)

Part III: The Experience of the Individual: Facets of Human Intelligence
  Chapter 6: Coping with Novelty
  Chapter 7: Automatizing Information Processing

Part IV: The External World of the Individual: Functions of Human Intelligence
  Chapter 8: Practical Intelligence
    1. Adapation to environmental contexts
    2. Shaping of environmental contexts
    3. Selection of environmental contexts

Part V: Personality, Motivation, and Intelligence
  Chapter 9: Why Intelligent People Fail (Too Often)

The Teacher's Guide
  Purpose of Chapter
  Chapter Outline
  Main Ideas
  Questions for Class Discussion
  Suggested Paper Topics
  Supplementary Activities
  Suggested Readings
  Suggested Time Allocation

relatively novel or else is in the process of becoming automatic. In sum, a theory of intelligence should specify how intelligence relates to the internal world of the individual, to the external world of the individual, and to experience.

In the triarchic theory, thinking skills and the intellectual skills that constitute intelligence overlap to a great extent. Most thinking skills are involved in intelligence, although there is more to intelligence than just thinking skills. For example, intelligence is involved in making information processing automatic, but thinking is not. To the contrary, information processing becomes automatic as the amount of thinking, or at least of conscious thinking, decreases. But the ties between thinking and intelligence are extremely close.

The Student's Text

The student's text is entitled *Intelligence Applied: Understanding and Increasing Your Intellectual Skills* (Sternberg, 1986) and is the heart of the triarchic program for training intellectual skills. The text, which is suitable for either a semester or year-long course at the high-school or college level, is divided into five main parts, each of which is described sequentially below.

Part I: Background

When one makes an important investment, such as buying a car, one usually does at least some research to make sure that one is getting the best car available, given one's financial and other resources. Such research might include searching for information about the car's features, performance, reputation, advantages and disadvantages, and so on. The research one does can have at least two beneficial aspects: First, it helps ensure that one does indeed purchase the best possible car, and second and less obviously, it motivates one to take pride in and do the most to take care of and get the most out of the car.

Undertaking a program for developing intellectual skills resembles purchasing a car. The more one learns about the program and how it compares to other programs, the more one is likely to have confidence in the program one undertakes and become convinced that the program will be beneficial. The confidence and pride that ensue are likely to result in performance that is better than if one simply undertakes a program blindly and without any knowledge of what the program is trying to accomplish, how it is trying to accomplish it, and why what it seeks to accomplish is indeed worth accomplishing in the first place.

It is not enough for the teacher to understand what the program does, how it does it, and why it does it. The success of a program depends at least as much upon student understanding and attitudes as it does upon teacher understanding and attitudes. Even if the teacher is convinced that a given program is acceptable or even optimal, the student may not be. One cannot assume that students will take the teacher's word, any more than one can assume that the car buyer will take the word of the car salesperson. Students perceive teachers as having vested interests, just as car purchasers perceive salespersons as having vested interests. These vested interests may or may not correspond to the self-perceived interests of the student. It is therefore essential to orient the student to the program he or she is about to undertake, as well as to the theory that underlies the program. The time spent in understanding intelligence will pay large dividends when it comes time to increase intelligence. Moreover, the knowledge students gain about intelligence is valuable in its own right, whether or not it is used as an introduction to a program for training intellectual skills.

Providing students with background information regarding theories of and programs for training intelligence has a second purpose. In learning background information, students are encouraged to apply to it the very analytical, interpretive, and evaluative skills that the program is designed to foster. In other words, the background chapters are not merely an introduction to the program—they are part of it. In their analyses and evaluations of theories and programs, students are practicing and developing the intellectual skills that will be addressed explicitly and in detail later in the program.

The first part of the student text contains two chapters that provide a brief, but not cursory, introduction to the nature of intelligence and attempts to train it.

Chapter 1: Some Historical Background on Views of Intelligence The first chapter of the text describes, at an elementary level, the major approaches to understanding intelligence: the definitional approach, the learning-theory approach, the psychometric approach, the Piagetian approach, and the cognitive approach. The goal of the chapter is to set the historical and theoretical stage for explaining to students the triarchic theory of intelligence, which motivates the training program. The text emphasizes that the alternative conventional approaches to understanding intelligence are largely complementary, emphasizing, as they do, different aspects of intelligent thought and behavior. A comprehensive theory and a training program built upon this theory attempt to bring together the best elements of these prior theories, without regard to the particular experimental paradigms or methods that gave rise to the theories, and to add to these theories the additional ingredients that are needed in order to construct a systematic and comprehensive theory that does justice to the full range of thought and behavior that constitutes intelligence. The triarchic theory will be presented later in the book as a step in this direction.

To understand and appreciate the background of a program for training intellectual skills, one must understand not only previous conceptions of intelligence, but previous (as well as other contemporary) conceptions of how intelligence can be taught. Chapter 1 describes two of the best such programs—Feuerstein's Instrumental Enrichment and Lipman's Philosophy for Children—to show both the main features of existing programs and how these programs are similar to and different from each other.

This chapter seeks not only to fill in background information, but also to encourage students to think critically about these programs. Thus, students find themselves being required to think critically about existing efforts to train intelligence—to find what is wrong with them and, just as important, what is right with them; to discover how they compare to and contrast with each other; and to think about how these programs could be improved. Students thus become active constructors, rather than passive recipients, of the training program. As will be described below, the Teacher's Guide contains activities that individualize the program to each student, so that the program is tailored to the individual, rather than merely to some nonexistent, hypothetical, average individual.

Chapter 2: The Triarchic Theory of Human Intelligence   This chapter introduces the triarchic theory of intelligence, which underlies and motivates the training program. The triarchic theory of intelligence seeks to understand intelligence in terms of (1) the internal world of the individual (i.e., the cognitive mechanisms underlying intelligent performance), (2) the external world of the individual (i.e., the environmental contexts in which intelligence operates), and (3) the experience of the individual in the world (i.e., the interface between the internal and external worlds over the individual's life span).

Students are taught the three parts of the theory. The first, componential part of the triarchic theory specifies three basic kinds of information-processing components: (1) metacomponents, which are executive processes used to plan, monitor, and evaluate one's strategy for solving problems; (2) performance components, which are nonexecutive processes used to execute the instructions of the metacomponents for solving problems; and (3) knowledge-acquisition components, which are nonexecutive processes used to learn how to solve the problems in the first place.

The three kinds of components are highly interactive, which means that they must be understood and trained in tandem. Metacomponents can be perceived as the stage directors that tell the actors—the performance components and the knowledge-acquisition components—how to act. The actors in turn provide feedback to the directors about how the show is going. This feedback may necessitate changes in directions for action or even changes in the script. An important part of metacomponential functioning is figuring out exactly what changes need to be made when, and how these changes should be implemented.

The contextual part of the triarchic theory specifies the functions to which components are applied in coping with the external world. These functions are (1) adaptation to existing environments, which involves changing oneself to fit better into these environments, (2) shaping existing environments, which involves changing the environments to adapt these environments more suitably to oneself, and (3) selecting new environments, which involves deselection of one or more current environments in favor of one or more new ones that are perceived to have more favorable characteristics for the individual.

The three functions of the components, like the components themselves, are highly interactive. Generally, one first seeks to adapt to the environment in which one finds oneself. Indeed, a critical aspect of intelligence is the application of the components of intelligence to adjust to a given environment. After a while, one may decide for any of a number of reasons that the given environment is nonoptimal. It may not suit one's values, interests, abilities, or preferences. In such instances, one may attempt to shape the environment so as to create a better fit to oneself. Thus, one seeks to change the environment itself, rather than, or in addition to, changing oneself. But sometimes, one's attempts to shape the environment are frustrated or only partially successful. One may eventually decide that one will never attain a satisfactory fit to the environment, despite one's efforts to adapt to or to shape that environment. In such instances, one may decide to leave that environment and select another. Alternatively, shaping may follow unsuccessful attempts at selection: After seeing that one is unable or unwilling to leave a given environment, one instead decides to shape it in a way that will make it maximally tolerable.

The experiential aspect of the triarchic theory specifies those regions—in the continuum of experience with tasks or situations (which ranges from totally unfamiliar to thoroughly familiar)—that most directly tap components that function intelligently. These two regions are those of (1) relative novelty and of (2) making information processing automatic. Relative novelty refers to the region of experience in which a task or situation is fairly, but not totally, new. Adapting to the mores of a foreign country one is visiting for the first time would be an example of relative novelty: One has some, but not a great deal of, relevant experience to bring to bear upon the situation. Making information processing automatic refers to the transition between conscious, controlled information processing and subconscious, automatic information processing. Examples are learning to read or drive. Initially, reading and driving are very deliberate, purposeful, and resource consuming. Eventually, reading and driving become essentially automatic, so that one scarcely has to think while doing them. At this point, they consume relatively few mental resources and can be done without conscious realization.

The two levels of experience in the application of components, like the components and the functions to which they are applied, are highly interactive. Better ability to cope with novelty enables one to begin making information processing automatic sooner and, perhaps, more effectively. Better ability to make a process automatic enables one to free more resources for coping with novelty, and hence for dealing with new kinds and levels of experience. Thus, superiority in dealing with novelty facilitates making a process automatic, and superiority in making a process automatic facilitates dealing with novelty.

The triarchic theory does not stand in opposition to most previous theories of intelligence. Rather, it integrates some of their most critical aspects, while dispensing with aspects that are idiosyncratic or simply wrong. The idea is not that this new theory will show other theories to be wrong, but rather that it will highlight what is right about these theories. The theory represents the best of previous theories, while at the same time incorporating new elements, including elements of integration, among the aspects of intelligence.

This integrationist view of conceptions of intelligence has an important implication for a training program based upon the triarchic theory: One is incorporating some of the best elements of past training programs, rather than repudiating these programs. A problem in selecting a program for intellectual-skills training is the fear that in buying into one theoretical approach, one misses the advantages of other theoretical approaches at the same time that one is saddled with the disadvantages (as well as the advantages) of the present theory. The triarchic theory does not leave one in this uncomfortable position. Rather, it leaves one in a position of having at least some of the best, and, one would hope, little of the worst of past theories and programs.

Part II: The Internal World of the Individual: Components of Human Intelligence

Part II consists of three chapters on each of the three kinds of information-processing components of intelligence: metacomponents, performance components, and knowledge-acquisition components. Each of these chapters will be considered in turn.

Chapter 3: Metacomponents This chapter specifies the metacomponents of intelligence and contains materials to develop skill in utilizing these metacomponents. The format for introducing and developing each metacomponent is parallel. Each section describing a metacomponent opens with some real-world examples of the metacomponent in action or inaction (and the consequences of this inaction). The purpose of this introductory section is to provide motivation for the material to follow and show how the metacomponents are important in one's everyday life, in addition to their academic importance. The next section provides several tips on how to increase the effectiveness with which one utilizes the metacomponent. The purpose of these tips is to provide concrete suggestions for improvement, rather than leaving it solely up to the learner to figure out just what changes in thought or behavior might result in more effective intellectual functioning. These concrete suggestions are followed by a set of problems, each of which requires the use of the metacomponential skill under consideration. Students are generally asked first to try to solve each problem on their own. They are then given the answer and shown how the metacomponent applies to solution of the problem.

The metacomponents dealt with in the chapter are

1. defining the nature of a problem,

2. selecting the components or steps needed to solve a problem,

3. selecting a strategy for ordering the components of problem solving,

4. selecting a mental representation for information,

5. allocating mental resources, and

6. monitoring the solution.

Let us consider some of the material pertinent to one of these metacomponents: defining the nature of a problem. This section opens with concrete examples of inadequate definitions of problems. One such example is in the personal arena, where an ethnographer has noted that, in a certain community she has observed, people frequently find themselves lacking the monetary resources they need to make ends meet. When this happens, they almost inevitably define the problem facing them as the need to earn more money: They thus take on second and even third jobs in order to support their life-style. Curiously, they almost never define the problem as one of living beyond their means, and thus fail to consider a second viable option: cutting their expenses so as to live within their means. A second example among the several provided is the curious case of the Watergate fiasco. In the early and, arguably, even the later phases of this fiasco, the Nixon administration perceived that its problem was to cover up what had happened. The result was a slow, tortuous, and painful sequence of discoveries, each of which put the administration in a successively worse predicament. An alternative way of defining the problem would have been one of disclosing just what had happened, albeit in a way that would minimize the damage, and then of letting the matter die a rapid death. This course of action seems never to have been seriously considered. It was certainly never pursued.

Three suggestions are given for improving one's definition of problems. The first is to reread or reconsider the question. Often, a problem seems insoluble because it has been misconstrued. The second suggestion is to redefine one's goals. If an initial problem is not soluble, often a more modest attempt to solve a series of subproblems can lead either to the whole solution or at least to a part of this solution. The third suggestion is to ask whether one's chosen goal really represents what one wants. In some instances, one will find an alternative goal with a different method of attack upon a different problem that will yield satisfactory results, even though the results are different from the ones originally sought.

Finally, three problems are presented that involve the metacomponent of defining the problem. The first of these is the classic nine–dot problem, in which one must connect a series of three dots placed in three rows and three columns using just four lines without lifting one's pencil from the page. Students often fail to solve this problem because they make an assumption about the nature of the problem that proves to be incorrect. This assumption is that the four lines must stay within the implicit perimeter defined by the three rows of three dots. In fact, solution of the problem depends upon extending each of the four lines beyond the periphery of the implicit borders defined by the dots.

The second problem is the monk problem. In this problem, a monk climbs a mountain one day, spends the night at a retreat, and goes down the mountain the second day. The monk does not descend the mountain at the same rate that he ascended it. The question is whether there must be a point on the mountain that the monk passes at exactly the same time of day on the two successive days of his ascent and descent. The easiest way to solve the problem is to reformulate it in an isomorphic way: Instead of imagining the same monk going up and down the mountain on successive days, one imagines two different monks, one of whom is ascending the mountain and the other of whom is descending the mountain, both on the same day. This reformulation makes it clear that there must be some point at which the two monks pass each other on the same day or at which the monk passes himself on the successive days.

The third problem is the hatrack problem, in which one must figure out how to make a hatrack, given two poles and a C-clamp, in a room of specified dimensions. Students have great difficulty in solving this problem. As in the nine-dot problem, part of the students' difficulty is in their assumed problem space for solving the problem. The students do not normally include the floor and ceiling of the room in their solution. Yet, solution of the problem depends upon wedging the two poles together against the floor and ceiling and using the C-clamp to hold the poles together.

The format of the remainder of this chapter is parallel to the format for the problem-definition metacomponent, with real-world examples, suggestions, and problems suitable for each of the respective metacomponents. By the time students have finished the chapter, they have a very good sense of how metacomponents can improve rather than impede their problem solving.

Chapter 4: Performance Components   The performance components of intelligence implement the plans that the metacomponents formulate. The number of performance components in the individual's repertoire is very large. Fortunately, for both theoretical and practical purposes, the number of performance components that is critical for intellectual performance is relatively small, because a small number of performance components crop up again and again in intellectual tasks. These general performance components are the most interesting ones from both a theoretical and a practical point of view.

Some of the most important performance components are

1. inferring relations between stimuli,

2. applying previously inferred relations to new stimuli,

3. mapping higher order relations between relations, and

4. comparing attributes of stimuli.

These are four of the six or so performance components that form the core of inductive-reasoning tasks, such as analogies, series extrapolations, and classifications.

Chapter 4 shows how to apply these and other performance components to a variety of different kinds of problems, ranging from quite academic to quite practical. Consider the instruction and exercises that constitute the section on the inference component. The section opens with a practical example of an inference: If one hears that a friend is in the hospital, one is likely to infer that the friend is either ill or injured, although there are, of course, alternative interpretations of the data. This and other inferences can be classified into several categories.

The first major subsection details the kinds of verbal inferences most frequently encountered, for example,

1. similarity inferences,

2. contrast inferences,

3. predication inferences,

4. subordination inferences, and

5. part-whole inferences.

Examples of each of the inferences are given, and then students are asked to classify each of 25 inferences as falling into one of the 13 categories given.

Next, students are shown how inferences can serve either constructive or destructive purposes. Inferences are destructive when they reflect inferential fallacies. Nineteen kinds of inferential fallacies are described, for example,

1. irrelevant conclusion (the conclusion has nothing to do with the reasoning),

2. division (the assumption that what is true of the whole is necessarily true of each individual part of the whole),

3. hasty generalization (assuming that what is true of exceptional cases is also true of typical cases), and

4. invalid disjunction (assuming that only two solutions to a question are possible when in fact more than two are possible).

Each inferential fallacy is described, and then an instance of the fallacy is given and explicated. Finally, another example of the inferential fallacy is given, and the student is asked to indicate why it is an example. After all of the inferences have been described, 25 vignettes are presented, some of which contain fallacies. The student must indicate whether there is a fallacy in each vignette, and if so, say of what kind it is. Here are two examples of such vignettes:

1. Chris refused to eat his peas, because, he said, "They are green." When Jack questioned this reason for disliking peas, Chris explained, "My mother

always made me eat a lot of green vegetables, and I came to dislike having green things at meals." (This is an example of an irrelevant conclusion.)

2. A medical researcher, Carol, had been taking hormone samples from 30 patients who had cancer of the liver. In three of the patients, she noticed unusually high concentrations of the hormone, DNG. She reported to her supervisor, "I think we've found a significant link between DNG and liver cancer, based on this evidence from three cancer patients." (This is an example of a hasty generalization.)

Later problems build upon the information contained in the inference section. After other components are introduced—for example, verbal and non-verbal analogy—classification and series extrapolation problems are presented that require exercise of the inference performance component. Later, more complex problems are presented that require inference in more ecologically relevant settings. For example, in one type of problem, students must infer which of two legal principles is relevant to solving a particular case. In a second type of problem, the students must infer which of two principles for interpreting Rorschach ink blot protocols is relevant for making a diagnosis in a particular case. (Of course, the students are informed that imaginary principles are used in both the legal and clinical inference items.) The goal in these problems, as in all the problems, is for students to use the various performance components in a wide variety of applications and recognize when the various kinds of components need to be used, irrespective of surface-structural difference between problem types that may mask the deep-structural similarities in the performance components of the solution.

Chapter 5: Knowledge-Acquisition Components This chapter deals with the topic of knowledge acquisition in general and vocabulary acquisition in particular. The training material is based upon a theory of verbal comprehension according to which there are three basic ingredients involved in learning vocabulary from context:

1. the processes used to figure out meanings of words from context,

2. the kinds of information—or cues—to which these processes can be applied, and

3. the mediating variables that affect how well the processes can be applied to the cues.

Each of these respective aspects of the training is considered below.

The three processes are those mentioned earlier: (1) selective encoding, (2) selective combination, and (3) selective comparison. Selective encoding is used to decide what information in a passage is relevant for figuring out the meaning of an unknown word. Selective combination is used to put together these informational cues into a unified definition. Selective comparison is used to relate the new word and its definition to information one already has, both about words in particular and about the world in general.

However, it is not enough just to be able to draw upon these three processes. One has to apply them to the particular content of a given passage through the use of different kinds of contextual cues. For example, setting cues specify the time, place, or situation in which a given concept appears. Class membership cues specify a class of which the unknown concept is a member. Value/affect cues describe evaluative connotations associated with the concept. Active-property cues specify actions performed by or to the concept. These and other cues serve as objects for the knowledge-acquisition processes: They are the stuff to which the processes are applied so that the meanings of new words can be inferred.

It is not always equally easy to apply the processes of knowledge acquisition to the contextual cues. The passages contain mediating variables that make application of the processes either easier or harder. For example, the distance of the cue from the unknown word is one such mediating variable. It is easier to apply the processes to the cues if the cues are in close proximity to the unknown word. A second mediating variable is the number of different contexts in which the word to be learned appears. It is easier to learn the meaning of the word if it appears in several contexts. More than one context is needed to get a fix on the word's meaning. But too many contexts can be confusing and actually impede learning the word's meaning.

Students are trained in all three aspects of the theory and are given concrete examples of each aspect of the theory as they go along. The training is incremental: Rather than attempting to teach the students the whole theory at once, students learn bits of it at a time and are then asked to apply it as they learn it.

The basic vehicle for giving the students experience in learning and applying the theory to defining new words is a set of reading passages in which one or more unknown words are embedded. Consider just one example of such a passage:

The *flitwite* was only one of the judicial remedies available to the justices of the Court of the King's Bench in the eleventh century, but it was perhaps the most important. Its frequent use added enormously to the treasury's coffers, and new royal expenditures were often financed by the issuance of an increased number of *flitwites*. However, even the most impartial of justices must have handed them down in multitudes, for the *flitwite* was as much a part of eleventh century society as the civil tort is of our own. Medieval men and women related in direct and personal ways; therefore, conflict was likely to take the form of actual fighting. In our litigious culture, the law must often deal with more subtle forms of conflict.

Students are presented with passages such as this one, and are shown how to use the aspects of the theory to figure out the unknown word or words, in this case, *flitwite* (which is a fine for fighting). For example, one might selectively encode in the first sentence that a relevant cue for figuring out the meaning of *flitwite* is that it was a judicial remedy. This is a stative-property (descriptive) cue. It is easily applied to partly figuring out the meaning of the unknown word because of the favorable circumstances generated by a mediating variable—the cue is in close proximity to the unknown word it can help define.

Part III: The Experience of the Individual: Facets of Human Intelligence

The triarchic training program deals with both facets of the relation between the individual's experience and his or her intelligence: coping with novelty and making information processing automatic. Let us consider the form that training for each of these facets takes.

Chapter 6: Coping with Novelty   This chapter extends the theory of the processes of knowledge acquisition to learning in novel domains. It opens with an overview of alternative views of insight and then quickly proceeds to the triarchic view of insight, according to which insights can involve one or more of the three processes of selective encoding, selective combination, and selective comparison.

Selectively encoding insights involves screening relevant from irrelevant information in unusual ways. A detective must decide which of the many pieces of information at the scene of a crime are relevant for solving the crime. A doctor must examine a patient and decide exactly which tests and results are relevant for making a diagnosis. A scientist often must take a voluminous computer printout and decide which elements of the printout are relevant for testing his or her hypothesis, or the scientist may have to decide what natural or experimental observations are relevant. Many important scientific discoveries, such as the discovery of penicillin, hinged upon selectively encoding the results of experiments that to many would have seemed trivial. Similarly, selective combination is important when a detective has to assemble the clues to reconstruct what happened at the scene of the crime or when a doctor has to assemble the results of the medical observations and tests to come up with a diagnosis. Selective comparison can also be critical to insightful discoveries: The detective may realize that the circumstances of a given crime closely resemble those of a previous crime that was solved in a particular way. Or a doctor may remember a related case in which the same set of presenting symptoms led to a diagnosis, say, of Rocky Mountain spotted fever. As the processes are explained to the students, examples of insights involving these processes are given to make the processes concrete and motivate the students to use the three processes of insight in their own thinking. Some tips are then given about how to use these insights. Finally, several kinds of problems are presented that challenge the students to apply these three forms of insightful thinking.

The first kind of problem is the arithmetical/logical word problem. A good example of such a problem is the socks problem:

Suppose you have brown socks and blue socks in a drawer, mixed in a ratio of 4 to 5. What is the maximum number of socks you have to take out of the drawer to be assured of having a pair of socks of the same color?

This simple problem involves both selective encoding and selective combination. Selective encoding is involved in deciding that the ratio information in the problem is irrelevant to the problem's solution. Less-insightful problem solvers tend to focus on this irrelevant information and attempt to use it in problem solving. Selective combination is involved in figuring out how to form the possible pairs of brown and blue socks to see that one never needs more than three socks to form a pair of the same color.

After the arithmetical/logical word problems come information-evaluation problems. Students are presented with a question, such as, "How do desert animals withstand the heat of the desert?" or "Why do television sets with cable connections get better reception than do televisions with antennas?" Following each question is a set of facts. Students must mark each fact as either relevant or irrelevant to answering the question. In response to the first question, for example, the fact, "Most desert animals cannot tolerate temperatures above 150 degrees Fahrenheit" is not relevant to answering the question, whereas the fact, "Desert animals are often nocturnal and live inside underground tunnels during the day" is relevant. These problems primarily involve selective encoding (figuring out which facts are relevant).

Next come mystery problems. A mystery problem is usually three to five paragraphs in length and presents a case for a detective to solve. Often, the detective (Ramirez) questions people at the scene of the crime. At the end, the detective figures out who committed the crime. The student has to figure out how the detective decided who perpetrated the crime. These problems involve extensive selective encoding, in that only a small portion of the presented information is relevant to solving the crime. Selective combination is involved in assembling the clues. Selective comparison is also involved, because the solution always entails at least some use of worldly knowledge.

The mystery problems are followed by conceptual-projection problems, in which students must predict future states of the world on the basis of limited information. For example, in the first set of problems, students are told about the planet Kyron, in a faraway galaxy, on which there are four kinds of people: A *twe* is a Kyronian who is born a child and remains a child through his lifetime; a *nel* is a Kyronian who is born an adult and remains an adult throughout his lifetime; a *bit* is a Kyronian who is born a child and becomes an adult; a *dek* is a Kyronian who is born an adult and becomes a child. In each conceptual-projection problem, the student is given partial information about a particular Kyronian. The student must figure out which of the four kinds of Kyronian the individual is and then predict what the state of the person will be (child or adult) in the future. These problems primarily require selective combination:

The student must take the given information, all of which is relevant to problem solution, and figure out how to combine it in order to determine which kind of Kyronian is represented by the described individual.

After the conceptual-projection problems come novel analogies. These are like ordinary analogies, except that in solving them the student must sometimes take into account an altered state of the world. The problem opens with a sentence that, in some instances, represents a counterfactual condition. The student must then solve the analogy as though that condition were true. Consider one such counterfactual analogy:

Villains are lovable.

HERO is to ADMIRATION as VILLAIN is to (a) contempt, (b) affection, (c) cruel, (d) kind.

The correct answer is (b) affection. Note that the counterfactual sentence changes the correct answer to the analogy. This is true only in some of the analogies, so that the student must determine for him- or herself whether or not the answer is changed, and if so, how.

The last kind of problem found in the chapter is the scientific-insight problem. Students are presented with a brief scientific problem. Some of the problems are more theoretical, others more practical. The student must then answer an insight question based upon the problem. Consider an example of such a problem:

There is at least one known instance of a jet fighter pilot shooting his own plane out of the air, using his own guns. Amazing as it seems, aeronautical engineers have made it possible for a supersonic jet fighter to catch up with the fire from its own guns with sufficient speed to shoot itself down. If a plane flying at 1000 mph fires a burst from 20 millimeter guns, the shells leave the plane with an airspeed of about 3000 mph.

Why won't a plane that continues to fly straight ahead fly into its own bullets?

In this case, the correct answer is that the bullets will fall due to gravity, whereas the plane that flies straight ahead will not fall. Problems of this kind involve various combinations of the three insight processes.

Chapter 7: Automatizing Information Processing   This chapter opens with a description of the difference between controlled and automatic information processing and discusses examples of each, as well as the relation between the two kinds of information processing. The chapter then explicates the ten principles for expediting the process of making information handling automatic. For example, one principle is that it helps to learn the task you wish to make automatic under moderate speed stress. Another principle is that making information processing automatic is likely to be more rapid if one is able to devote one's full attention to the task at hand. Students are encouraged to apply these principles to their own information processing to facilitate its becoming automatic.

Students are then presented with several relatively simple information-processing tasks in which they can use the principles to speed their functioning by making them automatic.

The first task, letter comparison, involves comparing pairs of letters and indicating whether or not they have the same name. For example, "j o" do not have the same name, whereas "A A" and "G g" do. Students receive four sets of 80 such problems and are encouraged to develop as much speed as possible, so long as they retain near 100 percent accuracy.

The second task, visual search, involves determining whether a target letter appears in a subsequent string of letters. An example of such a problem is "f   K n p C." In this problem, the letter does not appear in the subsequent string. In the problem, "B   L x B f," the target letter does appear. Students receive eight sets of 40 problems. The problems become more difficult as one goes along, with difficulty controlled by the number of letters in the subsequent string that has to be scanned.

The third task, digit-symbol, is similar to a task that appears on many intelligence tests. The student is presented with an initial pairing of digits and symbols, for example, "^1, (2, +3, %4." The student is then presented with a set of 120 symbols and must match digits to them as rapidly as possible. Thus, if the student sees the symbol "(" he or she must write "2" as rapidly as possible. There are eight sets of 120 items. Items become more difficult in successive sets as the number of digit-symbol matchings increases from 4 to 8.

The fourth and last task is complex letter scanning. This task is a more complex version of the visual search task. One is initially presented with from one to four target letters. For each problem, the student must indicate whether any of those letters appears in a two-dimensional array of letters. The two-dimensional array is unsystematic, so that the student must scan his or her visual field in order to find the letters, if they appear. A simple example of such a problem is the following:

r j

q   p

s

d

There are twelve sets of 40 items each. Problems become more difficult as the number of targets increases from two to four and as the number of letters in the subsequent visual array increases.

Part IV: The External World of the Individual: Functions of Human Intelligence

Chapter 8: Practical Intelligence   Part IV of the training program contains just a single chapter on practical intelligence. The chapter contains several kinds of material for the development of practical intellectual skills.

It opens with four motivating vignettes—one about a college student who is not admitted to the graduate program in her university, ostensibly because the faculty did not see her as having academic values, but actually because the faculty did not like her; a second about two students, one of whom seemed always to know the right thing to say and the other of whom did not; a third about a doctor with an unsafe diet plan who nevertheless managed repeatedly to get favorable promotion for himself and the diet plan; and a fourth about a teacher who is a solid lecturer, but is nevertheless unable to kindle the enthusiasm of her students. These vignettes point out that even people who are very intelligent in academic settings may have difficulty applying their intelligence to their lives.

The chapter continues with a definition of practical intelligence—as intelligence that operates upon real-world contexts through efforts to achieve adaptation to, shaping of, and selection of real-world environments. It then proceeds to a discussion of alternative means that have been used to assess practical intelligence, including

1. psychometric tests measuring everyday skills and abilities,

2. the in-basket (a simulation of executive performance),

3. behavioral checklists,

4. projective techniques (such as the Thematic Apperception Test), and

5. the measurement of tacit knowledge—knowledge that is needed to get ahead but that is not explicitly taught.

The chapter then moves on to several kinds of exercises to develop practical aspects of intelligence, each of which will be considered in turn.

The first kind of exercise involves a behavioral checklist. Students rate on a 1-to-9 scale the extent to which each of a set of behaviors characterizes their own behavior. The checklist contains a set of behaviors that has been found in my past research to measure three factors that laypersons and experts alike agree are central to intelligence: practical problem-solving ability, verbal ability, and social competence. Examples of behaviors measuring practical problem-solving ability are "reasons logically and well," "identifies connections among ideas," and "keeps an open mind." Examples of verbal ability are "speaks clearly and articulately," "reads widely," and "displays a good vocabulary." Examples of social competence are "accepts others for what they are," "admits mistakes," and "displays interest in the world at large." Note that gains in most of these behaviors are subject to self-motivated improvement and that a checklist of this kind can point out those behaviors in which individuals should seek such improvement.

A second and quite different type of exercise involves decoding of nonverbal cues. Students are shown two kinds of photographs, involving pictures of couples ostensibly involved in romantic relationships and pictures of pairs of workers, one of whom is the other's supervisor. For the first kind of photograph, the students' task is to guess which pictures represent genuine couples and which represent pairs of individuals posing as though they were romantically involved. For the second kind of photograph, the students' task is to guess which of the two individuals is the other's supervisor. In each case, students are invited to try the task, either with or without reading about the nonverbal cues that facilitate these decisions. For the pictures of couples, these cues include, among others, relaxation of the individuals, positioning of arms and legs, tension of hands, match in socioeconomic class, distance between bodies, amount of physical contact, and general similarity. For the second test, the cues include, among others, direction of eye gaze, formality of dress, age, tension of hands, and socioeconomic class.

A third task involves reading a vignette of an everyday situation and selecting a course of action to pursue in that situation. One course of action stresses adaptation to the environment, one stresses shaping of the environment, and one stresses selection of an environment. Students are encouraged to ask themselves certain questions to help decide which source of action is most appropriate. An example of such a vignette is the following:

Television reception in your area is hampered by a nearby mountain range. The reruns of "Bonanza," your favorite show, are hardly worth watching because of all the double images and static interference. Given that you value your leisure time highly, do you:
a. continue watching your favorite show in its crippled form. After all, the reception is not that bad? (adaptation)
b. buy a deep-dish antenna to improve reception? (shaping)
c. take up bridge? (selection)

A fourth kind of exercise involves the display of tacit knowledge. Students are asked to put themselves in the role of two individuals: a business manager and a professor of psychology. Their task is to answer a series of questions the way a successful executive or psychologist would. The questions assess a person's knowledge of what it takes to get ahead in a particular life course. The answer key provides the responses made by experts. An example of one of these problems—for an executive—is the following:

A number of factors enter into the establishment of a good reputation as manager of a company. Consider the following factors and rate their importance:
a. critical thinking ability
b. speaking ability
c. extent of college education and prestige of the school attended
d. no hesitation to take extraordinarily risky courses of action
e. a keen sense of what superiors can be sold on

The last kind of exercise involves a series of situations calling for resolution of conflicts. Some of these situations involve interpersonal conflicts, some involve organizational conflicts, and some involve international conflicts. The students' task is to read each conflict and then rate the suitability of each of a series of possible modes of conflict resolution for its appropriateness in resolving each of the given conflicts. The modes of conflict resolution involve seven different styles of resolution: physical action, economic pressure, undermining the esteem in which the other party is held, third-party mediation, accepting the situation, waiting to see what further developments transpire, and stepping down the conflict so as to reduce tension. The conflict-mitigating strategies are generally more adaptive than the conflict-exacerbating ones.

The chapter closes with a description of the Janis-Mann balance sheet technique, which is a useful aid for people who need to make difficult decisions. The balance sheet takes into account favorable and unfavorable potential outcomes of a decision both for oneself and for others and weighs these outcomes in terms of their positivity or negativity, as well as in terms of their importance.

Part V: Personality, Motivation, and Intelligence

Chapter 9: Why Intelligent People Fail (Too Often)   The final chapter discusses 20 impediments to the full realization of one's intelligence. Although these impediments are not, strictly speaking, intellectual, they interfere with the use of intelligence and hence are quite relevant to a course for training intellectual skills. Each impediment is defined and discussed and examples of each are given. The impediments are

1. lack of motivation,

2. lack of impulse control,

3. lack of perseverance, or perseveration,

4. capitalizing on the wrong abilities,

5. inability to translate thought into action,

6. lack of product orientation,

7. task completion problems and lack of follow-through,

8. failure to initiate,

9. fear of failure,

10. procrastination,

11. misattribution of blame,

12. excessive self-pity,

13. excessive dependency,

14. wallowing in personal difficulties,

15. distractibility and lack of concentration,

16. spreading oneself too thick or too thin,

17. inability to delay gratification,

18. inability or unwillingness to see the forest from the trees,

19. lack of balance between critical, analytic thinking, and creative, synthetic thinking, and

20. too little or too much self-confidence.

The Teacher's Guide

The Teacher's Guide helps the teacher implement the triarchic program for training intellectual skills. For each chapter, there are eight sections to the guide. For the sake of coherence, these sections will be illustrated with reference to a single chapter, that on Metacomponents (Chapter 3).

Purpose of Chapter

This section simply describes what the chapter seeks to accomplish. In Chapter 3, the metacomponents (executive processes) of intelligence are described and exercises for improving metacomponential skills are presented.

Chapter Outline

This section outlines the chapter, using two levels of headings. In Chapter 3, the main sections of the outline are an introduction, followed by headings corresponding to each of the metacomponents. The subsidiary sections show the format of the description for each metacomponent: examples, improving your execution of the metacomponent, and exercises on the metacomponent.

Main Ideas

This section summarizes the main ideas of the chapter and varies widely in length as a function of the particular chapter. A main idea in Chapter 3 is that metacomponents guide the functioning of the other kinds of components.

Questions for Class Discussion

These questions are intended to help students better understand the material, but also to help them apply the material in formulating and evaluating answers to the questions. Here are some examples of questions for discussion in Chapter 3:

1. What are some examples, in your own life, of situations in which inadequate or suboptimal metacomponential functioning resulted in a decision that you later regretted?

2. Is the execution of metacomponents always conscious, or can it be subconscious in some instances? If so, in what kinds of instances?

3. In what ways, if any, do psychometric theories of intelligence take metacomponents into account?

4. How do the programs of Feuerstein (Instrumental Enrichment) and Lipman (Philosophy for Children) train metacomponential skills?

5. What metacomponents might be used to help you memorize a story?

6. How might one go about testing experimentally a theory of metacomponential functioning in problem solving?

7. To what extent do metacomponents explain mental functioning, and to what extent do they merely describe it?

8. What roles do metacomponents play in scientific thought?

Suggested Paper Topics

This section presents topics for papers. It is strongly recommended that teachers require at least several short papers during the course of the term to stimulate thinking about the skills taught in the program. Some examples of suggested topics are:

1. Analyze in some detail a major decision you have made in your life, considering the metacomponential functioning that was involved and how it might have been improved.

2. Write a critical analysis of the role, whether explicit or implicit, of metacomponents in major theories of intelligence.

Supplementary Activities

Supplementary Activities are projects in which students can engage to improve their understanding and utilization of the content of the course. Some examples are:

1. Construct a test of metacomponential functioning, using at least some problem types other than those that occur in the text.

2. Cut out some advertisements from newspapers or magazines, and show how their appeal depends, in part, upon suspension of metacomponential thought.

Suggested Readings

This annotated bibliography suggests readings relevant to the topic of each chapter. These readings are appropriate for both students and teachers. The readings are important: A comprehensive course will go beyond the main text to other related readings that reinforce and elaborate upon points made in the main text.

Suggested Time Allocation

This section suggests the amount of time that should be allocated to each chapter, both for a year course and for a semester course. Suggested allocation for Chapter 3, for example, is three weeks in a year-long course and two weeks in a semester-long course.

CONCLUSION

Intelligence Applied presents a program for training intellectual skills based upon my triarchic theory of human intelligence. The program has two basic elements: a text and a teacher's guide. The text contains nine chapters divided into five main parts. The first part provides background information on views of intelligence, training intelligence, and the triarchic theory of intelligence that motivates the program. The second part contains three chapters, one each on each of the three kinds of information-processing components in the triarchic theory: metacomponents, performance components, and knowledge-acquisition components. The third part contains two chapters on the two facets of intelligence that relate it to experience: coping with novelty and making information processing automatic. The fourth part contains a single chapter on practical intelligence, and the fifth part contains a single chapter on sources of failure to utilize intellectual potential. The teacher's guide contains eight sections for each of the ten chapters: Purpose of Chapter, Chapter Outline, Main Ideas, Questions for Class Discussion, Suggested Paper Topics, Supplementary Activities, Suggested Readings, Suggested Time Allocation.

Strengths and Limitations of the Program

No doubt, others will decide upon the strengths and limitations of the triarchic program. However, I feel it incumbent to state what the main strengths and limitations are.

The program has eight main strengths:

1. The program is based on a theory that has been subjected to fairly extensive empirical testing. Although there exist many programs for training intellectual skills, few of them are theoretically based, and among those that are based on theories, for the most part, the theories have not been rigorously tested.

2. The theory and program are broad rather than narrow in scope. The range of intellectual skills covered is wide enough to provide a fairly complete basis for training intelligence.

3. The theory and program emphasize practical as well as academic intelligence. It is difficult to obtain transfer of training, and programs that do not cover practical as well as academic applications of material seem unlikely to yield significant transfer.

4. The program is process based. Other theories may be broad in scope, but because they do not always specify the processes of intelligence, they do not have clear implications for the training of intellectual skills. The triarchic theory does specify the processes of intelligence to be trained and contains training material directed toward the improvement of functioning of these processes.

5. There exists a triarchic test of intellectual skills in two forms that can be used, along with other tests, as a pretest and posttest for assessing training effects. The tests do not merely measure performance on the problems in the text, but they do measure performance on skills trained in the text. Assessment should always involve a control group as well as the trained experimental group.

6. The program includes a comprehensive Teacher's Guide as well as the main text.

7. The program teaches students about intelligence as well as teaching them intellectual skills. Students therefore understand why they are learning these particular skills. They are not merely asked to accept the program blindly. The learning of material on theories and programs exercises the very intellectual skills that the program teaches.

8. The program teaches synthetic as well as analytic skills. Existing analytical programs are heavily emphasized. Although analysis is important, most important contributions to knowledge involve going beyond the information given, not just evaluating that information.

A balanced account must indicate limitations as well as strengths. The main limitations of the program, at the present time, are the following:

1. The program is currently limited to the secondary and college levels. Although I hope to expand its scope, there do not exist, at present, any materials based on the triarchic theory that are appropriate for the elementary-school level.

2. The program has relatively little material on deductive thinking (traditional logic). The range of traditional logic is so broad that it requires a whole course in its own right. Usually, logic is taught as a separate course at the college level. I would strongly recommend a course in traditional logic to supplement the present program.

3. The program has not received the extensive empirical testing that a few programs, most notably Feuerstein's Instrumental Enrichment and Lipman's Philosophy for Children, have received. Although tests to date have yielded favorable results, these tests are much more limited than those that the other two programs have received.

4. Although the program deals with all three aspects of the triarchic theory, it probably does least justice to the contextual aspect. The domain of practical intelligence can scarcely be covered in one chapter. One problem in teaching practical intelligence is that we do not yet know a great deal about it. As we learn more about it, there will be a need to expand coverage of the practical side of intelligent functioning.

Intelligence Applied: Understanding and Increasing Your Intellectual Skills provides a new and exciting option for the development of intellectual skills in secondary and college-level programs. The program is ready to be used and will contribute substantially to the development of intellectual skills in those who follow it.

REFERENCES

Cole, M., Gay, J., Glick, J., & Sharp, D. W. (1971). *The cultural context of learning and thinking*. New York: Basic Books.

Davidson, J. E., & Sternberg, R. J. (1984). The role of insight in intellectual giftedness. *Gifted Child Quarterly*, 28:58–64.

Feuerstein, R. (1980). *Instrumental enrichment: An intervention program for cognitive modifiability*. Baltimore: University Park Press.

Sternberg, R. J. (1981). Intelligence and nonentrenchment. *Journal of Educational Psychology*, 73:1–16.

Sternberg, R. J. (1982). Natural, unnatural, and supernatural concepts. *Cognitive Psychology*, 14:451–488.

Sternberg, R. J. (1984). A contextualist view of the nature of intelligence. *International Journal of Psychology*, 19:307–334.

Sternberg, R. J. (1985). *Beyond IQ: A triarchic theory of human intelligence*. New York: Cambridge University Press.

Sternberg, R. J. (1986). *Intelligence applied: Understanding and increasing your intellectual skills*. San Diego: Harcourt, Brace, Jovanovich.

Sternberg, R. J. (In press). The psychology of verbal comprehension. In R. Glaser (Ed.), *Advances in instructional psychology* (Vol. 3). Hillsdale, N.J.: Erlbaum.

Sternberg, R. J., Conway, B. E., Ketron, J. L., & Bernstein, M. (1981). People's conceptions of intelligence. *Journal of Personality and Social Psychology*, 41:37–55.

Sternberg, R. J., & Nigro, G. (1980). Developmental patterns in the solution of verbal analogies. *Child Development*, 51:27–38.

Sternberg, R. J., & Powell, J. S. (1983). Comprehending verbal comprehension. *American Psychologist*, 38:878–893.

Sternberg, R. J., & Weil, E. M., (1980). An aptitude-strategy interaction in linear syllogistic reasoning. *Journal of Educational Psychology*, 72:226–234.

Wagner, R. K., & Sternberg, R. J. (1984). Alternative conceptions of intelligence and their implications for education. *Review of Educational Research*, 54:197–224.

Wagner, R. K., & Sternberg, R. J. (1985). Practical intelligence in real-world pursuits: The role of tacit knowledge. *Journal of Personality and Social Psychology*, 49:436–458.

Wagner, R. K., & Sternberg, R. J. (In press). Executive processes in reading. In B. Britton (Ed.), *Executive control processes in reading*. Hillsdale, N.J.: Erlbaum.

Preparation of this chapter was supported by a contract from El Dividendo Voluntario para la Comunidad, Caracas, Venezuela, and by contract N0001483K0013 from the Office of Naval Research and Army Research Institute.

Part IV

EVALUATING THINKING SKILLS

JOAN BOYKOFF BARON
Office of Research and Evaluation
Connecticut State Department of Education

Evaluating Thinking Skills
in the Classroom

The recent commitment to improve thinking skills has been accompanied by a growing need to evaluate those skills. This need is shared by educators working in a large variety of settings. Teachers trying to tailor their instructional activities and strategies to develop thinking skills often wonder whether they have succeeded in improving children's thinking. Sometimes, they are asked by their administrators to provide data. After providing professional development opportunities, securing time for teachers to develop materials, or possibly purchasing a thinking skills program, school administrators who have made a commitment to improving thinking skills may want to know whether their efforts were worthwhile. These administrators may also be motivated by the need to produce evidence for the local school board. State boards of education and consortia of national educators (e.g., National Assessment of Educational Progress (NAEP)), concerned about the recent preponderance of poor performance on higher order thinking skills in all subject areas, are striving to develop sensitive assessment procedures for monitoring changes in students' thinking over an extended period of time. Finally, program developers want to evaluate the success of their programs. As researchers, they are interested in the program's validity and as developers, they want to make justifiable claims about their program's impact on children's thinking.

Each of these groups is motivated by a combination of internal and external factors ranging from intellectual curiosity to the need for accountability. These motivations are closely linked to the purposes the evaluation will serve. This chapter is designed to address the full range of purposes that motivates educators working in different roles to develop evaluations of thinking skills and dispositions.

TYPES OF EVALUATIONS

The *purpose* of an evaluation should largely determine the *type* of evaluation that is most appropriate. A teacher who is experimenting with new approaches to enhance students' thinking skills and dispositions will require a very different kind and scale of evaluation from a large city school district that has implemented a new thinking skills pilot program in three of its schools and is deciding whether the program has been sufficiently successful to warrant purchasing it for the other fifteen schools. When an important decision is to be made that has a potentially major impact on students, it is advisable to plan a carefully controlled, broadly conceived, and well-documented evaluation study.

Four Evaluation Dimensions

In designing evaluations of thinking skills, there are four relevant dimensions that can be useful. These dimensions grow out of the distinctions between formative and summative evaluation, product and process evaluation, qualitative and quantitative evaluation, and experimental and quasi-experimental evaluations. These distinctions represent important dimensions on which evaluations differ.

Formative–Summative

The formative–summative distinction (Scriven, 1967) has to do with the basic purpose of the evaluation. As one might suspect, formative evaluations occur during the early stages when the main purpose of the evaluation is to improve the program. The major focus is on looking closely at the students' reactions while the learning events or program is being implemented so as to make necessary changes, assess the effect of those changes, make other required modifications, and so forth. When the major concern is to determine the net effectiveness of a program, the evaluation is called summative. This occurs when the fine tuning is over and a program is in place. For example the principal or superintendent wants to know whether a program should be continued or terminated. Both types of evaluations are important because they serve different yet important purposes required for efficient program development and sensible use.

Product–Process

A second distinction is between product evaluation and process evaluation. Product evaluations concentrate on what the students produce—their work samples, test scores, and self-report measures. In a process evaluation, the evaluator is concerned with the internal workings of the situation. How are the students responding to the learning events or program? Are students engaged in animated, probing discussions or are they sitting at their desks daydreaming? These studies are concerned with how an effect was achieved. An additional purpose of process evaluations is that they ensure that a program being evaluated is actually taking place. Both types of evaluation are important because programs have been judged to be ineffective when they in fact were never implemented. Similarly, without some product evaluation, it is quite possible to conclude that a program is effective because the students are enthusiastically engaged in discussion when very little actual learning is taking place.

Qualitative–Quantitative

The distinction between qualitative and quantitative evaluations is also important. Qualitative evaluations are concerned with capturing the depth and detail of experiences of people in the program. They are largely descriptive. Quantitative evaluations generally rely on tests, instruments, questionnaires, and surveys that provide a standardized format using the evaluator's predetermined categories. Quantitative data are often presented numerically rather than descriptively. Both kinds of evaluations are important. Educators not only want to know what percentage of students are improving certain skills, they also want to understand exactly what it means to attain those skills.

Experimental–Quasi-Experimental Designs

The distinction between experimental and quasi-experimental evaluation designs has been made by researchers and evaluators (see Campbell & Stanley, 1963). Experimental studies include a control group that is exactly like the group receiving the program. Because the two groups are randomly selected, the teachers and students are essentially the same. Therefore, if you introduce a change in one group and not the other and detect a change in the experimental group, that is considered strong evidence for the program's effectiveness. If this situation sounds unfamiliar, it is not surprising. Experimental designs are used effectively in laboratory settings but are rarely found in educational contexts because children and teachers are almost never randomly assigned to classes and experimental programs are almost never randomly assigned either. Rather, special needs, scheduling conflicts, personal requests, and a variety of other factors determine which children are placed with which teacher. Frequently, teachers volunteer to try out new programs. Therefore, it is often difficult to draw strong causal connections between the introduction of a program and results. Additional pitfalls and several possible quasi-experimental designs that educators can use to remedy—at least partly—the lack of randomization will be described in the second half of this chapter.

Characteristics of Effective Evaluations

As different as the small classroom study and large-scale district study appear on the surface, there are some common elements of sound evaluation design that appear in all good evaluation studies. They incorporate a concerted effort to understand both whether there were any meaningful changes in the students' thinking skills and dispositions and how those changes came about. Therefore, in conducting an effective evaluation, whether large or small, the evaluator will attend to the following ten concerns:

1. The evaluator should determine whether or not the program being evaluated took place.

2. The evaluator should compare the performance of the students before and after the program was introduced (and, if possible and appropriate, use a comparison group).

3. The evaluator should watch for unintended effects (or side effects) in addition to the program's desired effects.

4. The evaluator should gather data on a variety of measures and activities so as to allow the effects of the program every chance to be seen.

5. The evaluator should check all tests that are used to evaluate the program for their ability (i.e., sensitivity) to measure the desired changes.

6. The evaluator should try to use unobtrusive measures so that the mere fact of being evaluated doesn't actually bring about some of the desired changes.

7. The evaluator should look for changes that do not occur immediately.

8. The evaluator should look at whether the changes that occur early in the program are also sustained over time.

9. The evaluator should look for a transfer from the specific situations in which the thinking skills were taught to other more general situations.

10. The evaluator should question the meaning of the results—both positive and negative—to understand their implications and limitations for decision making.

Although there are similarities between well designed large- and small-scale evaluation studies, there are some essential differences resulting from the intimacy of the classroom on one hand and the variety of available resources used by larger-scale studies on the other. This chapter will now focus on evaluating thinking skills and dispositions within the classroom with the teacher as the primary audience. Then the needs of administrators, state and national test makers, and program developers will be addressed. An array of existing tests and instruments as well as some recent approaches developed by state departments of education to assess thinking skills in large-scale testing programs will be presented.

THE TEACHER AS THINKING SKILLS EVALUATOR

The thinking skills and attitudes to be evaluated in the classroom must be directly linked to the teacher's goals. If the teacher chooses an existing program, the goals are prescribed by that choice. If the teacher chooses to develop a series of learning activities and processes in an infusion model, the evaluation will be focused on the selected goals. However, in both types of situations, for maximum success, the teacher and students should be clear about the goals.

Developing and Using Criteria for Effective Thinking

To conduct an evaluation, it is necessary to develop a set of evaluative criteria. These criteria will specify the discernible behaviors and dispositions (or attitudes) that accompany effective thinking. The teacher can develop these criteria alone, with colleagues, or in collaboration with the students. Ideally, it should include the students, because until they both understand and internalize the evaluation criteria, they are less likely to incorporate them into their behavior. The primary source of the students' criteria for effective thinking is their own experience. Therefore, a very fruitful activity can be the generation of evaluation criteria that will allow each student to compare his or her own conceptions of effective thinking with the conceptions of other students and the teacher. Once the tentative criteria are established, each member of the class should test them against real-world life situations. Do people whom they consider to be good thinkers—in school, on television, in their neighborhood—display those skills? Do people whom they consider to be poor thinkers display evidence of deficiencies on those skills?

The participation of students in establishing criteria and trying them out is important for five reasons. The first is that in participating in the definition of good thinking and the development of standards, the teachers and students will develop a clear set of goals. Any misunderstandings can be clarified during discussions. This results in a second advantage—if the teacher and students agree on what good thinking is and how it can be recognized, chances are greater that students and teachers together can monitor their progress. A third reason is that it gives the students a sense of ownership—a genuine sense of having had a meaningful part in defining desirable behavior and setting standards for judging it. A fourth advantage stems from the application of these criteria to models that demonstrate good thinking. When students gain experience in applying the criteria to models of effective and less effective thinkers, they may enhance their own ability to apply effective thinking skills to a variety of real-life situations. Finally, having a clear idea of what behaviors and dispositions constitute effective thinking will result in evaluations that are less impressionistic and more accurate.

Using a Wide-Angle and Telephoto Lens

It is important to use at least two lenses in evaluating thinking skills and dispositions. The first is a wide-angle lens that will allow the teacher to look at the entire class. This might be particularly useful on occasions when the whole class is engaged in a discussion of an issue on which opinions differ. The second is a telephoto lens that allows the teacher to look carefully at the behavior of the individual students. This can occur either in a group setting, where the teacher focuses on a selected subset of the students, or in activities in which children are working individually to produce a piece of writing or artwork. Both perspectives are important because either alone can be misleading.

At the Connecticut Thinking Skills Conference (CTSC, 1985), both Bransford and Nickerson described examples of how, without specific criteria for evaluating thinking skills, one can look at the class through the wide-angle lens and be misled. In the first situation, Bransford described a classroom using the LOGO program designed by Papert (1980). In LOGO, children work individually to program a computer to make designs. The program is intended to develop a wide variety of thinking skills involved in creativity, problem solving, planning, and so forth. Bransford described his impressions upon entering the LOGO classroom. He noted that the students were involved in discovery learning, there was tremendous excitement in the room, there were no discipline problems, and the students were having fun. Through the wide-angle lens, he said that it was the kind of situation that looked idyllic. However, when he switched to the telephoto lens to look carefully at the behavior of individual students, he noted that some of them were not using appropriate thinking skills. Rather than planning ahead, some students were using trial and error to develop their designs. Those children required more assistance from the teacher to develop the skills and strategies needed to create designs more systematically.

Perkins shared some of his experiences in observing some of the Project Intelligence lessons designed for use in the Republic of Venezuela. He described situations in which the students looked active, were answering the questions the teacher asked, and reported liking the materials. He noted that often on the basis of just such behaviors, teachers and program designers conclude that the class went very well. Yet, when they looked at the individual students' performance on exercises based on the lesson, it became obvious that many students had not learned the skills required. In reflecting upon this example, Perkins noted that in most classroom lessons, chances are that only 20 or 30 percent of the students are responding and the rest are doing something else.

Using a wide-angle lens does not have to result in impressionistic evaluations. It is quite possible to use the criteria described earlier to look at the entire class systematically. If open-mindedness is a criterion for evaluating thinking, the teachers and students can look for the extent to which open-mindedness is reflected by the participants in the discussion. The same can be true for focusing on the extent to which the students are providing reasons and evidence for their opinions, building upon others' ideas, and making connections. Using either lens, it is possible to monitor how frequently the students ask each other for elaboration and clarification. The situations described by Bransford and Perkins reinforce the importance of applying specific and nonimpressionistic criteria to evaluating students' thinking through both lenses. Although being busy, being excited, being well behaved, and answering questions are generally desirable characteristics of effective classrooms, they do not guarantee that effective thinking is occurring. These examples alert us to the importance of evaluating the quality of students' products and listening carefully to the content of the discussion. If teachers and students have jointly developed the criteria for judging the success of an activity, this can help to prevent very noticeable effects like students' enthusiasm from blurring our vision of less obvious behaviors that truly reflect students' improved thinking skills and dispositions.

Evaluating Continually

The thinking skills and dispositions described throughout this book are not developed in a day or a month. They require continual attention and monitoring. Even though teachers might be very interested in looking at growth from the beginning of the year to the end of the year, they will need more than just a pretest and a posttest for evaluation to be useful. Teachers need to collect data over time and chart the progress of students on the important dimensions. In documenting samples of the group's behavior over time, videotapes and audiotapes of classroom discussions are useful. So are anecdotal notes made by teachers and students while discussing or silently reflecting on what went well and what went poorly during that day's activities. At the individual level, the teacher can use students' portfolios of writing and artwork. For example, students might keep daily journals in which they reflect upon their own progress and the progress of the group as a whole. Or they might fill out short questionnaires from time to time that apply the criteria to the day's events and their role in them.

This is akin to what Perkins (CTSC, 1985) has referred to as "taking the pulse" of the classroom on a regular basis. It also supports Quellmalz's (CTSC, 1985) view of classroom evaluation as a description of students' strengths and weaknesses. Furthermore, it is consistent with Arthur Costa's (1983) challenge to replace test scores with "individual cognitive maps" (p. 219). Costa advocates that teachers pay careful attention not only to what the child knows but also to how the child behaves when he or she doesn't know the answer to a question.

Looking for Sustained Effects

Continually monitoring behavior not only permits a look at new changes but enables us to assess the sustaining effects of the changes. Often educational programs are evaluated only immediately following their implementation, and any conclusions made about effectiveness are made on the basis of short-term results. Teachers are in a unique position to learn about the long-term effects of instruction. When teachers watch children's thinking over the course of the school year, they can see whether certain skills and dispositions are maintained or disappear. This long-term perspective will increase our understanding of the characteristics of those skills and dispositions that require interim reinforcement for maintenance and those that do not.

Looking for Transfer

One of the implications of Perkins' chapter on learning strategies in this volume is that once certain powerful strategies have been learned, they will be retained and applied in a variety of learning situations. Other less powerful skills and strategies will not be applied outside of the context in which they are learned. Looking for transfer may have the effect of increasing the probability of transfer. If providing evidence is an important criterion for evaluating thinking, students should be on the alert for opportunities to look for supportive evidence in their reading lesson, their social studies activity, the commercials they see on television, and the claims they hear made by candidates running for office. The more varied the tasks and situations used to apply the criteria of good thinking skills and strategies, the more likely is the student to internalize and transfer their use.

Looking for Side Effects

Having evaluation criteria based upon models of effective thinking does not necessarily mean that teachers and students need to be blind to side effects. Scriven (1972) described an approach to evaluation called goal-free evaluation, in which the evaluator does not have access to the objectives of the program. He claimed that this allows the evaluator to be open to seeing changes of all types—even those not explicitly addressed by the program. Even though there is much to be gained from a clear understanding of goals and criteria, there are advantages in remaining open to the unintended benefits and costs of programs. What if the discussions being implemented by the thinking-skills program are so interesting that students' attendance improves? What if students' curiosity has been so stimulated that they are using the library more frequently? What if there has been a dramatic improvement in the students' respect for one another? What if parents call to praise the school for long hours of individual research their children are engaged in at home? Or on a more controversial note, what if some parents are calling the school to complain that their children are asking them too many questions or to justify their positions? Remaining open to unintended changes may increase our appreciation of the potential impact of teaching thinking skills.

Looking for Metacognition

John Flavell (1976) has fostered a great deal of interest in metacognition, which refers to the awareness and control of one's own thinking. Some of his examples include taking note of what we have trouble learning, reminding ourselves to double-check something before accepting it as fact, being sure to scrutinize each alternative in a multiple-choice test before selecting an answer, and sensing that it is important to write something down before forgetting it. If teachers and students believe that being metacognitive is an aspect of effective thinking, they should look for examples of introspection, retrospection, and "futurespection." The evaluation should document examples of students' thinking out loud—describing how they plan, monitor, and evaluate, including how they represent and solve problems. It should capture examples of students' discussing their misconceptions and errors as well as their insights and strategies. It is important to document how students think they might have prevented certain problems and how they would approach similar problems differently in the future.

Using a Variety of Approaches

Teachers who have tried a variety of approaches to measure the progress of their students' thinking skills know that students often respond differently to different measures. Last spring, several teachers from four Connecticut school districts were developing curricula to improve the evaluative comprehension skills of their third- and fourth-grade students. Several of these teachers taught in schools where students' reading and writing achievement test scores were relatively low. These teachers observed that often their poorest readers and writers were among their best thinkers. In class discussions about real life problems, their poorer readers often provided some of the most creative and ingenious responses, often surprising the other students as well as the teacher. In fact, many of these students gained new respect as a result of these discussions. Unfortunately, when these same students had to write their responses to similar problems, they wrote very poorly and received poor evaluations.

Certainly, discussions and writing tasks are both rich forms of evaluating thinking. The fact that they can provide conflicting data about children's thinking may have to do with the fact that some students may be able to think clearly but have trouble writing down their ideas. Other students may write quite well, yet be shy about speaking in front of their classmates. These individual differences make it necessary for teachers to use different approaches in their assessment of thinking skills. The following sections will describe several categories of students' behaviors that provide rich opportunities for evaluating thinking. These include discussions, writing, and other sustained projects in art, science, social studies, math, and so on.

Using Discussions to Evaluate Thinking

Before describing some approaches to evaluating discussions, it is important to contrast two activities that are quite different but are often called by the same name. Brandt (1985) distinguishes between recitation and discussion. Recitation occurs when teachers ask students questions for which the teacher already has the right answer. A discussion, according to a definition provided by Bridges (1979), is used to develop knowledge, understanding, and/or judgment about the matter under discussion. It requires not only the advancing of multiple points of view, but also that the participants are disposed to examining those points of view.

This section will draw upon the evaluation experiences of Lipman's Philosophy for Children program for upper-elementary and middle-school children described in this volume and the critical thinking project developed by the Pittsburgh public schools. The Pittsburgh project, which focuses on generating philosophical discussions in high school draws from both the Saint John's College program in Annapolis, Maryland, and the Great Books program (Great Books Foundation, Chicago, Illinois). Both of these programs try to create a community of inquiry in which students discuss important philosophical issues for which there are no right and wrong answers.

Lipman (CTSC, 1985) suggested a variety of criteria to use in evaluating the community of inquiry that he strives to create through his Philosophy for Children program. These criteria can be used by students and teachers in reflecting upon the discussion as a whole or they can be used by each child to assess his or her own participation in the discussion.

Students challenge one another for reasons and examples.

Students offer counterexamples, counterinstances, and counterarguments.

Students piggyback on one another's comments.

Students identify the function of their comments (e.g., "I would like to comment on A, add to B, or disagree with C.").

Students view themselves as scholars discussing worthwhile materials.

Students search for and present relationships between the subject under discussion and other relevant school subjects and outside experiences.

Students relate the specific subject under discussion to more general principles.

Students ask relevant and sequential questions.

Students don't take things for granted, but ask for justification.

Students ask for clarification (e.g., "What do you mean?").

There is considerable overlap between the criteria suggested by Lipman and those being developed in Pittsburgh. The Pittsburgh program has only been in place since the beginning of the 1985–1986 school year and is being cited here as an example for how a teacher might go about evaluating discussions. Although the Pittsburgh group is currently mounting a large-scale evaluation using a variety of approaches, many of these can be employed on a small scale by teachers working alone or in pairs. The Pittsburgh system has arranged for each teacher in the program to videotape discussions at regular intervals. A nearby university is providing observers to code discussions for desirable behaviors such as student-generated questions, the use of the text as evidence, evidence of collaborative learning, students' interactions among themselves, examples of students complimenting each other, and so forth. Teachers are asking students to reflect upon the discussions following their completion by asking them to respond to open-ended questions such as, "What did you like or not like about the discussion?"

In addition, students are asked to fill out a checklist that evaluates both the discussions and their participation in them with particular reference to whether students felt that they backed up their opinions, strove for understanding, listened carefully, spoke up freely, and were courteous. The Pittsburgh program is still in the early stages of developing criteria, but it is obvious that the student checklist is beginning to move students in a direction of monitoring their own thinking skills and dispositions. Through an analysis of the videotapes, scripts, open-ended responses, and checklists, the Pittsburgh project hopes to develop a broad, multidimensional set of criteria. It is essential for the discussants to understand the criteria for judging sound evidence or the relevance of one's own experiences to those in the text. Similarly, when it comes to dispositional elements, students need to know precisely what it means to criticize in acceptable and responsible ways.

Finally, the Pittsburgh research and evaluation department will also look at the test scores of these students on subsets of standardized reading tests that are thought to be related to the program.

Using Writing to Evaluate Thinking

Over the past decade, there has been an increase in the attention paid to teaching and evaluating writing. Two of the important impetuses for this increase have been work on the writing process (See Hansen, Newkirk & Graves, 1985; Murray 1985) and recent large-scale assessment efforts growing out of the work of the NAEP and at least 13 state departments of education, which have incorporated direct measures of writing into their state-wide assessments (see Baron, 1984; Quellmalz, 1984; Williams, 1984). One of the major findings of these large-scale assessments is that students have difficulty writing persuasively. According to the NAEP (1981), during the period between 1974 and 1979, only 21 percent and 19 percent, respectively, of students in the United States were able to write an acceptable persuasive essay. The major difficulty is that students are not proficient in providing support for their beliefs. Many students make assertions and unwarranted generalizations without providing reasons and examples to illustrate their points.

Yet the problem is not limited to persuasive writing. One of the major differences between an effective and ineffective narrative essay is the degree of elaboration. Many children are not experienced in elaborating upon their ideas. Many classroom activities require listing rather than elaborating. This produces students who can easily generate many ideas, but find it much more difficult to provide details.

Writing can be used in many ways to help students and teachers clarify and evaluate their thinking. Conferencing with peers and teachers has been used quite effectively to improve children's thinking and writing (see Newkirk, 1985). Students read each other's work and describe to the writer what they think the message is. Where suitable, they might ask questions of clarification, elaboration, and justification. Through this proess, children begin to generate, apply, and internalize criteria of good thinking. They learn to focus and organize. And because they have an audience, they apply principles of appropriateness, credibility, and relevance. As a sustained activity, writing has the potential to develop many of the dispositions associated with the development of thinking skills. Certainly it can foster persistence and precision in both thought and the use of language. Therefore, writing provides opportunities for evaluating many of the dispositions and abilities that accompany good thinking.

A second and very different kind of writing allows other insights into children's thinking. Logs or journals that children keep can be used for a number of purposes. For example, at the end of a day, children might be asked to reflect upon the day's events. In Bristol, Connecticut, students were asked each day to use any of three ideas as a writing topic: what connections they can make between what happened during the day's class and other experiences; how someone with a different point of view might view the day's events; or what question they would like to have answered about the day's events. Such entries allow the teacher to evaluate whether students have internalized the basic principles of the lesson, whether they can transfer the principles appropriately, and/or what questions they still have. These daily glimpses into children's thought processes allow the teacher to make more strategic interventions than they might otherwise be able to make.

When evaluating children's ideas, it is desirable to provide them with specific feedback related to their thinking, including requests for further clarification, elaboration, justification; questions designed to help students change the scope of their focus; or suggestions for improving the organization. Teachers might ask questions about sequence, relevance, consistency, or precision. Furthermore, Lipman recommends that, when appropiate, teachers should indicate when a student's thinking made the teacher think. This could be accomplished through brief comments that build upon the child's thinking or provide another perspective on an issue being discussed.

Using Tests to Evaluate Thinking

Barry Beyer (1985) recommends that if teachers are serious about teaching thinking, their tests should evaluate thinking. His reason is simple—students always ask if what they are being taught is going to be on the test. Therefore, tests send clear signals to students about what is important. This alone is sufficient justification to include thinking skills on tests.

As noted earlier, writing, especially extended discourse, provides rich opportunities to evaluate and reinforce thinking skills. Essay examinations allow students to explain their reasons as well as state their conclusions. Teachers can use these evaluations to improve their understanding of students' reasoning processes and diagnose their misconceptions.

Many teachers wonder whether multiple-choice tests can be used effectively to measure thinking. The answer is a qualified yes. There are many thinking skills that are amenable to multiple-choice testing. For example, Ennis (CTSC, 1985) claimed that for testing deductive reasoning, multiple-choice tests are quite adequate. There are many types of questions that have only one correct answer and can be assessed on multiple-choice tests.

The selection of item formats is an issue that goes well beyond the classroom. State and national assessment developers have thought about the advantages and disadvantages of different types of items. Multiple-choice tests, though time consuming to construct, are very efficient to score and have a short turn-around time. In contrast, essay tests are more time consuming as well as expensive to score. In addition, they create logistical problems. If scores are returned to students, each paper is generally read twice, often creating the need for hundreds of trained scorers to score thousands of essays. Therefore, even though direct measures of writing have been used to assess writing skills, they are not frequently used to assess thinking skills. Two recent exceptions are California (see Kneedler, 1985; Quellmalz, 1985), which has integrated writing into the content areas, and Connecticut, which on its 1984–1985 science test, included some open-ended short essay responses into its sample testing program.

Infusing thinking skills into content-area tests creates some interesting interpretation problems. Specifically, if a multiple-choice item requires that students both have some knowledge of content and use that knowledge in some way and then students get the item wrong, it is hard to know why. In order to specifically address that problem, Connecticut has used an approach called "nesting" (see Baron and Kallick, 1985; Baron, 1986). Nesting requires the development of a series of questions. One question is designed to learn whether students know a concept; a second question is written to see whether they can apply that knowledge. It is then easy to find out how many more students have the knowledge than can apply that knowledge. Students might know what a veto is, but be unable to recognize an appropriate situation for its use. Without the knowledge question, it is not possible to know why the students got the application question wrong. In developing nesting designs, the work of Bloom, Englehart, Furst, Hill, and Krathwolh (1956) and Hunkins (1972) is quite useful.

A second approach is to evaluate thinking skills outside the context of academic subject matter. Ennis has developed several critical thinking tests (described later in this chapter) that try to isolate thinking skills from subject matter knowledge and embed them in common everyday situations. For teachers interested in using this approach, Ennis (CTSC, 1985) provided a few practical hints based on the fact that test takers have different background assumptions and different degrees of sophistication. Therefore, what might be credible for one person may not be credible for another. Ennis (CTSC, 1985) suggested:

> In testing for credibility of sources, ask for a *preference* rather than an absolute judgment of whether a particular source is credible. That is, ask which of two particular statements is more credible. A reasonable third choice might be "neither, they are equally credible."

> Similarly, with induction in judging hypotheses, instead of asking whether a particular hypothesis is justified, provide some evidence that bears on the hypothesis and then ask whether the evidence supports the hypothesis, is opposed to it, or neither.

> With identifying assumptions, don't ask whether an assumption is made; instead, ask which of the following possible statements is probably an assumption.

Of course, there are many thinking skills for which multiple-choice tests are not well suited. As Nickerson (CTSC, 1985) so aptly stated:

> There is something mildly incongruous about teaching dialectical reasoning on open-ended multilogical questions as Richard Paul has defined it and then testing what the student has learned by giving an objective test which presumes that all questions have a correct answer.

Each author in this book has described situations in which the correctness of a response depended upon the quality of the reasoning behind it. Such situations are not amenable to multiple-choice formats.

Using Other Performance Tasks to Evaluate Thinking

Because the present reward structure motivates students to prepare for evaluation activities, the challenge for teachers is to develop evaluation methods that as closely as possible mirror the behaviors that are sought. To the extent that teachers use rich, naturalistic, sustained, and somewhat novel tasks, having the evaluation activity serve as a motivator is desirable. Only when the evaluation tools are impoverished substitutes for the desired behaviors should one question the value of requiring students to prepare for such tests. The same logic applies to teaching to the test. If the test reflects what is truly desirable, teaching to the test (i.e., its objectives, not its answers) is optimal.

There are many other kinds of performance tasks that teachers can use to measure students' thinking. In science or social studies classes, students might be asked to design an experiment that can be evaluated in terms of the reliability of the findings. For example, did the students use careful controls? In mathematics, students could be asked to solve multistep problems and provide calculations to check their work. In art, they could be asked to design a building or an object according to certain specifications or to achieve certain purposes. In English, they could be asked to design a stage set or select the cast for a dramatic version of a piece of literature. Each of these tasks demands the use of a variety of critical and creative thinking skills.

Bransford (CTSC, 1985) suggests that teachers try to include some evaluation activities designed to assess the effectiveness of groups of children working together. At the Shoreham-Wading River School, students have many occasions to work on sustained group projects. Recently, a middle-school language arts class planned, developed, and presented a multimedia slide show on different aspects of nuclear war to audiences in the community. In a history class, each student took on the role of a person in Colonial times and simulated the dress and activities of that period. At the end of several weeks, the activity culminated in a debate and vote by each member of the Colonial community on whether the colonists should declare their independence.

Using Unobtrusive Measures

A variety of unobtrusive measures can be very useful in evaluating the effects of thinking skills programs. Such measures make use of already existing data. Two examples of unobtrusive measures used in other evaluation settings were the frequency with which the carpet needed to be replaced in front of the most popular exhibits in a museum and the rate of books checked out of a library following certain events. (Being unobtrusive does not mean that the measures will be impressionistic; it does mean that they do not interfere with students' performance and do not require additional instructional time for the purpose of evaluation.) Webb, Campbell, Schwartz, and Sechrest (1966) described some creative ways of using physical traces, archival data, and observations, many of which can be adapted to the classroom.

Interpreting Results

If the evaluation tasks are rich and the students do well on them, the teacher has reason to be pleased. It appears that the students understood what was expected of them and displayed the appropriate skills and dispositions. But what if the results are poor? Although there are many reasons why this might be true, several of them are more common than others. Teachers might begin with questions such as these:

Do the tasks truly promote the desired activities?

Is the time allowed sufficient for the students to attain the skills?

Do the classroom and school environments support the skills and dispositions sought?

If the teachers and students believe in the importance of the thinking skills and dispositions being fostered, it may be well worth the time and energy to try to understand why the evaluation is not demonstrating the desired changes. The very process of exploring the meaning of poor evaluation results may provide even more useful information for program improvement than the results themselves.

THE SCHOOL ADMINISTRATOR AND PROGRAM DEVELOPER AS THINKING SKILLS EVALUATOR

School administrators and program developers generally want to design a study that will provide the answer to one major question: Is this an effective thinking skills program? This question spawns three related questions. First, if a group of students showed improvement on a measure of thinking skills, was it due to an effective thinking skills program? Second, if a group of students did not show improvement on a measure of thinking skills, was it due to an ineffective thinking skills program? Third, is it appropriate to generalize from the experience of these students and assume that the same will be true for other students?

Designing the Evaluation

To answer these three questions with some degree of certainty one needs to collect pretest and posttest data on appropriate and sensitive instruments. To analyze the importance of any changes between the pretests and posttests, it is generally important to use a control group, ideally with random assignment of students and teachers to the experimental and control groups. As noted earlier educational settings generally do not permit such an ideal design. An appropriate control group permits the evaluator to know what changes might have taken place without the program. Although other comparison groups can be used, they require that attention be paid to ascertain whether the groups differ on any important factors. Were the students who received the treatment the same as those who didn't in their motivation, intelligence, and interest? Were the teachers in one group more motivated or experienced?

Quasi-experimental designs try to overcome what has been lost when randomization is not feasible. One possible solution strategy is to use a group as its own control. For such a procedure to be interpretable, it is necessary to secure stable information about what the group was like both before and immediately after the intervention. Specifically, one needs baseline information over an extended period of time, perhaps weeks or months before the program is introduced. One also needs an extended observation period after the program has been introduced. This general type of design is discussed by Cook and Campbell (1979) under the heading simple interrupted time series. If there is another class similar to the one that is receiving the program, Cook and Campbell recommended that the second group serve as an equivalent no-treatment control group, thereby making the design more powerful than if no such comparison is possible.

Another frequently asked question is whether the positive effect of the experimental group is due to the Hawthorne effect, that is, whether being singled out for some special treatment produces the positive effect or whether the content of the intended treatment produces the effect. To avoid this problem, the control group also needs to feel that it is receiving some kind of special treatment—not an easy feat when it is not yet receiving the program. One technique that has been used successfully is a lagged onset design in which the control group is told at the beginning of the study that it will be receiving the program at a later time. This also helps school administrators to respond to the desire of the control group to receive the program.

Another possible scenario concerns a program for which there are no changes observed on a measure of thinking skills. Should we conclude that the program was ineffective? Just as positive results are not clear proof of an effective program, the lack of positive results is not clear proof of an ineffective program. Instead, there are many questions the evaluator should ask. Many of these were raised earlier and have to do with whether or not the program was properly implemented in the experimental group. Also, one might look at whether the instruments are appropriate and sensitive enough to measure the potential changes brought about by the program. This critical question requires careful scrutiny of the instruments on the part of those who know both the intended and possible unintended effects of the program. A detailed discussion of this issue appears later in the chapter. The evaluation should consider whether the program allowed sufficient time for slowly developing changes to take place. The evaluator should assess effects that develop slowly as well as those that develop early but fade over time. This approach assumes the use of a reasonably long time frame.

Finally, administrators and program developers must give thought to the question of generalizing from the specific context they are studying to others. If the students and teachers are randomly selected from the general population and there are no obvious extenuating circumstances, the results should be generalizable. However, if these are gifted students or learning disabled students, or if the teachers are particularly enthusiastic or experienced, these factors should be presented with the evaluation results and cited as possible limitations to the generalizability of the findings. It may prove helpful at the inception of the program to try it out in a context that is close to the one for which it is intended, that is, with the kinds of students and teachers with whom the program will ultimately be used.

Criteria for Selecting Appropriate Tests

Just as a teacher's testing program tells students a great deal about what the teacher values, a school's testing program tells the entire educational community what that school values. If a school places a high value on teaching for thinking, the tests used to assess students should reflect that commitment. If, on the other hand, the school's goals emphasize thinking skills but the testing program does not, this mixed message creates discomfort for teachers who may be striving to create lessons that match the school's goals but who worry that their students' progress may not be reflected in higher test scores. Therefore, it is important for the teaching of thinking skills that a school's goals, curriculum, and assessment be consistent with one another. If they are not, to the extent that the assessment is viewed as important, it may become the driving force in classrooms and result in an educational program that is more impoverished than the stated goals.

Frederiksen (1984) has called this "the real test bias." He expressed concern that schools often choose efficient tests over less efficient tests, leaving many important abilities untested—and untaught. He urged educators to develop instruments that would better reflect the whole domain of educational goals and then use those tests to improve education.

Unfortunately, in many schools the tests are not in synchrony with either the school's goals or the individual teacher's desire to teach for thinking. This section will describe criteria to use in selecting and developing tests to evaluate thinking at a school level. At the end, it will describe some of the existing instruments and scales that can be used and conclude with an echo of Frederickson's call for more comprehensive measures of children's thinking.

Reliability and Validity

Any test used to measure students' thinking should be reliable and valid. Reliability and validity have quite specific meanings when applied to measurement and evaluation. *Test-retest reliability* has to do with the extent to which results are replicable. Would a student receive the same score on the test if he or she took it several times? Would a student get the same score if two colleagues graded the same essay independently? *Internal consistency reliability* reflects the extent to which all of the items on the test are measuring the same construct.

In testing, there are several types of validity. What they share in common is a concern with what the test measures. *Content validity* refers to the extent to which the items sufficiently represent the domain of all possible items that might have been selected. Is the breadth of the thinking skills that have been taught reflected in the tests? There is a big difference between tests designed to measure thinking skills and tests that inadvertently measure thinking skills. This difference has to do with domain coverage. Furthermore, to the extent that representative items like the ones students will encounter in life are used, the evaluation will have sufficient content validity.

Construct validity has to do with whether the test measures what it purports to measure. That is why the teacher's definition of good thinking should be incorporated in both the instructional tasks and the evaluation instruments. This concept is elusive, and very few test publishers ever adequately demonstrate construct validity for their tests. Also, it is highly unlikely that administrators or teachers will have sufficient time or resources to do so. Yet it might be interesting to understand how it might be done. Psychometric approaches to measuring construct validity consider both convergent and discriminant information. First, they observe the degree to which the test results of students on the newly developed measures are consistent with those of other known and accepted measures of the same trait; then, they look at the extent to which the newly developed measures are inconsistent with those of known measures that test related yet different traits. Using a variety of evaluation approaches will assist in establishing construct validity.

A third type of validity is *predictive validity*. Sternberg (CTSC, 1985) suggests that teachers concern themselves with whether their evaluation results really do predict (or distinguish) which students are good thinkers. If they do not, he suggests finding or developing other measures.

A fourth type of validity could be called *validity of purpose*. One of the important questions administrators should ask is whether the test is a valid assessment of the purposes for which they are using it. For example, a reading test may be a very valid measure of reading, but it may not be a very sensitive measure of many of the children's thinking skills. An understanding of the limits inherent in using tests for purposes they were not intended to serve may prevent administrators from overinterpreting or misinterpreting test results. To avoid using a test to evaluate something for which it was not originally intended, it must be scrutinized for its sensitivity to the new purpose. Content, construct, and predictive validity for a test are limited to the context and purpose for which they were established; one test is not valid for everything.

Sensitivity to Change

In establishing the validity of a test for assessing thinking skills, administrators need to determine whether the test is sensitive enough to measure improvement in children's thinking. Sensitivity has two aspects—whether the test taps the skills taught and whether the children possess the enabling skills required by the test.

To assess the test's sensitivity, Ennis (CTSC, 1985) recommended that teachers and administrators actually take the test themselves. That would enable them to see if the test really measures the skills they are teaching in the classroom. If the thinking skills emphasized require making inferences and evaluating evidence, does the test under consideration (e.g., a standardized reading test) contain a substantial number of test questions that would be sensitive to improvement in those areas? Often, such analyses force teachers to conclude that many standardized reading tests contain a preponderance of questions at the literal comprehension level. If the test does not measure what is being taught, the test scores will not reveal that changes have taken place even when they have.

Another issue has to do with whether the children have the requisite enabling skills to perform the tasks required by the test. A test may include the desired thinking skills and children may have improved on those same skills, but if children cannot display their learning because of the way in which those skills are assessed, the conclusions reached will underestimate the true growth. To respond to reading questions that require making inferences, children must be able to understand the passages. An inability to read with understanding will interfere with the measurement of their critical thinking skills.

Utilizing Information

Another criterion for selecting a test is whether the information obtained about children's thinking is provided in a useful form for program improvement. Does the test provide a profile of students' strengths and weaknesses? Unless a test is specifically designed to provide information about students' thinking, the results may be represented in a form too general to be useful. A higher-order thinking score on a standardized reading test that clusters all nonliteral test items may not provide enough useful information for program improvement.

Can Standardized Norm-Referenced Achievement Tests Be Used to Measure Thinking Skills?

Standardized norm-referenced achievement tests play a very important role in most of our nation's schools. These tests are valid and reliable for their originally intended purpose—the assessment of reading and mathematics skills. If the school is going to use these instruments for an expanded purpose—one for which these tests were not originally intended—it is imperative that the administrators and teachers apply many of the criteria listed above.

Whimbey (1985) recently asserted that because there were strong correlations between standardized reading, mathematics, and ability tests and most tests of critical thinking, these tests were all measuring a common factor—one that has been called intelligence. Therefore, he stated that the latter group of tests— the ones measuring critical thinking—were essentially redundant and could be replaced by standardized tests. To illustrate this, he cited a study reported by Zenke and Alexander (1984) in which the Strategic Reasoning program was used with Chapter I students in Tulsa, Oklahoma. The program was evaluated by using the Educational Abilities Scale of the S.R.A. test battery, the Gates MacGinity reading test, and the Iowa Test of Basic Skills mathematics test. Because in a two-and-one-half-month instructional period, the experimental group gained four intelligence quotient points, seven months of growth on the reading test, and five months of growth in mathematics, the Strategic Reasoning program was judged by the authors to be successful.

Articles like Whimbey's and studies like Zenke and Alexander's raise some interesting methodological and conceptual questions. First of all, what does it mean to evaluate a thinking-skills program? If its sole purpose is to raise students' standardized test scores, then it appears as though the program has been successful. (Methodologically the reader should use caution in interpreting grade-equivalent scores to measure longitudinal change; see Hills, 1983.) However, if there are additional purposes of the thinking skills programs that are not measured on the basic skills tests, additional information is necessary to judge the success of students on those skills. The criteria of content, construct, and predictive validity, as well as sensitivity, help teachers to recognize important gaps.

The Zenke and Alexander situation is a pleasant one—people generally don't want to argue with success. But what about those situations in which teachers are convinced that the children's thinking has improved, but the norm referenced standardized tests scores have not? In these situations, issues of validity, sensitivity, sufficiency, and utility are of particular concern. If the tests are not sensitive to the instruction either because of lack of test coverage or deficiencies in the children's enabling skills, this mismatch must be understood. Otherwise, misattributions to the thinking-skills program are possible and unnecessary frustration will result.

Even if standardized tests were to meet the criteria of sensitivity and sufficiency, there are two additional limitations that administrators might want to consider. First, there are some thinking skills that cannot be assessed on multiple choice tests. Divergent skills such as those used to generate several possible hypotheses or different ways to test those hypotheses are not appropriate for standardized multiple-choice tests. Second, standardized tests do not directly measure changes in dispositions and attitudes. If a student becomes more open-minded and curious, it is unlikely that the standardized test will measure those changes.

Therefore, given the potential limitations in the sensitivity, breadth, and diagnosticity of standardized reading and math tests in the measurement of thinking skills, school administrators may want to diversify their evaluation resources.

Using General Tests of Critical Thinking

For the past several years Robert Ennis has been compiling a list of general and aspect-specific critical thinking tests. Ennis (1985) noted that his criterion for inclusion on the general list was that half of their items be critical thinking items with critical thinking being defined as "reasonable reflective thinking that is focused on deciding what to believe or do" (p. 303). The most recent version of Ennis's list of general tests is presented in Table 11-1. Ennis emphasizes that "anyone considering using any of these tests should examine the items with great care."

Evaluating Appropriate Attitudes and Dispositions

Program goals for teaching thinking too rarely include references to changes in student's attitudes and dispositions. Hartman and Barell (1985) found that only twelve of the fifty-four schools identified with thinking programs listed in the Association for Supervision and Curriculum Development Network Directory included attitudes or dispositions in their list of major program goals. (For lists of dispositions, see the chapters by Ennis and Nickerson in this book; Feuerstein, 1980; Costa, 1984; Duckworth, 1978; Brandt, 1985; Bolt, Beranak, & Newman and The Republic of Venezuela, 1986; and Hartman, 1985). These lists of attitudes and dispositions that accompany good thinking generally include being reflective, openminded, curious, persevering, precise, able to tolerate ambiguity, and so forth. Some sources (Hartman, 1985) also include internal locus of control and self-esteem as attitudes accompanying effective thinking. These lists were developed by first evaluating the characteristics of good thinkers and then by determining that these dispositions could be altered by systematic instruction and support. Teachers can help students acquire and refine these dispositions as well as evaluate the extent to which they are being displayed.

The topic of attitudes and dispositions has received recent attention from both philosophers and psychologists. Ennis (CTSC, 1985) advised, "as far as evaluating the critical thinking dispositions, I think the best way is to watch your students very closely. I don't know of any good paper and pencil way to evaluate dispositions and the dispositions are terribly important."

This area is ripe for teacher creativity and invention. If teachers (and perhaps students) can develop observational scales and other measures of dispositions and attitudes, they may be able to amass some very compelling data about the changes in students' dispositions and the effectiveness of instructional programs. Certainly, the idea of measuring students' attitudes is not new. Psychologists have successfully created attitude scales for many decades. In fact, many existing scales may prove useful for teachers who are interested in monitoring changes resulting from an emphasis on thinking skills. There currently exist instruments for measuring curiosity in children (Maw & Maw, 1971) and measuring closed-mindedness in young children (Figart, 1965, and Dommert, 1967, both contain versions of the Rokeach Dogmatism Scale). The School Attitude Measure (1980) assesses locus of control and self-concept and Covington's (1966) Childhood Attitude Inventory for Problem Solving (CAPS) measures another important dimension.

Nickerson, Perkins, and Smith (1985) in reviewing evaluation studies of the Instrumental Enrichment Program listed several other instruments used to

Table 11-1 Tests That Could Be Called Critical Thinking Tests, at Least in Part

Multiple choice

Basic Skills for Critical Thinking (1979, 5 forms) by Gary E. McCuen. Greenhaven Press, Inc., 577 Shoreview Park Rd., St. Paul, MN 55112.

Aimed at high school students; sections on source of information, primary and secondary sources, fact and opinion, prejudice and reason, stereotypes, ethnocentrism, library card catalogue, and *Reader's Guide to Periodical Literature*.

Cornell Critical Thinking Test, Level X (1985) by Robert H. Ennis and Jason Millman. Midwest Publications, PO Box 448, Pacific Grove, CA 93950.

Aimed at grades 4–14; sections on induction, credibility, observation, deduction, and assumption identification.

Cornell Critical Thinking Test, Level Z (1985) by Robert H. Ennis and Jason Millman. Midwest Publications, PO Box 448, Pacific Grove, CA 93950.

Aimed at advanced or gifted high school students, college students, and other adults; sections on induction, credibility, prediction and experimental planning, fallacies [especially equivocation], deduction, definition, and assumption identification.

New Jersey Test of Reasoning Skills (1983) developed by Virginia Shipman. IAPC, Test Division, Montclair State College, Upper Montclair, NJ 08043.

Aimed at grades 4–college; syllogism [including A,E,I,O statements] heavily represented; several items apiece on assumption identification, induction, good reasons, and kind and degree.

Ross Test of Higher Cognitive Processes (1976) by John D. Ross and Catherine M. Ross. Academic Therapy Publications, 20 Commercial Blvd., Novato, CA 94947.

Aimed at grades 4–college; sections on verbal analogies, deduction, assumption identification, word relationships, sentence sequencing, interpreting answers to questions, information sufficiency and relevance in mathematics problems, and analysis of attributes of complex stick figures.

Watson-Glaser Critical Thinking Appraisal (1980, 2 forms) by Goodwin Watson and Edward Maynard Glaser. The Psychological Corporation, a subsidiary of Harcourt Brace Jovanovich, 7500 Old Oak Boulevard, Cleveland, OH 44130.

Aimed at grade 9 through adulthood; sections on induction, assumption identification, deduction, conclusion-logically-following-beyond-a-reasonable-doubt, and argument evaluation.

Essay

The Ennis-Weir Critical Thinking Essay Test (1985) by Robert H. Ennis and Eric Weir. Midwest Publications, PO Box 448, Pacific Grove, CA 93950.

Aimed at grade 7 through college; also intended to be used as a teaching material; incorporates getting the point, seeing the reasons and assumptions, stating one's point, offering good reasons, seeing other possibilities [including other possible explanations], and responding appropriately to/avoiding equivocation, irrelevance, circularity, reversal of an if-then [or other conditional] relationship, overgeneralization, credibility questions, and the use of emotive language to persuade.

Compiled by Robert H. Ennis, 1985.

measure attitudes and dispositions thought to have been enhanced by that program. They included the Intellectual Achievement Responsibility Questionnaire (Crandall, Katkovsky, & Crandall, 1965), the Rosenberg (1965) Self-Esteem Scale, the Piers-Harris (1969) Self-Concept Scale, the Picture Motivation Scale (Haywood, 1971), the Nowicki-Strickland (1973) Locus of Control Scale, and the Student's Environmental Preference Survey (Gordon, 1975). Two additional sources of attitude scales are Cohen (1976) and Robinson and Shaver (1973).

The idea of measuring dispositions and attitudes holds great promise for the evaluation of a thinking skills program. This is being explored by members of both the Connecticut Statewide Thinking Skills Committee and several participants in a staff seminar coordinated by Robert Swartz at the University of Massachusetts, Boston Harbor Campus. Furthermore, the Groton-Dunstable Regional School District in Massachusetts has begun to develop some observable behavioral criteria for some of these dispositions. To evaluate a student's flexibility in thinking, they look at whether a student:

can be heard considering, expressing, or paraphrasing another's point of view or rationale;

can state several ways of solving the same problem and can evaluate the merits and consequences of two or more alternate courses of action; and

when making decisions, uses such words as "however," "on the other hand," "if you look at it another way . . ." or "John's idea is. . . , but Mary's idea is. . . ."

CONCLUSIONS

As noted earlier, what the evaluator chooses to measure sends an important message. We are becoming increasingly more sophisticated about what constitutes good thinking. We are gaining a better understanding of the dispositions and attitudes good thinkers display. We know that good thinking includes a large number of skills and strategies as diverse as philosophical inquiry, problem solving, dialogical reasoning and spatial analogies. We know that good thinking includes creative as well as critical thinking.

The challenge for evaluators is to move from an intellectual understanding of the breadth of good thinking to an evaluation design that reflects that same breadth through its choice of instruments and tasks. To restrict oneself to those skills that are easily measured will do a serious disservice to the children and the teachers whose programs are being evaluated. The real test bias today is the one Frederiksen described, the tendency to measure what can easily be defined on multiple-choice tests. If we take seriously Costa's statement that real thinking goes on when the student does not know the answer to a question, it confirms the fact that, as evaluators, we have a lot of good thinking ahead of us.

REFERENCES

Baron, J. (1984). Writing assessment in Connecticut—a holistic eye toward identification and an analytic eye toward instruction. *Educational Measurement: Issues and Practice*, 33:27–28,35.

Baron, J. (1986). Assessing higher order thinking skills in Connecticut: Lessons from Connecticut. In C. P. Kearney (Ed.), *Assessing higher order thinking skills*. ERIC/TME Report 90. Princeton, N.J.: Educational Testing Service.

Baron, J., & Kallick, B. (1985). Assessing thinking: What are we looking for? And how can we find it? In A. L. Costa (Eds.), *Developing minds: A resource book for teaching thinking*. Alexandria, Virginia: Association for Supervision and Curriculum Development.

Beyer, B. (1985). Presentation at The State of Thinking Conference. Detroit, Mich.

Bloom, B. S., Englehart, M. D., Furst, E. J., Hill, W. H., and Krathwohl, D. R. (1956). In B. S. Bloom (Ed.), *Taxonomy of educational objectives: the classification of educational goals. Handbook I: Cognitive domain*. New York: McKay.

Bolt, Beranek, & Newman and The Republic of Venezuela (1986). *Odyssey: A curriculum for thinking*. Watertown, Mass.: Mastery Education Corporation.

Brandt, R. (1985). A preliminary synthesis of teaching thinking. Mimeograph, distributed in Fairfield, Connecticut.

Bridges, D. (1979). *Education, democracy and discussion*. Windsor, Berks: National Foundation for Educational Research in England and Wales.

Campbell, D. T., and Stanley, J. C. (1963). Experimental and quasi-experimental designs for research on teaching. In N. L. Gage (Ed.), *Handbook of research on teaching*. Chicago: Rand McNally.

Cohen, L. (1976). *Educational research in classrooms and schools: A manual of materials and methods*. London: Harper & Row.

Connecticut Thinking Skills Conference (CTSC). (1985). Sponsored by the Connecticut State Department of Education and the Institute for Teaching and Learning, Wallingford, Conn.

Cook, T. D., & Campbell, T. D. (1979). *Quasi-experimentation: Design and analysis issues for field settings*. Chicago: Rand McNally.

Costa, A. L. (1983). Teaching toward intelligent behavior. In W. Maxwell (Ed.), *Thinking: The expanding frontiers*. Philadelphia: Franklin.

Costa, A. L. (1984). Thinking: How do we know students are getting better at it? Mimeograph, distributed at the Harvard Conference on Thinking, Cambridge, Mass.

Covington, M. V. (1966). Childhood attitude inventory for problem solving (CAPS). Berkeley: Department of Psychology, University of California.

Crandall, V.C., Katkovsky, W., & Crandall, V. J. (1965). Intellectual achievement responsibility questionnaire. Chicago: University of Chicago Press.

Dommert, E. M. (1967). An adaptation of Rokeach's dogmatism scale for use with elementary school children. M. A. thesis, Texas Woman's University, Denton, Texas.

Duckworth, E. (1978). *The African primary science program: An evaluation and extended thoughts*. Grand Forks: University of North Dakota.

Ennis, R. (1985). Tests that could be called critical thinking tests. In A. L. Costa (Ed.), *Developing minds: A resource book for teaching thinking*. Alexandria, Virginia: Association for Supervision and Curriculum Development.

Feuerstein, R. (1980). *Instrumental enrichment: An intervention program for cognitive modifiability.* Baltimore: University Park.

Flavell, J. H. (1976). Metacognitive aspects of problem solving. In L. B. Resnick (Ed.), *The nature of intelligence.* Hillsdale, N.J.: Erlbaum.

Figart, R. L. (1965). An elementary school form of the dogmatism scale: development of an instrument for use in studies of belief-disbelief systems of children in grades 4, 5, and 6. Ed.D. dissertation, Ball State University.

Frederiksen, N. (1984). The real test bias. *American Psychologist,* 39:1–10.

Gordon, L. V. (1975). Student's environmental preference survey. *In measures of psychological assessment: A guide to 3,000 original sources and their applications.* Ann Arbor: Survey Research Center, Institute for Social Research, University of Michigan.

Hanson, J., Newkirk, T., & Graves, D. (Eds.). (1985). *Breaking ground: Relating reading and writing in the elementary school.* Portsmouth, N.H.: Heinemann Educational Books.

Hartman, H. (1985). Developing thinking holistically. Annual Conference of Educators and Scholars, Hackensack, N.J.

Hartman, H., & Barell, J. (1985). The flip side of cognition: Attitudes which foster thinking. International Society for Individualized Instruction Conference on Teaching Thinking Skills, Newark, N.J.

Haywood, H. C. (1971). Individual differences in motivational orientation: A trait approach. In H. I. Day, D. E. Berlyne, & D. E. Hunt (Eds.), *Intrinsic motivation: A new direction in education.* Toronto: Holt, Rinehart and Winston.

Hills, J. R. (1983). Interpreting grade-equivalent scores. *Educational Measurement: Issues and Practice,* 2:15, 21.

Hunkins, F. P. (1972). *Questioning strategies and techniques.* Boston: Allyn & Bacon.

Kneedler, P. E. (1985). *Assessment of the critical thinking skills in history-social science.* California State Department of Education.

Maw, W. H., & Maw, A. J. (1971). The curiosity dimension of fifth grade children. *Child Development,* 42:2023–2031.

Murray, D. (1985). *A writer teaches writing* (2nd ed.). Boston: Houghton Mifflin.

National Assessment of Educational Progress (NAEP). (1981). *Reading, thinking, and writing.* Denver, Colo.: Education Commission of the States.

Newkirk, T. (Ed.). (1985). *To compose: Teaching writing in the high school.* Chelmsford, Mass.: Northeast Regional Exchange.

Nickerson, R. S., Perkins, D. N., & Smith, E. E. (1985). *The teaching of thinking.* Hillsdale, N.J.: Erlbaum.

Nowicki, S., & Strickland, B. R., (1973). A locus of control scale for children. *Journal of Consulting Clinical Psychology,* 40:148.

Papert, S. (1980). *Mindstorms.* New York: Basic Books.

Piers, E. V., & Harris, D. B. (1969). The Piers-Harris children's self-concept scale. Nashville: Counselor Recordings and Tests.

Quellmalz, E. S. (1984). Toward successful large-scale writing assessment: Where are we? Where do we go from here? *Educational Measurement: Issues and Practice,* 33:29–32, 35.

Quellmalz, E. S. (1985). Needed: Better methods for testing higher-order thinking skills. *Educational Leadership,* 43:29–36.

Robinson, J. P., & Shaver, P. R. (1973). *Measures of social psychological attitudes, Appendix B.* Ann Arbor: Survey Research Center, Institute for Social Research, University of Michigan.

Rosenberg, M. (1965). *Society and the adolescent self-image*. Princeton, N.J.: Princeton University Press.

Scriven, M. (1967). The methodology of evaluation. In R. W. Tyler, R. M. Gagne, & M. Scriven (Eds.), *Perspectives of curriculum evaluation*. American Educational Research Association Monograph Series on Curriculum Evaluation, No. 1. Chicago: Rand McNally.

Scriven, M. (1972). Pros and cons about goal-free evaluation. *Evaluation Comment*, 3:1–7.

School Attitude Measure 4/6. (1980). Glenview, Ill.: Scott, Foresman Test Division.

Webb, E. J., & Campbell, D. T., Schwartz, R. D., Sechrest, L. (1966). *Unobtrusive measures: Nonreactive research in the social sciences*. Chicago: Rand McNally.

Whimbey, A. (1985). You don't need a special "reasoning" test to implement and evaluate reasoning training. *Educational Leadership*, 43:37–39.

Williams, P. L. (1984). The application of direct writing assessments in five states. *Educational Measurement: Issues and Practice*, 33:19–28, 35.

Zenke, L., & Alexander, L. (1984). Teaching thinking in Tulsa. *Educational Leadership*, 42:81–84.

The idea for this chapter began with a symposium entitled, "Assessing Thinking Skills in the Classroom" held on March 13, 1985 at the Connecticut Thinking Skills Conference in Wallingford, Connecticut. The other nine authors represented in this volume spoke on this topic. I have referenced this symposium as (CTSC, 1985). The author wishes to thank Martin Espinola, Michael Galluzzo, Hope J. Hartman, Bena Kallick, Hannah Kruglanski, Steve Leinward, John P. Rickards, and Robert J. Sternberg for their helpful suggestions on this and earlier drafts of this chapter.

Part V

INTEGRATION

12

Robert J. Sternberg
Department of Psychology
Yale University

Questions and Answers about the Nature and Teaching of Thinking Skills

Anyone who has made it through 11 chapters on the nature and teaching of thinking skills might find it difficult to organize his or her thinking about thinking. The purpose of this chapter is to assist in this organization, and in particular, to discuss some of the major questions that were raised earlier. At the same time, I will attempt to integrate the ideas raised throughout the book, without making any claims to supply final answers. We simply do not have many, if any, final answers at this time, and perhaps we never will.

WHAT IS THE STRUCTURE OF THINKING SKILLS?

Someone once counted the number of personality traits that had been written about in the research literature on personality and found that the number was pushing 1000. After perusing this book, the reader might come to the same conclusion about the number of thinking skills that have been written about. The problem, of course, is not that there are close to 1000 personality traits or thinking skills (at least, that we know about), but that there are many different names for the same thing, with each investigator having his or her own preferred set of names.

When this problem occurs in the natural sciences, there are usually fairly direct means of resolution. For example, new chemical elements can be assigned unique atomic numbers, so that even if there is a dispute regarding their name, at least the chemists are able to recognize they are arguing about alternative names for a unique element. In the biological sciences, molecular structures can be compared. When scientists in both France and the United States claimed to have identified the virus that causes acquired immune deficiency syndrome (AIDS), it was possible to compare the molecular structures of the two viruses to determine that they were the same. In psychology, too, there exist techniques for identification of constructs, such as factor analysis and multidimensional scaling. But they provide nowhere near the same degree of definitive resolution as do the techniques in the physical and biological sciences. Although some have hoped that factor analysis would provide a periodic table of the mind, we have yet to identify a unique factorial structure upon which psychologists can agree in the same way that chemists agree on the periodic table.

Regardless of the particular scheme one prefers, I believe it useful to divide thinking skills into three kinds: executive processes (which I call metacomponents), nonexecutive performance processes (which I call performance components), and nonexecutive learning processes (which I call knowledge-acquisition components). Executive processes are used to plan, monitor, and evaluate one's thinking; performance processes are used actually to carry out the thinking; learning processes are used to learn how to think in the first place.

In Ennis's scheme, for example, "identifying or formulating a question," "identifying or formulating criteria for judging possible answers," and "keeping the situation in mind" would be examples of executive processes; "seeing similarities and differences," "deducing," and "making value judgments" would be examples of performance processes; and "asking and answering questions of clarification" such as "Why?," "What is your main point?," and "What do you mean by that?" are examples of learning processes. In Nickerson's scheme, "organizing thoughts" and "attempting to anticipate the probable consequences of alternative actions before choosing among them" would be examples of executive processes; "distinguishing between logically valid and invalid inferences" and "seeing similarities and analogies that are not readily apparent" would be performance processes; and "learning on one's own" and "listening carefully to other people's ideas" would be examples of learning processes.

One could go on, but I wish only to make the point that the various processes about which our theorists talk seem to be classifiable into the three categories of executive, nonexecutive performance, and nonexecutive learning processes, and that this distinction is useful in terms of the psychology of human thought because it points out that thinking skills are not of a single kind, and moreover, that they are not all equal. Executive processes are needed to decide upon, to keep track of, and, later, to evaluate the results of nonexecutive ones. Without executive processes, we would be like the proverbial chicken with its head cut off: We would be able to do things, but not to know why we should do them. Without performance processes, we would be perpetual planners—always planning what we should do but never getting any of it done. Without learning processes, we would never be able to learn how to do any of the things we do to begin with.

Although all of the chapters deal with the processes of human thinking, the chapters written by Ennis, Nickerson, Quellmalz, Lipman, Bransford et al., and Sternberg are particularly concerned with spelling out what some of these processes might be. Although their lists of processes are different, all seem to fit into the scheme outlined here.

IS HAVING THE RIGHT THOUGHT PROCESSES TANTAMOUNT TO BEING A GOOD THINKER?

The chapters in this volume make it clear that the answer to this question is a resounding no. There is much more to being a good thinker than just having the right thought processes. What else is involved? Consider four elements.

Strategies

Good thinkers not only have the right thought processes, but know how to combine them into workable strategies for solving problems. Virtually no problems can be solved by single processes of thought in isolation, so one must learn to combine these processes in a way that gets things done effectively. Consider Ennis's example of the jury trial or Perkins's analysis of knowledge as design. In order to reach a successful verdict in a trial or to complete an analysis of knowledge as design, one must combine a complex set of processes in a way that makes sense, not just jumble them together in a way that may not lead to anything concrete.

Mental Representations

Processes act on mental representations of the information in our environment. If these representations are inadequate, the processes will fail to solve the problems at hand. The case study mentioned in Swartz's chapter on the Battle of Lexington is a good example of the importance of mental representations. A major point of the lesson is to teach students to engage in what Paul calls dialogical thinking—to see things from multiple points of view, and especially in this case, the respective points of view of the Americans and the British. Unless one is able to represent information from both points of view, the lesson will fail dismally, regardless of the process used to handle the information about the battle.

Knowledge Base

Thinking cannot occur in the absence of knowledge. One needs something to think about. It is a mistake to concentrate only upon knowledge to the exclusion of thinking skills, because such concentration risks generating students who know a lot but who are unable to evaluate their knowledge. It is equally a mistake to concentrate only on thinking skills, because the result may be students who know how to think but who have nothing to think about.

Motivation to Use Thinking Skills

All of the finely honed thinking skills in the world will be for naught if they are not actually used. Students need to be encouraged to employ thinking skills and monitored in the actual use of these skills. Programs such as Quellmalz's HOT program and Lipman's Philosophy for Children are designed to bring thinking skills into the everyday lives of children, blurring as much as possible the distinction between thinking as a subject for academic study and thinking as a part of one's everyday life.

SHOULD THE TEACHING OF THINKING SKILLS BE SEPARATED FROM OR INFUSED INTO THE REST OF THE CURRICULUM?

The never-ending story of the thinking-skills business seems to be whether thinking skills should be separated from or infused into existing curricula. Among the present authors who have developed thinking-skills programs of one sort or another, Nickerson, Lipman, Bransford, and Sternberg have developed separated programs, whereas Quellmalz, Perkins, Swartz, and Paul have developed infused programs. Each kind of program has its advantages. Separate programs (1) are less likely to be overpowered by knowledge-based curriculum and hence become nonprograms, (2) allow students to get a clear sense of just what the thinking skills are, with less danger of their simply being mixed in with other learning processes and hence losing their identities, and (3) can be evaluated more easily outside of specific content areas. Infused programs (1) do not require a wholly separate course, which may not fit into school priorities, (2) seem to run less risk of fostering inert knowledge about thinking skills—that is, knowledge that is never applied outside the thinking-skills classroom, and (3) reinforce the thinking skills throughout the curriculum, rather than conveying the message that thinking skills are something apart from other curriculum.

So long as the issue of infusion versus separation is presented as a contest, the debate is likely to continue. I doubt, however, that the model of a contest is ideal in this case. The points raised by both sides are persuasive enough to argue for a mixed model in which thinking skills are taught as a separate course at the same time that they are infused and reinforced throughout the entire curriculum. I believe that the burden of teaching thinking entirely within existing curriculum is just too great: One cannot expect all teachers to be experts on thinking skills, any more than they are all experts on science or social studies or mathematics. Expertise in teaching thinking skills is no shorter an order than expertise in any other discipline. Ideally, it requires general liberal arts training, as well as training in psychology and philosophy. At the same time, unless all teachers in a given school are at least aware of what is being taught and can reinforce what is being taught, then the teaching is likely to be for naught. Indeed, teachers in other disciplines can undermine thinking-skills training if they think or teach in a way that counters the spirit of inquiry fostered in a thinking-skills curriculum. Hence, I believe that if a school system is serious about teaching thinking, it should dedicate special time to it, at the same time that workshops and seminars should be made available to all teachers so that they can reinforce rather than extinguish or even undermine what is being taught in the thinking-skills curriculum.

SHOULD THINKING SKILLS BE TAUGHT VIA A PREESTABLISHED PROGRAM OR A TEACHER-MADE ONE?

Here again, we find an area of controversy among the experts. Perkins, Quellmalz, Swartz, Paul, and Baron describe curricular strategies that can be used for the construction of a teacher-made program for teaching thinking skills. Lipman, Bransford et al., and Sternberg also describe such principles, but emphasize the implementation of these principles within their own, preestablished programs. Of the latter authors, Bransford and Sternberg seem more neutral with respect to the benefits of the one kind of program versus the other, whereas Lipman feels rather strongly that a preestablished program such as his own is likely to be of greater benefit than are teacher-made ones. After all, his program and others like it—for example, Feuerstein's Instrumental Enrichment—are based upon elaborate theories of thought; have been extensively tested, revised, and evaluated; and have been shown to work in a number of different kinds of settings. On the one hand, teacher-made programs run the risk of being amateurish and misguided; on the other hand, preestablished programs are not necessarily any better, and even those that are better may not be appropriate for a particular school system or setting.

Again, I think the either-or contest mentality is probably less than expedient. If a school system can afford a preestablished program, fit it into its own schedule, assure adequate time and funds for teacher training, and tailor the program to fit its own needs, then I think a good preexisting program can work well. On the other hand, if these conditions are not met, then teacher-made programs may be preferable. Moreover, there is no difference between a bad teacher-made program and a bad premade one—and there are plenty of bad programs available on the market. Hence, no matter what program is used, careful selection should be made, taking into consideration the needs of the school district and the children. We must remember that some programs emphasize certain sets of skills, other programs emphasize other sets of skills, and the selection should take into account just what the goals are for the children once they have completed the program.

NEED A FORMAL EVALUATION OF THE PROGRAM BE CONDUCTED?

Baron's chapter describes a variety of formal and informal strategies teachers and administrators can use to evaluate programs for teaching thinking skills. Other chapters also refer to either informal or formal evaluation. It is important to realize that when programs are implemented at a school (or grade) level, informal evaluations are never substitutes for formal evaluations, and indeed, that there is no substitute for a formal evaluation. Rather, informal evaluations complement formal ones. If a district or school is going to invest the time and effort—both of students and teachers—in the implementation of a thinking-skills program, then that district or school owes it to everyone to conduct a formal, comprehensive evaluation of the program. All too often, those involved in the programs feel like things worked, when in fact no documentable gains can be shown. In other cases, there may be gains that elude informal evaluations and can only come to light through a broad-ranging formal evaluation. Having been involved in interventions with many school districts, I know that districts are often more reluctant to evaluate programs than they are to implement them. Yet, without evaluation, the programs may be continued when they are, in fact, worth little or nothing.

A poorly designed formal evaluation is worse than no formal evaluation at all. Simply giving a few intelligence tests as a pretest and a posttest does not constitute an adequate formal evaluation, especially if they are given without an untrained control group. A comprehensive formal evaluation should include measures based upon just what it is that the program is supposed to teach, standardized thinking-skills and intelligence tests, measures of achievement, measures of attitudes toward thinking and learning, measures of study habits, and the like. Evaluations will almost always require specialists trained in evaluation as well as specialists trained in teaching and assessing thinking skills; it may not be possible for the two sets of specialists to be composed of the same people. But an evaluation should always be done in an expert and carefully planned way, rather than haphazardly or as a seat-of-the-pants operation.

IS THERE SUFFICIENT EVIDENCE AT THIS TIME TO SELECT ONE THINKING-SKILLS TRAINING PROGRAM AS THE BEST OF THE BUNCH?

This is a question I am often asked when I lecture or consult: Teachers and administrators want to know if, after all is said and done, there is one program that is superior to the others. This question rather misses the point: Teachers and administrators have to apply the same thinking skills they ultimately plan to teach to their own selection of a thinking-skills program. There is no one program that is best for everybody or every place. Some programs are more suited to older children, some to younger; some are more suited to urban children, others to rural children; some programs are more suited to brighter students, others to less-bright students; some programs emphasize analytic thinking skills, others emphasize synthetic thinking skills; some programs require extensive teacher training, others require very little teacher training; some programs require multiple-year interventions, others require as little as a semester. The point is that in general the question of which program is best is unanswerable. One must learn about the principles of thinking and the programs available for teaching it through books such as this one, as well as through workshops, journal articles, and seminars, and then make a carefully thought out decision as to what will work best in a given setting—first-hand proof that there is no substitute for thinking skills in the lives of teachers and administrators, just as there is no substitute for them in the lives of students.

WHAT IS THE MINIMUM INVESTMENT OF TIME POSSIBLE TO ATTAIN A MEANINGFUL PROGRAM FOR TEACHING THINKING SKILLS?

Although there is no consensus upon this question, I doubt that a program that is of less than a semester in duration is worthy of serious consideration, and I would strongly urge planning that includes at least a year of instruction, with the time devoted to the instruction commensurate to that devoted to other courses of instruction. Of the programs described in this book, that of Bransford and Stein is probably the shortest, and even that one could not be done adequately in less than a semester. In contrast, Lipman's program could range from the lower elementary grades all the way through high school.

Ideally, I would view thinking-skills instruction as something that continues throughout schooling, much as would instruction in mathematics or social studies. If there is one thing we have learned about thinking skills, it is that there is no quick fix. Shorter-term programs may produce increases in test scores by teaching to specific tests; they will not produce long-term gains in thinking skills, nor should they be expected to produce such gains.

WHAT CAN ONE DO TO MAXIMIZE TRANSFER OF TRAINING FOR THINKING SKILLS TO STUDENTS' EVERYDAY LIVES?

I believe this to be *the* fundamental question in the teaching of thinking skills. Without far-spreading transfer of training, instruction in thinking skills is not terribly meaningful. And psychological research has shown that transfer of training does not come easily. One must teach for transfer, rather than merely hoping or even praying that it will occur.

I believe that there are several things one can do to maximize the probability of transfer in a thinking-skills training program. First, training must include development of executive, or metacomponential, skills, as well as of nonexecutive skills. Research in the 1960s showed that without training of executive processing, transfer does not occur. Of course, training of executive processes is necessary but not sufficient for facilitating transfer. Unless students can learn to think flexibly, look for opportunities to transfer their skills, and seek analogies between past and future situations, transfer is most unlikely to ensue.

Second, principles and rules of thinking must be presented in the context of a variety of academic disciplines. Whether the thinking-skills program is infused into or separated from other curricula, the examples that are used in conjunction with the program must cross disciplines, so that students can see directly the relevance of these principles across subject-matter areas. One cannot expect students to transfer unless they are shown just how the principles do transfer across domains.

Third, principles and rules should be presented in contexts that vary from the very abstract to the very concrete. On the one hand, it is important for students to understand how principles of thinking apply abstractly, without regard to particular content. On the other hand, they need to see how the principles can be instantiated in particular, concrete kinds of settings.

Fourth, principles and rules should be presented in contexts that vary from the academic to the practical. Again, one should not expect transfer to occur outside the classroom through some kind of miracle. Students apply principles of thought to their everyday lives because they are given examples of how these principles apply in such situations. Unless the program models the type of transfer that is expected to everyday situations, transfer probably will not occur.

Fifth, the program should involve multiple media of instruction, such as classroom lecture, discussion, reading, papers, individual projects, group projects, and the like. The greater the variety in media, the more likely students will internalize what they are taught in the program.

Finally, the program should be individualized sufficiently to meet the varying needs of students in any classroom setting. Although full individualization is probably only an ideal, some individualization will always be needed. No two students start with the same ability pattern or knowledge base. A given program will never be equally meaningful to any two students. The teacher is responsible for making the program as meaningful as possible to each individual student.

WHAT'S TO BE DONE WHEN THERE ARE SOME VERY INTERESTED TEACHERS AND SOME VERY UNINTERESTED ADMINISTRATORS?

Convince the administrators. If you can't, send them to state or regional meetings of organizations such as ASCD (Association for Supervision and Curriculum Development), AERA (American Educational Research Association), or similar groups. Try to convince them to read recent issues of journals such as *Phi Delta Kappan* or *Educational Leadership*. Show them reports of program implementations. Many administrators are still unaware that a revolution is afoot in the teaching of thinking, and a considerable effort may be required to bring them into the present. I believe that convincing the administrators is of the utmost importance, however, because in my own experience, programs initiated without administrative support or in an atmosphere of administrative hostility tend neither to work nor to be sustained for very long. The same is true for teachers: They must support a program fully in order for it to work. Many teachers need the same kind of intervention I have recommended for administrators.

WHAT SHOULD OUR ULTIMATE GOAL FOR THINKING-SKILLS PROGRAMS BE, ANYWAY?

As I mentioned above, specific goals have to be decided upon at a district-wide or school-wide level. Different programs emphasize different skills, and no one program is all inclusive. But at a more general level, the goal of thinking-skills programs should be (1) to make students better all-around thinkers, as well as better thinkers in specific disciplines, (2) to help students capitalize upon their strengths, (3) to remedy their deficiencies in thinking skills, and (4) to make students realize whatever potentials they have, rather than letting these potentials drain away through lack of concerted development. If the goal of the school is just to improve test scores, you don't need this book and you don't need these programs. Send the students to professional test-preparation courses which specialize in improving scores rather than in improving minds. If the goal is to improve minds, then the investment you have made in reading this book should be well worth the time you put into it, and the investment put into a good thinking-skills program will be well worth the time of students and teachers alike. Much knowledge is ephemeral; thinking skills never are. And it is the ability to think that will enable students to acquire new knowledge, replace old knowledge, and recognize what knowledge is worth acquiring in the first place.

Name Index

Subject Index